Praise for *Start in Your Own Backyard*

"*Start in Your Own Backyard* is an extraordinary true-life story of transformation with worldwide implications. Serenbe integrates community, design, biology, and nature. It is not a proposal or set of solutions—it is genius and brilliance in action."

—Paul Hawken, *New York Times* Bestselling Author, *Carbon*

"Serenbe is a model of leadership and commonsense design that is applicable to communities everywhere. It is also testimony to the fact that the world is still rich in possibilities and that 'hope, indeed, is a verb with its sleeves rolled up.' As told by Serenbe's legendary founder, this book is an inspiring story of one man's vision. It's also full of practical possibilities for resettling America in a way that allows nature, people, and communities to flourish together."

—David W. Orr, Paul Sears Distinguished Professor Emeritus, Oberlin College, and Author, *Dangerous Years*

"Everyone plays a role in reinventing our farming system. That's because, at the deepest level, each one of us participates in agriculture. The critical question is, *How?* In *Start in Your Own Backyard*, Steve Nygren brings the spirit of regenerative organic agriculture to life and lays out a blueprint for how people can heal the planet starting in their own backyards."

—Jeff Tkach, CEO, Rodale Institute

"Steve Nygren's new book is a remarkable story about a unique person and a special place. The person is a visionary and pioneer who found a better way to live in harmony with nature. The place, Serenbe, has grown from a grand experiment to a trendsetting model. Serenbe, a nature- and farm-based community outside of Atlanta, gives us hope for the land and shows us there are better ways to build that are more healthy, beautiful, and resilient than the cookie-cutter subdivisions so common throughout America. Communities like Serenbe give residents a reason to love where they live. Nygren teaches us how small, commonsense changes can transform our neighborhoods and our relationships with each other."

—Ed McMahon, Charles E. Fraser Chair on Sustainable Development and Senior Fellow for Sustainable Development, Urban Land Institute

"Visionaries Marie and Steve Nygren have designed a model for smart residential development that works to conserve and protect trees, green space, farmland, and animal habitat. It's a Garden of Eden! I absolutely love Serenbe, and so do my family and friends who have either moved there or visited. Even if you don't move to Serenbe, this book gives us a blueprint of changes we can all make in our communities that will lead to a healthier, more sustainable lifestyle for our families."

—Laura Turner Seydel, Director, Turner Foundation, and Chair Emeritus, Captain Planet Foundation

"Combine a visionary leader, an inspiring idea, and a beautiful place . . . and magic happens. This story of Serenbe provides an uplifting model of a community that promotes social connectedness, health, and happiness, while protecting the natural world. It's a model we need to emulate widely on the path to sustainability and planetary health. Read this book, take it to heart, and get started in your own backyard!"

—Howard Frumkin, MD, DrPH, former Dean, University of Washington School of Public Health, and former Director, National Center for Environmental Health, US Centers for Disease Control and Prevention

"Steve Nygren knows that change in the world must begin first in our own neighborhoods and communities. A master builder and placemaker extraordinaire, Nygren knows we must engage with others in the timeless and sacred commitment to creating places that we will love deeply and that allow both humans and nature to flourish. He has done this in compelling fashion at Serenbe in Georgia, an inspiring community that blends innovative and creative design, deep commitment to place, and an essential connection to the daily rhythms and delights of the natural world. Nygren has become the pied piper for a new kind of city that inspires and uplifts, that nurtures our hearts and our souls, and that connects us to the magic of the natural world. There is another way to grow and build (and live), one where we care about each other and the larger ecological community that sustains us. He believes it is possible to design places that regenerate both landscape and spirit, and shows the way for others in this insightful book."

—Timothy Beatley, PhD, Teresa Heinz Professor of Sustainable Communities, School of Architecture, University of Virginia

"Steve is a true visionary. He left a successful career in the restaurant business to do something most thought couldn't be done. The real estate elite discounted his ability to execute on Serenbe, and they were wrong. He found an idea he believed in and built a team around him, and people became believers when they started to see him succeed. He worked through macro challenges in capital markets but stayed the course. He paid the tuition and now is offering what he learned tuition-free. That is the mark of a great leader: that he is willing to freely share best practices so we can make the world a better place."

—Mark C. Toro, Founder, Principal, and Chief Vision Officer, Toro Development Company

"I'm so happy Steve Nygren wrote this book—and you will be too. Worried that Atlanta's suburban sprawl would soon destroy the beloved rural landscape surrounding his farm, he and his neighbors on 40,000 acres enabled transfer of development rights to direct growth into walkable, mixed-use towns while conserving 70 percent of the land to remain unbuilt. Students, professionals, and other would-be 'accidental developers' will enjoy learning how Steve turned his own farm into Serenbe, a beautiful, experimental biophilic community that continues to grow, innovate, and inspire."

—Ellen Dunham-Jones, Professor of Urban Design, Georgia Institute of Technology

"The kind of change we need in our built environment begins with people like Nygren—with the good and active participants of community life: creative doers who find within themselves not only the inspiration, capacity, and energy to shape something different but the language to share their compelling story. *Start in Your Own Backyard* captures Serenbe's essential lessons for a new way of life."

—Ryan Gravel, Visionary behind the Atlanta Beltline Project; Founder and President, Sixpitch; and Author, *Where We Want to Live*

"This is one of those rare books that combines aspirational vision with practical action. Steve Nygren shows us that we can both dream big and do big, simply by committing ourselves to purposeful action. In a time when everything impinging on us seems so overwhelming, Steve Nygren shows that we can start in our own backyards to create the change we want to see in our own lives, and, in the process, we can have outsized impact in our neighborhoods, our communities, and our nation."

—Colonel Mark Mykleby, USMC (Ret.), Executive Director, Human Fusions Institute, Case Western Reserve University, and Coauthor, *The New Grand Strategy*

"It's a remarkable thing to fall in love with a place. If you've never experienced it, I hope you do one day. If you have, I hope you treasure it. Either way, Steve Nygren and this book will help you find and nurture places of connection to nature and to each other. These are the places worth falling in love with."

—John A. Lanier, Executive Director, Ray C. Anderson Foundation

START
IN YOUR
OWN
BACKYARD

Transforming Where We Live with Radical Common Sense

STEVE NYGREN

MATT HOLT

Matt Holt Books
An Imprint of BenBella Books, Inc.
Dallas, TX

Photos courtesy of Serenbe unless otherwise indicated.

Matt Holt is an imprint of BenBella Books, Inc.
8080 N. Central Expressway
Suite 1700
Dallas, TX 75206
benbellabooks.com
Send feedback to feedback@benbellabooks.com

BenBella and *Matt Holt* are federally registered trademarks.

Printed in the United States of America
10 9 8 7 6 5 4 3 2 1

Library of Congress Control Number: 2025016170
ISBN 9781637747438 (hardcover)
ISBN 9781637747445 (electronic)

Editing by Greg Brown
Copyediting by Amy Handy
Proofreading by Karen Wise and W. Brock Foreman
Text design and composition by PerfecType, Nashville, TN
Cover design by Brigid Pearson
Cover photo by Ali Harper
Printed by Versa Press

Special discounts for bulk sales are available. Please contact bulkorders@benbellabooks.com.

To my family,
who stood by me through my Don Quixote moment.

And to my grandchildren, and future generations,
for whom I wrote this book,
in the hope that common sense will guide us
in shaping the communities of tomorrow.

CONTENTS

FOREWORD

n the 1970s, the environmentalists' rallying cry was "Give Earth a Chance." In the decades since, we've been urged to "save the whales," "reduce acid rain," "give a hoot, don't pollute," "reduce, reuse, recycle," and much more. Understandably—and urgently—many of today's environmental efforts, including my own, revolve around nature and the climate emergency. In fact, as I write this foreword, I'm preparing to convene a climate forum at the Rockefeller Foundation's Bellagio Center in Italy.

Over the years, I've noticed that while the focus of environmental campaigns and PSAs may shift, there's a consistent undercurrent that runs through them all: The way we live isn't working. It isn't working for our communities, our country, or our planet. It isn't working for our children, our elders, our food systems, or our health. It certainly isn't working for underprivileged and marginalized communities at home and around the world.

I came to climate activism—and a deeper understanding of my own role in it—when I recognized how deeply interconnected gender and racial justice are with all social justice issues, and how they are all tied to the urgent planetary crisis threatening our collective future. My work had long focused on equity, but this realization broadened my perspective and deepened my commitment. I joined a group of women leaders to launch a global campaign we called *Project Dandelion*, inviting everyone—regardless of their specific passions or causes—to embody the dandelion: climate-resilient, growing on every continent; healing, with every part usable and nothing wasted; interconnected at the roots so it cannot be stopped; and regenerative, spreading through the wind.

In my work as an activist for climate justice, I've often struggled with how to balance modern convenience with sustainable, eco-friendly, and soul-filling living. While there has been a lot of fresh thinking in this area, the message we often hear is that in order to prioritize one value, we must sacrifice the other.

But that doesn't have to be the case. What Steve Nygren has demonstrated through his work is that it's possible to create a harmonious balance between development and conservation, comfort and sustainability, personal fulfillment and environmental responsibility. His story is not just about creating a thriving community—it's about rethinking how we live and challenging the systems that drive urban sprawl, environmental degradation, and social disconnection.

Steve didn't set out to become a developer. What started as a simple effort to protect a beloved farm from encroaching development became a journey to create a new model for sustainable, human-centered living. Along the way, Steve learned how to work with local landowners, residents, and policymakers to apply commonsense solutions that challenge the "bigger, faster, cheaper" mentality driving so much of modern development.

My husband Scott Seydel (who is a lifelong environmentalist) and I have experienced the results of this approach firsthand. While our primary residence is in Atlanta, we have a second home at Serenbe, and we spend as much time there as we can. Our weekends at Serenbe have become longer and more frequent, drawn in by the peace of the natural surroundings, the genuine connections with neighbors, and the sense of balance that comes from being part of a community intentionally designed to live in harmony with nature.

It's not just the beauty of the place that draws us back—it's the feeling of being part of something different. Serenbe embodies a shift away from the rapid, thoughtless development that has come to define so many communities. Instead of paving over nature, Serenbe works with it. Trails wind through forests and fields, farms supply fresh food to local restaurants, and neighbors greet one another by name. There's a palpable sense of balance—not just between people and nature, but between convenience and sustainability, comfort and responsibility.

What stands out to me most about Steve's approach is that it isn't about grand gestures or sweeping policy changes—it's about practical, incremental changes rooted in respect for nature and community. Just like those dandelions I mentioned earlier, there are dandelions growing all over Serenbe, and Steve has sown the "seeds" for many ways for all of us to live in greater harmony with nature, to protect what we love, to envision the clearer, safer, more sustainable future that we can begin in our own backyards!

The ideas in this book are not limited to any one place. You don't have to live in a biophilic community to embrace these principles in your own life. Whether you're a developer, an elected official, an activist, a business owner, or a concerned individual, the lessons Steve shares here are accessible and actionable. Small, thoughtful changes in how we build, connect, and live can have a ripple effect, transforming not only our neighborhoods but also our collective future.

Steve's work serves as a reminder that protecting the environment and fostering human connection are not mutually exclusive. When we create spaces where people can live in harmony with nature, we create healthier, more vibrant, and more equitable communities. This book offers a road map for how to begin that process—starting in your own backyard.

—Pat Mitchell
Former CEO of PBS, cofounder of TEDWomen,
and author of *Becoming a Dangerous Woman*

"DIDN'T I READ THIS SOMEWHERE ELSE?"
A Note on Repetition in This Book

While *Start in Your Own Backyard* can be read straight through cover to cover, it may not always happen that way. A biophilic approach to community building is holistic and nonlinear. Thus, readers might gravitate toward certain chapters that address specific topics of interest—either on the first read-through or on subsequent ones. That's why I've structured each chapter as a stand-alone reference. Don't be surprised if you notice that some tips, best practices, and stories are repeated across several chapters.

However you choose to read this book, I am grateful!

—Steve Nygren

WHY WE INCLUDED QR CODES

f you want to dig deeper into certain topics, we've made it easy for you to access supplemental materials. At the end of the chapters, you'll find QR codes linking to helpful resources. You'll also find "image gallery" QR codes, which will direct you to full-color versions of many of the black-and-white images included in each chapter.

INTRODUCTION
Start by Saving Your Own Backyard

This is a book about the emergence of a place called Serenbe, a two-thousand-acre neighborhood community located in the city of Chattahoochee Hills, Georgia—and a pioneering model of biophilic living. But it's also a book about empowerment, optimism, hope, and finding solutions rooted in simple common sense.

It's a book about changing your life by starting in your own backyard, or your sphere of influence.

That's what happened to me, and that's what I want for you.

It's a paradox that light is often born out of darkness. As you'll soon learn, the idea that eventually took root and grew into Serenbe was sparked by a moment of fear, anger, dismay, and that deeply embedded human trait (that gets an undeserved bad rap): self-interest. Yet what came of it was something amazing—a place that honors the Earth and brings so many people rewarding, healthy, joyful lives.

The key word in that last paragraph is *self-interest*. It's not a bad thing. In fact, more often than we realize, it's a powerful impetus for innovation. If I had to choose a single takeaway from this book it would be: *If you want to change the world, start by tending to your own backyard.*

My "backyard" journey started in the early '90s, when it slowly dawned on me that I needed a change. I was living in Atlanta at the time, fully invested in (and trapped by) what I call "the treadmill of life"—long hours at work, deep civic engagement, and (when I could fit them in) family. I kept my head down and powered through, trying to continuously grasp the next rung up on the ladder that society labels "success."

I ran hard on that treadmill until one weekend when my family and I somewhat spontaneously bought a farm in the Chattahoochee Hill Country in south Fulton County, thirty miles from our home. I kept working in the city, and, while I liked my daily life, I realized I was really living for those weekends on the farm. Breathing fresh air and doing honest physical labor, I felt alive and energetic, connected to nature and to my body's rhythms.

I soon realized I was experiencing a values shift. Those weekends gave me space to slow down, catch my breath, grow my own food, and truly connect with people—especially my family, but also friends and neighbors. These, I realized, were the things that fed my soul. And that's when, with my family's blessing, I decided to step off the treadmill, sell my businesses, and move to the farm full time. It was a frightening decision—yet once made, it opened the door to paradise.

People use words like "bucolic" or "idyllic" or "pastoral" to describe country living, but such words can't capture the profound transformation I experienced. My life, perhaps for the first time, *worked*. My family and I slowed down, dug in the dirt, climbed trees, read books, talked. There was a real sense that this is how life was always meant to be.

One day, after six years of blissful living on the farm, I heard the harsh grind of a motor as I was out running on one of the trails in the woods. To my horror, it was a bulldozer taking down trees. Although it turned out not to be the start of a tract housing development as I instantly assumed, this shocking event sparked a fear deep in my soul: Was suburban sprawl coming for our country paradise? If so, what could I do to preserve the land I lived on and limit how much others disrupted it?

This was my entry point into becoming an accidental developer. It all stemmed from the sudden urge to protect my own backyard. As you'll see in the following chapter, there was a steep learning curve. No wise expert came in and figured it out for me—I had to do it myself. I hope my "bulldozer moment" will help inspire your own. If something about your way of life isn't working, you can change it. At the very least, you can try. And that change usually begins in our own backyards.

When I started down the path that led to Serenbe, I wasn't setting out on a journey to change the world. I was simply tending to my own backyard. Had I understood the magnitude of the undertaking, I'm pretty sure I never would have begun. But, as environmental activist Erin Brockovich said, "Superman is not coming." So over the last twenty-plus years, with the help of many talented individuals, we built a community based on thoughtful principles that, when viewed decades down the road, will likely not make us regret the development decisions.

We each have our own "spheres of influence"—backyards of many, many different shapes, scopes, and sizes. Do you run a household? If so, how does it operate? Do you check labels for chemicals? Is your refrigerator stocked with fruits and vegetable or canned soda? Is your pantry shelf brimming with preservative-filled foods or fresh and dried items? Do you put chemical fertilizer and weed killer on your lawn, spraying the air you breathe with poisons to kill irritating bugs? Do you volunteer, run for office, or directly address any of the problems you complain about?

No matter how bad things might seem right now, you (and the world) are better served by taking positive action locally instead of handwringing. It's natural and depressingly easy to fall into a negative mindset, but if we really want things to change, we must resist that urge. As executive coach Bruce Kasanoff writes, "Being relentlessly positive means that you are a powerful, nearly unstoppable force for what is good and right. Even when it's hard. No, strike that. ESPECIALLY when it's hard."[1] In other words, we must get intentional—and relentless—about saving our respective backyards.

As you read this book, think about where you might start. Your diet? Your family's diet? Removing the lawn and planting edible landscaping? Buying an electric car? Accepting a position in your homeowners association or your building's oversight committee? Running for the school board or city council? What are your talents? Are you willing to step into an uncomfortable role to change the things you feel are destructive to your life, to our society? If we all step forward into our sphere of influence, take charge of our literal or metaphorical backyard, together we can change the world for ourselves and the generations that follow.

The first step is to change the conversation. This book is a good starting point. It's a blueprint of sorts that unpacks what biophilic design is and how to implement it in your own backyard, no matter its size.

The first chapter of this book will unpack how—collectively and individually—we've made decades' worth of choices that were meant to drive progress, but instead have had unintended consequences that harm our health, local economies, the natural world, and our sense of community. After all, to improve our backyards, we need to understand why our current way of life isn't working, and where we may have gotten it wrong.

Chapter 2 will focus on my personal story of leaving a corporate career, choosing a full-time life on the farm despite the complicated emotions that brought up based on my childhood, and ultimately starting Serenbe, which was framed around the philosophy of biophilic design—and which was the inspiration for this book.

In chapter 3, we'll look more closely at the various principles of biophilic design.

From there, each chapter will focus on exploring one or two of those principles by looking at how they can improve our health and well-being, how we implemented them at Serenbe, and how they can be applied in your backyard. Each chapter delves into practical aspects of creating a more connected, natural, and supportive environment.

More than anything, I hope that this book (and our story at Serenbe) is a source of inspiration for you and your community. It shows us that we *can* do life differently and that the status quo is changeable if enough people reject apathy, stop outsourcing what matters, begin critically thinking about whether development practices of the past are right for the present and future, and fully engage in life. Engagement is what makes community *community*, after all.

This book focuses on "community" in a literal sense. Yet "community" isn't only where you live. It's also where you work, where you socialize, where you gather with others to worship or meditate, or otherwise serve humanity and the Earth. It is my hope that you will start living by your heart and take action to impact any aspect of your life that needs it. It can be easy to default to thinking that all of the big societal and environmental issues are global, and only addressable by governments and corporations. It's not true! We all want a healthier Earth, healthier minds and bodies, and healthier lives for ourselves and our loved ones. When we start taking steps toward creating these things *right in our own backyards,* our neighbors see what we're doing and want to join in. One small win leads to another. Momentum grows. Before you know it, we're making real progress.

In short, start in your own backyard and do what you can. If your journey is anything like mine, you'll find it's a lot more than you ever could have imagined.

1

Life Isn't Working:
The State of the World Today

've just finished talking about the power of optimism and how it drives transformation on a local level. Now as we pull back and look at the bigger picture, we're going to see exactly why we need this optimism more than ever. Collectively, as a nation, we're not doing well. This is true on all levels: individual, cultural, and environmental.

As I write these words, the 2024 "World Happiness Report" has just come out.[1] It may not surprise you to learn that the United States is far from being at the top of the list of the happiest countries—we're now at number 23, having fallen from number 15 in last year's report.[2] We have a deep and profound longing for more joy in our lives, and it's not hard to see why.

Look around you. People are struggling in numerous ways. The CDC estimates that four of every ten Americans are obese.[3] Not surprisingly, chronic diseases related to obesity, like heart disease, diabetes, and some forms of cancer, are rampant. One in twelve US citizens suffer from asthma, including 4.5 million children.[4] Mental health issues, too, are on the rise, impacting one in five US adults and one in six US young people.[5] We are a nation of stressed-out, burned-out, overworked people grappling with loneliness.

Culturally, too, we are in trouble. The middle class is slowly shrinking as costs rise across the board.[6] Families are overwhelmed and crunched for time, forced to make tough choices around child-raising and elder care. Substance abuse and addiction (including reliance on prescription drugs) are burgeoning, sparking crime waves in our cities. Stories of political division, intolerance for differences, and incivility have taken over our media. It seems there's a breakdown of (and loss of trust in) the systems and institutions that should be our sources of stability. Education. Healthcare. Government. Religion. The criminal justice system.

Meanwhile, our environment is being relentlessly destroyed. The climate is heating up. The ice caps are melting. The oceans are dying. Pollution abounds. Our natural resources—forests, clean water, energy—are being rapidly depleted. Our food supply is in dismal shape, farmed with chemicals, highly processed, and filled with preservatives: the natural result of seven decades of focus on growing more food for less money.

Here's the thing: All these issues are intertwined. It's not that hard to see how obesity is connected to lack of access to nutritious foods and lack of time to exercise. How depression in our elders stems from their isolation. How poor mental health can lead to substance abuse, which can lead to hopelessness and crime. But is there a common factor at the center that causes (or at least exacerbates) *all* of these issues? Yes. *It's where—and how—we live.*

Our connection to nature and our connection to each other are the two most healing components to our physical and mental health, and we are missing out on both. Much of this disconnect is rooted in the development practices of the second half of the twentieth century, which focused on making space for the proliferation of the automobile and keeping commercial and residential areas separate for a fast-booming, post–World War II population.

When we start paying attention to how we've been conditioned to live, the hidden links between seemingly unrelated problems begin to reveal themselves. For instance:

- The proliferation of subdivisions with huge front lawns and no front porches discourages walking and socializing and creating neighborly relationships—which leads to a sedentary, lonely, disconnected populace that doesn't look out for each other.

- Nuclear families in car-centric suburbs are effectively cut off from the support systems that nourish the emotional well-being of everyone—which in turn can lead to lonely and neglected grandparents, stressed working parents worn out by long commutes, and children who lack meaningful relationships with adults who love them.

- Surrounding our homes with chemically treated (and HOA-approved) lawns prevents us from planting veggie gardens, blueberry bushes, ornamental shrubs, and wildflowers. This keeps us disconnected from our food and perpetuates our reliance on processed, preservative-laden, factory-farmed fare—which promotes obesity and a slew of health issues both physical and mental.

- When we live in ways that force us to compartmentalize our kids' lives and cut them off from nature—driving them to sports practices and structured play dates rather than emphasizing outdoor play with friends—it harms them on a multitude of fronts. Mental health, social skills, and academic performance may be compromised. (Bonding with nature improves learning. Bonding with other kids in free play builds a plethora of life skills.) Add to this the many deficits in our broken school system and it's not hard to see why our kids are sick, depressed, tech-obsessed, and ill-equipped to build relationships and solve problems.

Richard Louv's book *Last Child in the Woods* is a great resource on the importance of nature for child brain development. Scan QR code 1.1 at the end of this chapter to learn more.

The Children & Nature Network also does fantastic work in this space. Scan QR code 1.2 at the end of this chapter to visit their website.

We've been boxed into certain boundaries that have harmed our health and well-being. These are just a few examples of how we've built the places where we live, work, and play (in other words, the artificial boundaries we place between one part of life and another) to negatively impact our bodies, psyches, and relationships. This brokenness ultimately manifests in the organizations and institutions we create. How could it not?

As we've severed these vital connections, we've outsourced so many pieces of our lives: the raising of the food that nourishes us, the education of our children, the care of our elders. In a way, we've even outsourced friendship, replacing time spent in conversation and fellowship with texts and—maybe on special occasions—a FaceTime call. All of these elements are fundamental to the human experience. They are the things that bring us joy.

What's worse, we've been conditioned to think of all of this as "normal," even though in our heart of hearts we know it's anything but. In fact, today's American lifestyle goes against our human urge to interact with nature and with each other in a holistic, integrated way. The fact that we've accepted this dismal reality is the perfect example of how we allow our brains to overpower our hearts. The truth is the heart has its own ancient, profound, and life-affirming brand of intelligence, and we ignore it at our peril.

If you're interested in learning more about heart intelligence, scan QR codes 1.3 and 1.4 at the end of this chapter for two thought-provoking resources.

Intellectually and instinctively, we know that our diet, lack of exercise, loneliness, and stress are killing us. We know we need human connection. We know our kids are suffering. We know our climate is being destroyed. We know all these things. We've never had more research than we do right now. So why can't we make a change? It's because everything in society is working against us. It's so much easier to stay stuck in a rut thinking that this is just how it has to be.

But to build a new world, we need to build in a new way.

How We Got Here: A History of Unintended Consequences

So how did we find ourselves stuck in this unhealthy way of life? Volumes could be written on this subject. With unlimited time, ink, and paper, I might be able to untangle all the motives, economic forces, sociological changes, trends, and other factors that led us to this place. However, that really isn't the point of this book, and so I'll keep this part brief.

Many of the homes and communities we've built in the last seventy years, and what we did to create space for them, are the product of thinking that was shortsighted and expedient, or nature-abhorrent, or driven by greed and corruption. Today, few individuals or entities have the breadth of understanding to (a) comprehend what has happened with the built environment, and (b) know how to fix it. Most of the accumulated information and knowledge is siloed. Government doesn't appreciate the way systems are connected. Corporations don't. The public doesn't.

The darker realities of human nature notwithstanding, I believe the consequences we are experiencing are and were, for the most part, unintended. While there have always been (and always will be) callous individuals who don't mind harming others (or the Earth) for personal gain, most people want clean water to drink, fresh air to breathe, nutritious food to eat. We want well-being, strong relationships, happiness. We want these basics for ourselves and the people we love.

In other words, we haven't damaged the Earth and ruined our mental health *on purpose*. And it didn't happen overnight. Like the frog in the pot of water that's slowly heated to a boil, we only gradually realized we were in trouble.

It used to be that cities were built around walking. They gradually, organically grew over hundreds or even thousands of years. Because they evolved slowly and adapted in ways that made sense along the way, they were strong and productive—and they met the needs of the people who lived there.

Needless to say, this is no longer the case. For the last seven decades, the United States expanded housing without much forethought. Then, to address the unintended consequences of rapid sprawl, we added all kinds of regulations in an effort to organize the chaos. For example:

- Commercial and residential areas were separated. There was an attitude that retail and especially hospitality caused activity and noise, and that housing should be in quiet spaces.

- With the disappearance of the small mom-and-pop-type neighborhood businesses, larger national retail conglomerates began to emerge. As demand increased for large swaths of square footage, the suburban mall was born. Note the anti-nature language in *A Brief History of the Mall*: "The first enclosed mall was developed in a suburb of Minneapolis in 1956. Designed to get the shopper out of the harsh weather, it introduced the world to shopping complexes as worlds unto themselves—free from bad weather, life, crime, dirt and troubles."[7]

- Around the same time came parking regulations to allow stores to accommodate the high peak demand of the Christmas shopping season. Merchants saw convenient parking as a draw, so the commercial community jumped on board with the idea of asphalting the nature around them.

- Zoning regulations aimed at providing ample parking have led to asphalt jungles, creating urban heat islands and promoting obesity as our culture embraced the practice of driving to the front door of everything.

- Pasteurization regulations led to a very regulated food system. In addition, the competitive race for cheap food resulted in the birth of "Big Ag" and the proliferation of chemical-saturated food designed for extended shelf life. As a result, our food supply has become far less nutritious. A landmark study from 2004 attributes this to "the trade-offs between yield and nutrient content."[8] Other experts point to the rise in CO_2 in the atmosphere.[9] What we do know is that perhaps for the first time in civilization we are finding malnutrition and obesity in the same bodies.[10]

This shift toward suburbanization and all the problems that came with it can be traced back to the end of World War II. Americans started moving away from the cities and into the suburbs. This outmigration was fueled by a GI bill that allowed veterans to get home loans easily. The postwar economy was good, and jobs were plentiful. Plus, mass production techniques made it easier to build homes fast and cheap, leading to housing developments like those created by William Levitt (sometimes called "Levittowns") to spring up.

The interstate system, conceived by President Eisenhower from his experience as a war general, made this possible. Designed to move tanks across the country in the event of a war on our soil, this national pavement system was also a network of black asphalt veins spreading across America, fueling development that consumed our farms and forests.

Meanwhile, America's love affair with the automobile was in full swing. Cars had been around for decades when the 1950s rolled around, but demand for them skyrocketed in the new suburban economy. There is simply no way the suburbs could have sprawled without widespread car ownership. This "car centricity" seems disproportionate when you consider the average vehicle sits idle twenty-three hours a day.[11] As Lyft co-founder John Zimmer put it, "Cars weren't just shaping my worldview; they were shaping the world itself."[12]

During this same time, front porches began to disappear. Various factors contributed: The car craze meant people could leave their neighborhoods for entertainment, air conditioning meant they could stay inside instead of seeking cool breezes on the porch, television lured them in for entertainment. (Side note: Interestingly, porch use surged during

COVID-19 as people sought some form of [socially distanced] connection with neighbors.)[13] Meanwhile, postwar prosperity meant people could afford more space, and big front lawns and backyards became a status symbol.[14]

Innocent as all this may sound (and no doubt felt at the time), it set our nation on the path to where we are now. The developers, inventors, designers, and capitalists of the past simply did what we as flawed humans all tend to do. They used the materials at their disposal, and in creating their version of progress, they often spawned new, bigger problems. They very often kicked the can down the generational road. And consumers followed the path of least resistance.

If we had a crystal ball with a view into the future, I suspect we wouldn't be experiencing the environmental and health issues of today. We wouldn't be suffering the unintended consequences of urban sprawl on our bodies, psyches, and relationships. Our children wouldn't be suffering those consequences on their behavior and development. Our education system and national infrastructure and healthcare system would surely be superior. We wouldn't have replaced local farms with industrialized monoculture. We wouldn't be eating cheap, processed fast food. We wouldn't have so much noise and distraction.

Today's world is suffering the consequences of yesterday's decisions. By plowing ahead with good intentions, we became our own worst enemies. Siloed thinking became the norm. We became oblivious to the fact that when we destroy the natural landscape to build a highway system or a massive housing development or a gargantuan corporate farm, there is serious fallout in other areas. Our health. Our local economies. Our sense of community.

Now we are stuck in a rut. For example, any time development is proposed, there must be a feasibility study to fund it. This is rearview-mirror thinking. It leads to more of the same types of development with all the same negative consequences.

The great news is it doesn't have to be this way. We *can* take control of our own lives. We *can* build (or rebuild) our communities in a way that supports our health and happiness rather than detracting from them. We have the power to change our world. The story of Serenbe shows that it can be done.

Chapter 1 QR Codes

**Richard Louv
QR Code 1.1**

**C&N Network
QR Code 1.2**

**Heart Facts
QR Code 1.3**

**Heart Math
QR Code 1.4**

2

The Farm That Changed My Life

Gravel road from the Serenbe community to
The Inn at Serenbe. *Photo by Ali Harper.*

I t all began, not surprisingly, in our own family backyard.

In 1991, my wife, Marie, and I took a drive in the country. We stopped at a historic farm that was for sale because we wanted our daughters, Garnie, Kara, and Quinn—then seven, five, and three years old—to see some farm animals.

When we arrived, the farm had the Shetland pony saddled and ready to go. And as for us? Well, we bought the farm.

The farm and historic house were in not-yet-named Chattahoochee Hill Country, a mere thirty miles from our home in downtown Atlanta, but it felt like ten thousand miles or (more accurately) fifty years away. We began a routine that would last for years: leaving Atlanta for the farm every weekend. When we arrived on Friday afternoons, our first stop was at the caught-in-a-time-machine gas station to fill up and get the windows washed, and the attendant always gave each girl a stick of bubble gum. I felt like I had returned to the country farms of my youth. I'd grown up in rural Colorado on a farm, but my farmland childhood had often been anything but bucolic or holistic. In the fresh air and open vistas of this farm, *our farm*, I felt alive and energetic, connected to my family, connected to the world, the land, the food I ate, and connected to my own body's rhythms. I loved the physical labor, the joy of being outside. The more time I spent there, the more clearly I understood what fed me emotionally and physically.

My "weekday" life was blessed: I had experienced a great deal of success in the hospitality business, and my company of several midsized restaurants had been acquired by New York investors. Now, I oversaw two of the brands in the company's portfolio of restaurants. It wasn't why I got into the business, but what did I have to complain about? Except that my new nature-connected life was calling me. Until then, I hadn't realized that my life before the farm was making me tired, frustrated, and often unhappy.

After three years of weekends and holidays spent connecting with nature and each other, Marie, the girls, and I found ourselves driving back into Atlanta one Monday morning. Sitting in traffic with smog settling over the city, I felt a profound desire to change my life permanently and fully commit to the country.

But how could I give up what I had worked so hard to achieve? I'd come a long way from the rural Colorado farm, the outhouse until I was twelve, the alcoholic father who couldn't provide financial or emotional support. I was on a steadfast path to having a life very different from the one I'd known as a child. And here I was thinking about surrendering it to life on our farm, where nature nourished me but also caused painful flashbacks.

The call to change had snuck up on me, and it deserved an answer.

On that Monday morning drive back into downtown Atlanta thirty years ago, I resolved to make a change. Marie and the girls agreed. We would make the country home our permanent home. I gathered the courage to quit my job, sell what I considered my life's work, and abandon people who counted on me to turn on the lights and grow our company. As difficult as it was, I needed to be true to myself and give my children what I didn't have—a present, engaged father.

I was aware and grateful that my success had given me the luxury of this move without financial risk. Still, no matter a person's financial or emotional state, it takes strength to change. You do best when there's a brighter light ahead. (I didn't know that, come 2020, a global pandemic would force so many of my fellow humans to evaluate their lives and look for that light as well.)

When my family and I retreated to the country, we experienced a total lifestyle shift, one that made us realize exactly how disconnected we had been from each other and from our values for years. For instance, shortly after we moved to the farm, something surprising happened: Marie and I relaxed as parents. We had never thought of ourselves as helicopter parents, but in hindsight, we might have been (at least a little). About six months after our move, I asked our daughters, "Are you glad we left the city?"

Expecting them to mention the farm animals we'd added to our lives, I was caught off guard by Garnie, our oldest, who was eleven at the time. She glanced at her sisters, then confidently replied, "Yes, we are free here."

Curious, I asked what she meant. She explained, "In the city, even when we played in the backyard, we always knew you were watching from the window. But here, we feel free. No fences, just nature."

And what a slice of the natural world it was! Although we'd initially moved with plans for just a horse and a couple of rabbits, the farm quickly grew into something much bigger. We were soon gifted goats and pigs, and as our animal family expanded, so did the lessons of responsibility for our daughters. They eagerly took on the tasks of feeding and watering the animals, learning care and compassion in ways that city life had never offered.

The move didn't just give the girls freedom and a sense of responsibility, though; it gave all of us a chance to slow down and reconnect. While we had always tried to have dinner together in the city, our schedules often clashed with work meetings and other commitments. On the farm those conflicts disappeared, and family dinners became a cherished part of our daily routine. Many evenings began with harvesting fresh vegetables from the garden we had started and ended with long conversations around the table.

Our intergenerational family dynamic also blossomed. Shortly after we settled, Marie's mother decided to move into our guesthouse. Later, we built her a home on the farm, strengthening the bonds along our family tree and further enriching the experience of extended family life.

The farmhouse itself became a central character in our story. At its heart was a potbelly stove, a relic of the home's original design, which we chose to keep during the farmhouse's expansion and renovation. Positioned near the kitchen and dining nook, the stove became the centerpiece of cozy winter evenings. Its radiant warmth often kept us lingering at the table long after dinner was finished, sharing stories and laughter as the fire crackled in the background. As the months and years passed, our gatherings came to include our farm's neighbors—who became cherished friends—as well as our own family members.

At this point, the only gray clouds hanging over me were the literal ones I could see, about to deliver a beautiful afternoon rain. For the next six years, we enjoyed a bucolic lifestyle. Surrounded as we were by fields, forests, and open spaces, natural beauty and serenity were an intrinsic part of daily life. The quiet rhythm of the countryside, far removed from urban noise and crowds, soothed our nervous systems.

In particular, planting a garden was grounding and energizing. Working with the earth transformed ordinary days into opportunities for physical engagement. The digging, planting, weeding, and nurturing of plants felt as though it was revitalizing my body from the inside out. Even the sun seemed different here. The glow it imparted on my skin felt richer and healthier; distinct from the tans I once associated with days spent by the pool or at the beach.

A reporter who visited our farm to write about our transition to rural life and the later opening of Serenbe's bed-and-breakfast commented on the polished appearance of my nails, assuming I must be indulging in manicures. She never suspected that their natural glow came not from salon visits but from working in the garden. It turns out that soil itself is teeming with life; beneficial microbes like *Mycobacterium vaccae* not only support immune health but also stimulate serotonin production, reduce inflammation, and promote gut health. These invisible allies in the dirt became part of the transformation I experienced.

When I wasn't cultivating crops or coaxing flowers to grow, morning runs and afternoon walks through the natural landscape brought a meditative calm that I had never before experienced. This daily practice predated the popularity of Japanese forest bathing in the United States, which would later highlight the profound benefits of time spent immersed in nature, such as reduced stress and lower cortisol levels. Back then, I simply knew that time outdoors gave me a clarity and peace I'd never felt in the city.

After lunch on most weekdays, while the kids were at school, I would retreat to the daybed swing on our screened porch to read the papers. Inevitably, my reading would be interrupted by the weight of my eyelids, and I'd drift into an afternoon nap, lulled by the sounds of rustling leaves and birdsong. Somehow, I always woke in time to head out for carpool, feeling refreshed, present, and ready for engaging conversation on the way home.

Then came the significant day in 2000 when the bulldozer rolled onto the scene.

That morning, while running with Garnie, we heard an unpleasant, menacing noise coming from just over a rise in the road. When we got to the top, we saw the bulldozer, growling, eager to wipe out a forest of trees. I feared that the clearing would be used for tract housing. It didn't make me feel much better when, weeks later, I found out it was for a landing strip for the neighbor's prop plane.

This was my "backyard" they were encroaching on. Self-interest snapped me awake to the fact that seclusion from the world was bound to end once profit-motivated, shortsighted development (commonly called "progress") found us. I wanted no change to my surroundings. I wanted to stop this angry yellow machine from razing acres of trees.

But just wanting it to stop would not make it so. That moment turned into something so much bigger for me—a bridge to the way I would ultimately think and act.

I had to do something to protect and honor the natural environment that had sustained me and my family—and so many others—over the years. I could buy up a certain amount of acreage, but I knew that hoarding land was no long-term solution. I began investigating alternatives to what I saw as reckless development and discovered a great division between developers driven by economic interest and conservationists concerned about ecological balance. I pondered why these had to be opposing camps. This is where the concept of building something else, Serenbe, came into being.

Conceptualizing a New Kind of Community

The seed of an idea had been planted, but I still had to build the place and, more accurately, the *community*, that I was envisioning.

I had thought simply moving full-time to the farm was enough to find fulfillment. Again, it turned out that life isn't so simple. For the first time since our relocation, conflict and doubt had entered our pastoral little corner, and I was forced to consider: What really matters to me? What matters to my family? What is sustainable, durable—what's a way of building and living that would have no reason to someday get bulldozed?

Since I was conceptualizing an entirely new community—one where we could develop without destroying nature—how could we make it foster an actual better way of living? Did a road map for such a place exist? Did I need to create my own?

I gradually came to the realization that yes, a vision for what I wanted to create did exist in the form of design and development based on biophilic principles (more on that in the next chapter). However, someone would need to take the initiative in applying those principles to the built environment on a community scale. And that someone was me.

I began to research and visit various models that aimed to challenge conventional development norms. Seaside, Florida, and Prairie Crossing, Illinois, stood out as successful examples of integrating pre-automobile development patterns into modern contexts. However, these projects also unintentionally hastened the degradation of the surrounding land by allowing conventional development practices to take root at their edges.

Returning home, I recognized the need for a more regional approach. How would my actions impact my neighbors? Could we create a mutually acceptable plan to balance preservation and development across *all* our properties? With these questions in mind, I began a conversation at my neighbor Ned Peek's kitchen table. Ned, a sixth-generation steward of the land, was raising his son and grandchildren on the same property he'd grown up on. My initial discussion with Ned sparked the organization of five hundred landowners—both pro-development and conservation-minded—to rethink the future of our forty thousand collective acres that, though unincorporated then, would eventually make up the bulk of Chattahoochee Hills when the city was incorporated in

2007. Simultaneously, I was exploring how I could develop my own nine hundred acres as a model for sustainable growth. (These nine hundred acres would eventually form the footprint of Serenbe, which has since grown to two thousand acres.)

Fortunately, my longtime friend Ray C. Anderson, founder of Interface, one of the world's largest manufacturers of modular carpet and a green business pioneer, suggested a valuable next step. Ray, who had served as co-chair of the President's Council on Sustainable Development, became a valuable guide to me throughout the process of conceptualizing Serenbe, and I largely credit him with pushing me through the "door of passion." Back then, Ray invited the nonprofit organization Rocky Mountain Institute to assemble thought leaders over two days in September 2000 for a charette (basically, a group brainstorm). These were leading experts in specific areas of climate, land use, water, energy, and so forth, but they were *not* developers.

Realizing I had to step into the role of developer, my first move was to find a land planner. Because I was leading with environmental responsibility, I found there were not many viable candidates. My first hire oversaw all the assessments of the land, as well as archaeological digs that discovered the remnants of Indigenous cultures and early American farmsteaders who had been on the land over the past centuries. Unfortunately, this gentleman did not believe in density, which was a problem because I wanted to build a community balancing density and preservation using the hamlets in the English countryside as inspiration.

In the months that followed, Bill Browning with the Rocky Mountain Institute referred me to Dr. Phillip J. Tabb, who had conducted his doctoral research on the English countryside and was also well-versed in incorporating sacred geometry into land planning. At the time, Dr. Tabb was head of the architecture department at Texas A&M. Interested to hear Dr. Tabb's perspective on how sacred geometric principles might apply to our land, I invited him to lead a morning presentation at one of our monthly planning meetings. At the conclusion of the two-day meeting, Dr. Tabb shared that he understood what I was trying to create and suggested that he could bring some students to explore what a village in the woods might look like. This conversation launched him as our land planner for the next twenty years (continuing today). It felt as if Dr. Tabb had dropped from the heavens! When he retired from his university position, he moved to Serenbe and is now part of our consulting team.

Next, I had to find a civil engineer. I hired a team that I knew through political connections. They seemed an ideal fit because they could not only handle the civil drawings but could also expedite the permit process. Midway through the construction of our first phase of forty lots, I realized their skill was more about navigating political circles than doing civil drawings and once again I was on a search for a replacement. From there I found Southeastern Engineering, who continue to be our civil engineers today and have moved their environmental office to Serenbe.

Three Lessons from These Early Days

We learned three lessons from our rocky start:

1. Be clear on your vision. If you aren't you might easily be swayed by someone else's vision.
2. Don't be afraid to say, "I made a mistake." When you make a mistake with whom you hire or what you launch, course-correct the minute your gut tells you change is needed.
3. Look past the established regulations, perceptions, and habits regarding how things are done. Do consider commonsense solutions. Many times, these solutions are found in the way we did things a century ago.

Too many people start overthinking such decisions and end up compromising early on—and then the whole project gets off track. Better to cut your losses and move on.

And so we were off . . . and Serenbe started coming together.

If you'd like more detail on how Serenbe came to be, scan QR code 2.1 at the end of this chapter. It will take you to a series of Facebook posts I shared around the passage of the unique zoning overlay for the 40,000-acre Chattahoochee Hill Country's twentieth anniversary in 2022. I hope you enjoy reading it as much as I enjoyed recounting it.

Just because we were off doesn't mean it was easy. What enabled us to get from this auspicious starting point to a community renowned for its community health, connection, and closeness to nature twenty years later was a continued commitment to collaborating with like-minded visionaries while remaining focused on the principles of biophilic design. (We'll look at these principles more closely in the next chapter.)

You may not know how to transform your backyard yet, but it's my hope that these principles—as they were for me—can be the spark of inspiration that leads you through your own door of passion.

Chapter 2 QR Codes

History
QR Code 2.1

3

What Is Biophilic Design?

first heard the word "biophilia" from the Rocky Mountain Institute's Bill Browning during Serenbe's first charette in September 2000. At this point, I was just beginning the process of conceptualizing what the community of Serenbe might become. While I was intrigued by Bill's description of biophilia, the concept didn't really "click" for me until several years later.

As plans for Serenbe began to grow from blueprint to reality, people started to ask me what "type" of community Serenbe was supposed to be. New Urbanist? No, New Urbanist developments don't necessarily prioritize enforcement of environmental principles. An "environmental community"? Sort of. In 2010, the Urban Land Institute featured Serenbe in its book *Conservation Communities: Creating Value with Nature, Open Space, and Agriculture* by Ed McMahon, but Serenbe's commitment to incorporating clustered development to preserve the natural landscape made it unique even among that group. At one point, a *New York Times* reporter covering Serenbe even coined a new term to describe the trend of integrating organic farms into dense communities: "Agrihood." But in my opinion, that still didn't fully capture Serenbe's essence.

Then, while speaking at a conference in 2012, I heard Tim Beatley, a professor at the University of Virginia's Department of Urban and Environmental Planning, present on biophilic cities. *That's it!* I thought. *This concept perfectly embodies Serenbe's intent: the appreciation and love for all living systems, and the recognition of their interconnectedness—especially when creating spaces for people to live alongside and* inside *the natural world.*

My realization that Serenbe's ethos had a name, and that exploration and adoption of this concept could further enrich our community, led us to adopt biophilic design as a defining term.

Biophilia (popularized by Harvard biologist E. O. Wilson in 1984) is the idea that humans have an innate tendency to seek connection with nature. After all, humans have lived immersed in the natural world for hundreds of thousands of years. It just makes sense that modern humans have retained this genetic preference for dwelling amid the shapes, colors, sounds, and fragrances of nature. There's an instinctive bond between human beings and all other living systems. We simply do better when we live this way.

To embrace biophilia requires integrated (and to my mind, commonsense) thinking. Unfortunately, most developers are stuck in siloed thinking. Here's an example of what I mean. Generally, land planners look primarily at efficiency: Either (a) they try to maximize housing (or commercial) units per square foot, or (b) they do the reverse and create lots that feel like an estate, with minimal connection to neighbors. Neither approach considers the disruption to nature, such as the damage done to our tributaries and rivers when stormwater is artificially diverted from the homesite through pipes.

The biophilic principles I've briefly outlined below provide a framework for breaking down the silos and promoting a more integrated way of thinking. As the book unfolds, you'll learn more about these principles. For now, know that they are meant to work together to protect our Earth and help those who live by them create a sense of good health, emotional well-being, and community engagement. Here, I'll briefly explain how Serenbe incorporates each principle as we pursue our overarching goal to preserve and live in connection with nature.

The Twelve Biophilic Principles for Community Design

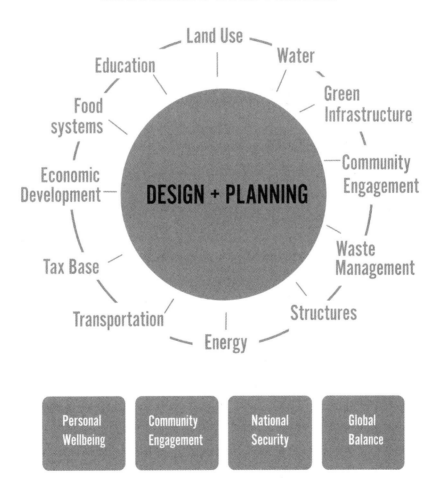

Land Use

Understanding that sprawl is not only expensive but also destructive to the environment and harmful to humans—who are biologically wired to live in community—we set out to develop Serenbe in harmony with nature. For example, when planning and developing Serenbe, I spearheaded the creation of a progressive zoning regulation for the greater 40,000-acre area requiring 70 percent of any land designated for development to be preserved for agricultural or conservation purposes. This approach allows all potential development to be concentrated within the remaining 30 percent of the land. Furthermore, it promotes a sense of community and requires less dirt to be moved via mass grading (saving money and resources).

How Does Mass Grading Harm the Environment?

Mass grading, or the process of reshaping large tracts of land for development, is a common practice in large-scale construction projects due to its efficiency. However, it carries significant environmental, economic, and social drawbacks, often causing long-term damage that outweighs its initial convenience.

This practice frequently involves the removal of vegetation and topsoil, leading to the displacement of wildlife and the destruction of ecosystems. As habitats for plants, insects, and animals are lost, biodiversity declines. Additionally, the exposed soil becomes highly vulnerable to erosion by wind and water, depositing sediment into nearby waterways. The natural soil structure is disrupted, reducing fertility and making it challenging for vegetation to reestablish.

Mass grading also interrupts natural drainage patterns, increasing the risk of flooding in surrounding areas. Stormwater runoff from graded sites often carries pollutants into streams and rivers, further degrading water quality. The removal of vegetation eliminates natural carbon sequestration, contributing to elevated atmospheric carbon dioxide levels. Moreover, dust and particulate matter from exposed soil exacerbate air pollution, affecting both environmental and human health.

While development projects that employ mass grading may attempt to mitigate the damage by revegetating the disturbed land after construction, this process is costly and often results in landscapes dominated by water-intensive, chemically enhanced lawns. These unnatural garden landscapes contribute to ongoing environmental strain, making mass grading a less sustainable choice for land development.

By considering alternative approaches that preserve natural features and minimize disturbance, developers can reduce these impacts, creating more sustainable and resilient communities.

To promote responsible land use and long-term conservation while minimizing the need for grading, Serenbe led an initiative to introduce transferable development rights (TDRs) as part of the new overlay for the 40,000-acre area now known as Chattahoochee Hills. TDR programs are a particularly useful tool in biophilic land use, because they allow for multiple owners to economically participate in the development of an area where the majority of land is protected for farms or open space, and for easy forest access for residents.

What Are Transferable Development Rights?

TDRs are an innovative zoning tool that allows landowners to transfer their development rights from one parcel of land to another within the same jurisdiction. This mechanism enables higher-density development in designated growth areas while preserving valuable open spaces, farmland, historic sites, or environmentally sensitive land. Landowners in the "sending areas" can voluntarily sell or transfer their development rights, often placing their property under a conservation easement to ensure it remains protected. Meanwhile, developers in "receiving areas" can purchase these rights to build at higher density levels.

The program is particularly effective in compensating smaller land-owners in the path of development, ensuring they benefit financially while guiding growth toward more suitable locations. By integrating TDRs into the planning framework, Chattahoochee Hills has set a model for balancing conservation and thoughtful development.

Green Infrastructure

This principle encompasses many aspects of development, from reducing energy demand through energy-efficient building practices and products to how energy is generated through the use of solar, wind, or geothermal systems for heating and cooling homes. As you'll learn later in this book, Serenbe established a geothermal utility in an effort to make geother-mal mandatory throughout the community, and as of this writing, all new residences are constructed with solar power compatibility in mind. Green infrastructure can also include utilizing porous hardscapes (e.g., walkways, roads, and parking areas) constructed using gravel or asphalt made from recycled tires.

Another piece of the green infrastructure puzzle is the edible land-scapes we build into Serenbe, from blueberry bushes planted at the cross-walks to the presence of medicinal and herb gardens. Everything we do is designed to conserve and celebrate the gifts of nature.

As a side note, the next three biophilic principles—water, waste-water management, and energy—are closely intertwined with green infrastructure and can even be viewed as subcategories of it. However, they are crucial enough to command their own focus.

Water

Rather than relying on stormwater regulations that emerged during the post-1950s mass grading building boom (which, as I explained earlier, pollutes and erodes local streams and tributaries), Serenbe turned to more natural solutions that contribute to water conservation. Instead of building hard pipes to divert the flow of rainwater to local tributaries or retention ponds, Serenbe focuses on landscaping that naturally retains water, including rain gardens, bioswales, pervious pavers, gutter chains, and engineered wetlands. By requiring water conservation fixtures and disallowing the use of potable water for lawns, we've reduced the average water use by 50 percent per household (compared to US standards on average household use).

Wastewater Management

Instead of building large tunnels to carry sewer water to be chemically processed, Serenbe has created a waste treatment facility that uses natural techniques to clean and conserve the black water, which is then used for irrigation. As a bonus, the natural treatment facility, which is composed of constructed wetlands, is strikingly beautiful—and the most photographed spot in Serenbe.

Other Options for Biophilic Wastewater Management

Serenbe's natural treatment facility is just one of many options for biophilic wastewater management. If acreage is limited, "living machines" can be a good option. These are a series of tanks or cells that contain plants, bacteria, algae, snails, and sometimes fish. They treat black water through biological processes in stages, including aerobic and anaerobic digestion.

Anaerobic digesters with biogas collection are another option for communities with limited space. This process uses sealed anaerobic tanks where microbes break down waste in the absence of oxygen. The organic matter is converted into methane (biogas), which can be used as renewable energy. The leftover nutrient-rich sludge can be integrated into greenhouses, farms, gardens, and landscaping, connecting technology and natural systems.

For single residences, installing composting toilets is a fantastic way to manage wastewater. These toilets collect black water in a dry or low-water composting system, where microbial and fungal activity breaks down waste. The resulting compost can then be used to amend soil.

If you're interested in learning more, I encourage you to research other biophilic methods of treating black water, which include aquatic treatment systems (lagoons and ponds), vermifiltration (worm-based systems), bioremediation gardens, solar evaporation with reservoir, tree-based systems (nutrient uptake via agroforestry), and biochar treatment systems.

Energy

When considering biophilic energy solutions for a home or community, the first priority should be reducing energy demand through thoughtful design and the use of energy-efficient materials during construction. Once energy efficiency is maximized, the choice of energy source depends largely on the geographical location and available natural resources:

- **Coastal or waterfront communities:** Tidal and wave energy harnesses the natural motion of ocean tides and waves to generate electricity.
- **Areas with agricultural or plant waste:** Biogas digesters and biomass stoves or power generators utilize organic materials such as plant waste or agricultural residues to produce energy. These systems mirror natural decomposition processes and offer a sustainable energy solution.
- **Communities near streams or rivers:** Micro-hydro turbines, which convert the flow of water into electricity, are an excellent choice for rural or biophilic communities. These systems are small-scale and integrate seamlessly with natural surroundings.

- **Western and midwestern United States:** Wind power is a practical option in areas with consistent wind. Small-scale or aesthetically designed wind turbines generate clean electricity and can be incorporated into residential or community settings.
- **Anywhere with stable underground temperatures:** Geothermal (ground-source heat pumps) take advantage of the Earth's constant underground temperature (around 50–60°F or 10–16°C) for heating, cooling, and hot water. These systems circulate a heat-transfer fluid through a series of underground pipes, which can be buried vertically, horizontally, or submerged in a water body. The heat pump, installed in a small space like a basement or attic, transfers heat between the ground and the building, distributing it via ducts or radiant flooring. In addition to reduced energy costs, these systems are silent and eliminate the need for noisy outdoor compressors.
- **Areas with consistent sun:** One of the most common and accessible sources of biophilic energy is solar power, which is widely available and versatile. Solar panels or solar roof tiles harness energy directly from the sun, offering a clean, renewable source of electricity. Solar systems can be designed to blend seamlessly with architecture, maintaining aesthetic harmony while supporting sustainability.

By tailoring energy solutions to the unique characteristics of a location, we can create systems that are both environmentally friendly and highly efficient, fostering harmony between the built environment and the natural world.

All homes in Serenbe are EarthCraft certified, meaning they are built to the standards of one of the nation's most successful regional green building programs. Serenbe invests in renewable energy sources by incorporating geothermal heating and cooling in its homes and ensuring they are solar-ready. Additionally, several net-zero-energy homes have already been built.

Community Engagement

The term "biophilia" comes from the Greek words *bios* (life) and *philia* (love or affection), meaning "love of life" or "love of living systems." This concept reflects the idea that humans have an inherent connection to nature—and also to one another. At Serenbe, we embrace this connection by designing spaces that encourage community, foster strong relationships, and promote engagement.

The community is laid out with a pedestrian-friendly grid, naturally incorporating paths through the landscape that lead to social hubs and gathering areas, seamlessly blending nature with opportunities for connection. Homes are designed with front porches that are close to the sidewalk, encouraging interaction with neighbors. Gathering spaces are thoughtfully scattered throughout, from central mail stations to hospitality centers within walking distance of each home. We take pride in offering a variety of restaurants, bakeries, wine and cocktail bars, and cafes—many with outdoor seating—where people can gather and connect. For a full listing, scan QR code 3.1 at the end of this chapter.

We also focus heavily on programming, creating a steady stream of arts and cultural events, seasonal celebrations, sports offerings, and so forth, all designed to encourage people to gather.

Structures

The 1970s introduced postmodern architecture, emphasizing efficiency and function over aesthetics. In contrast, Serenbe embraces a diverse range of architectural styles with a deliberate focus on beauty: the visual harmony of each home, its relationship with neighboring houses, and its integration with the surrounding natural environment. Many homes at Serenbe have a Southern vernacular while drawing inspiration from the romantic European styles of the nineteenth and twentieth centuries.

Across all architectural styles, key elements of biophilic design are thoughtfully incorporated to connect residents with nature, enhance well-being, and promote sustainable living. Features include abundant natural light through large windows, skylights, and clerestories, along with cross-ventilation to improve air quality and reduce reliance on mechanical systems. Homes are oriented to provide views of trees, water, or gardens and seamlessly integrate indoor-outdoor living with patios, balconies, and courtyards. Construction prioritizes natural materials (locally sourced when possible) like wood, stone, and bamboo, with interiors designed to foster a connection to outdoor spaces through sliding glass doors, French doors, verandas, and open floor plans.

Even the streetscape design that connects Serenbe's structures reflects our biophilic ethos. By placing homes within a shared garden environment (instead of taking a conventional approach that relies on individual houses with separate yards), we create a sense of community and harmony with nature.

Research now highlights that our perception of beauty directly impacts mental health, reinforcing the idea that what we build profoundly matters. By harmonizing architecture with the natural world, Serenbe strives to foster physical and mental health while reducing environmental impact, showcasing the profound connection between design and well-being.

Transportation

Make it more convenient to walk than to drive, and people will walk. Serenbe is a highly walkable (and bikeable) community. We've placed schools, shops, restaurants, and other necessities throughout the community, reducing the need for outside trips. There are ample sidewalks, pedestrian paths, and more than twenty miles of walking trails connecting all of Serenbe's hamlets and acres of undisturbed nature. ("Hamlet" is a zoning term that refers to a type of clustered housing district. Throughout this book, you'll see it used more colloquially to describe our community's various distinct neighborhoods.) Easy-to-use bike stands and an on-site bike shop contribute to a bike-friendly culture. Due to the fifteen-mile-per-hour speed limit, electric golf carts are a standard mode of transportation within the larger Serenbe community. Further, in seeking to reduce fossil fuel usage, we've designed all homes to be compatible with electric vehicles, with charging conduits leading to garages and under sidewalks for those parking on the street. And plans are in the works for a shuttle system and car share system to further reduce the dependency on cars.

Tax Base

The natural world functions best when in balance. This is also true for our human habitats, which are run mostly through governments funded by a tax base. A balanced range of home values, both affordable and higher-priced executive housing, is needed to create a sustainable tax base. When affordable housing is displaced, it becomes news, but when executive housing (and the corresponding taxes!) disappear, services are reduced. This creates anger but little media coverage.

Before Serenbe, the greater area of south Fulton County had a serious lack of executive housing and was not functioning well; it had low-performing schools, lack of police and other emergency responders, and poor infrastructure maintenance. With the construction of executive housing and the arrival of more affluent taxpayers, Serenbe has contributed to a more balanced tax base that has helped form a new city with services including fire, police, parks, and road works.

Economic Development

In the wild, there must be a supply of food for calm to exist. This balance is also true in our developed world. However, few connect the dots to understand that for a healthy local economy, there needs to be development. It brings in jobs and services. Due to decades of poor planning and design, most people are anti-development. This is in stark contrast to attitudes in the early twentieth century, when it was desirable to have jobs and service within walking distance of where you lived. By providing a well-thought-out example of development—including the live-work model of apartments above retail establishments—Serenbe hopes to change hearts and minds.

Food Systems

An important part of biophilia is reconnecting people with their food supply. As the local farm economy has disappeared over the past five or six decades, fresh, healthful foods have been replaced by nutritionally empty processed fare. One of Serenbe's main goals is to put people in touch with natural growing seasons and ensure they have good food to eat. We have an organic farm that produces more than three hundred varieties of fruits, vegetables, herbs, and flowers as well as a farmers market and other educational programs. There are community herb and medicinal gardens as well as fruit-bearing plants alongside paths and sidewalks. Five farm-to-table restaurants (with more planned) and multiple other food outlets give people a taste of fresh local produce and gourmet culinary experiences. Finally, we support a communitywide agrarian system with regional farms and value-added producers by partnering with state and national organizations like Rodale Institute, Georgia Organics, the Conservation Fund/Working Farms Fund, and American Farmland Trust. In coordination with these efforts, the Chattahoochee Hill Country Conservancy is developing a model to reestablish a local agrarian economy.

Education

Much evidence shows that children learn best when they are exposed to nature and natural environments. Unlike traditional schools, which operate like a factory with bells, strict schedules, and enclosed classrooms, Serenbe has taken a biophilic approach to education—helping children learn through exposure to nature. Terra School at Serenbe is a Montessori-style STEAM-based school. And the public Chatt Hills Charter School, which is a close neighbor to Serenbe, teaches a rigorous curriculum that integrates the wonders of the natural world. Both campuses' designs blend indoor and outdoor learning spaces and are inspired by the teachings of Richard Louv, author of *Last Child in the Woods*. Best of all, parents and the community in general are deeply engaged in the education of Serenbe's children.

Starting out, I was just doing what I felt was right for my family and community. But as the plans for Serenbe began to unfold, it became clear that biophilia best described what was at the heart of my inspiration. Today, Serenbe is a model for biophilic design. In fact, we believed the principles were so vital that we helped establish the nonprofit Biophilic Institute, whose mission is to educate people on the principles of biophilia and share how they can be implemented in anyone's communities.

All of this works. The people living here are thriving. Their health is stabilizing. They are losing excess weight and getting fit. They are making friends and enjoying a vibrant new social life. Their kids are happy and healthy. Serenbe isn't just a place to live; it's a lifestyle changer. People move here and find that the problems created (or at least exacerbated) by the dysfunctional built environment they came from begin to fade away. I could not be prouder of this place, the people who built it, and the families who call it home.

Best of all, our people are highly engaged in making Serenbe the best community it can be. When they see a need (such as a better school), they step up and fill it. They don't want to outsource their relationships with their children, their elders, and the natural world itself. They know these are the things that make life worth living. And they know, from experience, that their efforts make a powerful difference. Serenbe serves as a testament to how thoughtful planning and intentional design can inspire people to connect and bring out their best selves.

Before we move on to the "how to" part of the book, I'd like to assert that Serenbe is a viable model—not just for the well-off but for people in any economic strata. Real places can be built or improved by applying some of what my incredible team and I have learned over the past two decades. Lives can be reset and immeasurably improved by inviting nature into our lives, in many initially small but transformative ways. (It started with my backyard; it can start with your flower boxes.) Environments can be meaningfully altered by understanding how local decisions are made and getting to know the people who make them. The lessons of Serenbe can be applied to people living in different environments, with different resources, and different traditions and tastes.

People sometimes deride Serenbe as a "utopia" because sadly, places where people know, support, and regularly connect with their neighbors have disappeared over the last hundred years—making Serenbe unique by today's standards. But biophilic living makes far more sense than how most people live: hiding away in their self-imposed compounds and cutting themselves off from the woods, the gardens, and the streams. Buying into this approach doesn't require some great leap of faith. It merely takes common sense. We want and need to be close to nature and to each other. And when we are, it positively benefits all parts of our lives. I'm eager to share these principles with you and to help you, your family, and your community achieve the well-being that is your birthright.

Chapter 3 QR Codes

**Businesses
QR Code 3.1**

4

Building a Community While Respecting Nature

My ancestors emigrated to the United States from Sweden in the mid-1800s, joining the pioneers who established farms along the Front Range of Boulder County in Colorado. I was the fifth generation to grow up on that land, surrounded by open vistas of the Rocky Mountains. Today, the fields, slopes, and streams I explored as a boy have been overtaken by the northern sprawl of Denver. Later on, during my career as a restaurateur, I opened an eatery in a historic building in Roswell, Georgia, a small town north of Atlanta. In 1975, I drove through miles of countryside to reach it. Today, Atlanta's relentless sprawl has consumed that farmland, erasing the distinctions between Roswell and the surrounding suburbs. Chances are, you have similar recollections.

Experiences like these highlight how swiftly natural landscapes can vanish. They help us understand the fragility of our rural paradises. The rolling hills, forests, plains, and pastures that we love—and that once defined entire regions of our country—can so quickly be replaced by asphalt and rows of indistinguishable structures.

The fact that so many green spaces are vanishing is a problem, because spending time in nature does us good, mentally and physically (more on that later). The truth is, many Americans are chronically disconnected from the natural world. Often, this isn't entirely our fault—to some extent, we are all products of our (largely manmade) environments.

I'd like to share a brief (but far from comprehensive) list of reasons why so many people in our society are disconnected from nature:

- **We spend more time indoors than ever.** According to one oft-cited survey funded by the EPA, Americans spend 87 percent of their time indoors, plus about 6 percent in a vehicle.[1] Some of this is by necessity; after all, many people go to school or work indoors, which takes them out of the natural world for eight or more hours a day. But even in our downtime, many of us gravitate toward indoor environments, whether we're shopping, exercising, socializing, or relaxing.

- **And often, we're focused on our screens.** You'd have to be living under a rock (which, incidentally, would be out in nature) not to know how pervasive our smartphones, tablets, TVs, gaming systems, and other gadgets are. But the numbers might still surprise you: Worldwide, internet users spend almost seven hours each day online, which adds up to over seventeen years of one's adult life.[2] I'm not saying you shouldn't scroll social media, send an email, or check your bank balance while you're sitting on a park bench, for instance. I'm saying that focusing on a screen will inevitably pull your attention away from the green space around you and might blunt some of the "nature benefits" you'd otherwise receive.

- **More people live in urban rather than rural areas.** According to the Census Bureau, around 80 percent of Americans live in urban areas, which are defined as "densely developed residential, commercial, and other nonresidential areas."[3] While some urban areas have more green space than others, for many people the natural environment just isn't present (or at least, easily accessible) in everyday life. Many communities unintentionally limit access to green space with a lack of sidewalks, busy streets, uninviting spaces, or no natural areas set aside for recreational or leisure use. Nature seems to be an optional amenity or even a luxury, rather than a beneficial public service, in many highly developed areas.

- **Most of us don't live in walkable environments.** Because of the way our communities are designed, most people rely on vehicles to get from place to place. Whether we're driving an automobile or using public transportation, we're inside a metal box hurtling down a strip of asphalt or a set of tracks. Odds are, we're traveling from one paved parking lot to another and will enter a building immediately after arrival. Where in this equation is the opportunity to engage with nature?

All of this disconnection from nature has taken a massive toll.

Richard Louv, author of *Last Child in the Woods*, *The Nature Principle* (which features a chapter about Serenbe), and *Our Wild Calling*, calls this disconnection "nature-deficit disorder." He says a lack of time spent in the natural world affects our ability to find meaning in life and reduces our awareness of the world around us. In particular, Louv's work highlights how highly structured environments—both social and physical—can adversely affect children's brain development, imagination, problem-solving, and emotional resilience. We'll take a closer look at nature-deficit disorder and how it impacts children in chapter 10.

What Are the Benefits of Being More Connected to Nature?

If you saw yourself in the descriptions above, you might be thinking, *Okay, it's true that I don't spend much time in nature—especially without distractions. But is this so-called "nature-deficit disorder" really having that big an impact on my life?*

Well . . . yes. When people and communities are disconnected from nature, they are losing out on a myriad of potential benefits.

On an individual level, being connected to nature has far-reaching positive effects on physical and mental health. For instance, being in nature can improve mood, lower anxiety, reduce stress, improve memory, boost creativity, and regulate the nervous system. Over time, these benefits can help manage mental health conditions like PTSD and ADHD.[4] They can also lower risk or help manage chronic diseases. In fact, Richard Louv and Dr. Howard Frumkin (an internist, environmental and occupational medicine specialist, and epidemiologist at the University of Washington School of Public Health) assert, "increasingly the evidence suggests that people benefit so much from contact with nature that land conservation can now be viewed as a public health strategy."[5]

Nature Supercharges Your Exercise

You may think that exercise gives you the same benefits regardless of where you're working out, but that's not necessarily true! Movement done outdoors may bring greater benefits than the same action done indoors. For instance, one study found that cognitive function (such as attention and memory) is enhanced after an outdoor walk compared to an indoor one.[6]

Beyond the benefit to our bodies, on a community level, green space is good for business. Proximity to protected land and "conservation development," which seeks to leave as much land as possible in its natural state, attracts residents and businesses to communities, cuts development costs, and increases property value.[7] Contrary to popular belief, conserving the natural environment is not a financial negative. People commonly use excuses like "It costs too much" or "We can't afford it," but authorities on conservation development are proving otherwise. Consider the following:

- Using conservation development on eighty residential lots in Texas, grading costs were cut from $300,000 to $50,000.

Twenty-three of the twenty-four large oak trees that would otherwise have been cut down were saved.[8]

- One study that compared two subdivisions in Amherst, Massachusetts—one conventional and one built using conservation development—found that homes in the conservation development sold for an average of 13 percent more, even though lots in the conventional development were twice as large.[9]
- Serenbe has demonstrated the cost to both install and maintain infrastructure on clustered development is 40 percent of traditional sprawl development.

But the benefit expands far beyond us and our communities. On a global level, green space encourages appreciation, conservation, and protection of the natural world. When people don't spend time in nature, they might take it for granted, see it only as a resource to be consumed, or even believe it is inferior to manmade environments (this is known as biophobia). We are surrounded by the evidence of what happens when we don't prioritize the health of our planet, community, and backyard: global warming, pollution, unsustainable use of resources . . . the list goes on. The more people experience nature for themselves, the more they will appreciate it, understand the services it provides, and be motivated to protect it. We owe this to ourselves, and especially to future generations.

Throughout my life, I've been drawn to green space.

Growing up on a farm, nature was everywhere—it wasn't something I consciously thought about, much like the air we breathe or the natural rhythm of day turning to night. Nature was simply part of life, ever-present and inseparable from my surroundings. As a teenager, however, I found the open land on the farm began to represent work more than wonder, and I eagerly looked forward to leaving it behind. Yet even during those long, grueling days on our Colorado farm—just 20 miles from the Rocky Mountain foothills—pausing to take in the majesty of those rugged peaks rising from the plains was always a refreshing and grounding escape.

When I entered the workforce, I was eager to live in the city. Reflecting on my choices, though, I realize I was always drawn to urban areas with access to green spaces. My first apartments in Denver were near Cheesman Park. In St. Louis, I chose an apartment overlooking Gateway Arch National Park, and later, one near Forest Park. Over my many years in Atlanta, my homes—whether apartments or houses—were consistently near Piedmont Park.

When Marie and I decided on a home to raise our family, we chose to remodel a historic house in Ansley Park, a neighborhood renowned for its lush greenery, landscaped medians, open spaces, and numerous pocket parks. The neighborhood borders Piedmont Park's 200 acres on one side and Peachtree Street's vibrant mix of restaurants, museums, and cultural venues on the other. It was the perfect place to call home—until we bought the farm.

Looking back, I now recognize how deeply nature influenced my sense of well-being, even when I wasn't consciously aware of it. Cities across the country provide incredible opportunities to live near urban green spaces, but we need to prioritize making these spaces accessible to all. Every neighborhood deserves green spaces within walking distance, ensuring that nature remains an integral part of our lives, no matter where we live.

Scan QR code 4.1 at the end of this chapter to see a full-color image of Serenbe's master plan.

What Serenbe Is Doing Differently

As I shared in chapter 2, my family bought and moved to a farm in the woods, then decided to invite others to join us in creating the community of Serenbe. Our reasoning was at once simple and complex: Being immersed in nature changed our lives. We wanted to preserve the benefits we had found in this new lifestyle and invite others into the same transformative experience.

As part of its biophilic ethos, Serenbe incorporates nature as an integral part of the community. Nature is something that people organically experience as a part of daily life here—not something "out there" that they need to go visit. Various types of green space—often predating development—are integrated into Serenbe's city design. People live, work, and play in the outdoors. Even in residential and commercial areas they can see and touch plants and trees. They might hear birdsong or spot a lizard. They might walk on a wooded trail or cross a pond to get from one place to another. As described in chapter 8, they can see (and maybe even participate in) their produce being grown.

Here are a few ways we've helped to ensure that nature and green space are a natural part of life in Serenbe.

Go 70-30 on Land Use

Traditional development models encourage and even rely on sprawl. Unfortunately, in this outdated way of developing, natural features are amended or erased entirely to make way for manicured residential lots and heavily built-up commercial districts—all of which are connected by an ever-growing network of roads, peppered with paved parking areas, and feature very few, if any, sidewalks.

Aerial view of Serenbe.

At Serenbe, we've gone in the opposite direction. We adhere to a 70-30 development model that preserves 70 percent of the land and develops 30 percent. This percentage split has been codified in the zoning laws of our city, Chattahoochee Hills, and has proven to be a fantastic balance between land preservation and economic return. (Traditionally, the preservationists and developers are at odds.)

In Serenbe and the surrounding Chattahoochee Hills area, the preserved 70 percent of land can be used for agriculture or recreation or can be kept completely natural—all of which adds greater value to the developed land. We also strive to achieve as much preservation as possible within our developed areas by leaving nature in place and building around it. (I'll share a few examples of this later in the chapter.)

Serenbe's 30 percent of developed areas are high-density and clustered. When newcomers hear those words, negative associations often spring to mind. I've received many comments like "Doesn't it feel crowded? Don't residents want more space? I don't think I would enjoy being crammed in so close to neighbors and businesses."

But the truth is, our clustered high-density development brings numerous benefits:

- Because homes and commercial areas are clustered close to one another, we have been able to design our community so that every home has access to some part of our preserved 70 percent. Each of Serenbe's neighborhoods opens up to nature, whether that's a preserved forest, a wildflower meadow, a pond, a pasture, or our organic farm. Residents can see, step out into, and stay connected with the natural world. Most say they would never want to trade that access for a bigger private lot.
- Clustered high-density development facilitates several of Serenbe's other priorities, like fostering human connection and incorporating fitness into everyday life. (We'll look more closely at these elements in future chapters.)

- As Serenbe grows, we're finding that clustered high-density development is attracting a steady stream of (surprisingly diverse) new residents. For instance, many younger people are drawn to the convenience and eco-friendliness of our walkable community—in fact, some are even choosing not to own a car. Likewise, as aging baby boomers lose the ability or the desire to drive, they too are gravitating toward our walkable community.

- We don't need to sacrifice the number of homes for nature preservation. In fact, due to density, Serenbe can accommodate 20 percent more housing per square mile than most traditional development styles.

- As Serenbe continues to grow, it is estimated that we will save 60 percent of the development costs of installing and maintaining roads, utilities, and other infrastructure, versus spreading this development out over 80+ percent of the land in a traditional "sprawl" model. It is common sense when you think about it.

Have You Considered Cluster Communities?

If you've visited the English countryside, you probably noticed that most villages are densely clustered and tend to have "hard" edges (i.e., there's a fairly clear line between buildings and countryside). Most also include a community gathering place (like a pub) and footpaths. This contrasts with many towns and cities in the United States, where development is more spread out and buildings follow the roads out of town. In some areas, one town blends into the next without clear delineation between the two.

Serenbe was the first community developed under Chatta-hoochee Hills' innovative zoning, modeled after English villages to cluster development, preserve open land, and naturally integrate homes, businesses, and nature into a walkable, connected environment.

Don't Fight the Natural Flow

Traditional development tends to mold nature to fit humans' needs and desires—and when that's not possible, developers work around (or simply obliterate)—nature.

Again, Serenbe took the opposite approach. We try to minimize disturbance and contour the development to the land. The goal is to maintain natural beauty while building modern infrastructure. When you look at Serenbe from the ground or from the air, it's still primarily a forest. You can clearly see that we have placed buildings and roads in relationship with nature, rather than "allowing" nature to exist around them. Our philosophy is "We build with nature, not against it."

Here are a few tactics we've used to do so:

- **Integrating streams.** The "accepted" development rule is to place roads and footpaths on ridges and other elevated areas in order to avoid streams and other bodies of water, and to claim the best views for a few chosen homesites. I see this as turning your back to ecology, thereby removing natural water features from most people's everyday lives. Instead, Serenbe brings people to ecology by inviting them to interact with our streams and ponds via paths and bridges. In fact, bridges are often the shortest route between two points.

- **Keeping hills instead of grading the land flat.** Our first civil engineer wanted to flatten some of the hills and fill the valleys, because that's how traditional development has done things for the last several decades. This approach provides a flat area for utilities to be installed, flat pads for homes to be built on, and flat surfaces for trucks and equipment to get to the site easily. Maybe it's efficient, but I said, "Boring!" Plus, making these changes to the topography destroys the land. Instead, I explained that I wanted to maintain the natural elevation by building steeper roads and retaining walls where necessary.

Eventually Serenbe executed on this new vision—but not without overcoming challenges. For instance, when we discovered that grading a hill to the required 12 percent grade would cause habitat loss, loss of mature trees, erosion, and runoff to the stream below, we applied for and were granted a two-foot variance to a 14 percent grade. When the road was completed, the grade ended up being 15 percent—and is very natural and easy to navigate—plus we managed to avoid heavy earth cuts and additional tree removal. A definite win in my biophilic world!

Side note: In my career as an "accidental developer," I've found that there is often an acceptable solution after you're initially told, "It can't be done." The key is to stop, question, think, and push the limits instead of blindly following the rules. At the time, I naively didn't understand the traditional development "rules," but that turned out to be an asset. It allowed me to think outside the box and challenge practices I saw as destructive. Sometimes, approaching something you know nothing about can be an advantage, because ignorance of the usual constraints might open the door to creative solutions rather than hold you back.

- **Preserving mature trees.** When developing Serenbe, we tried to save as many trees as possible instead of clearing each landscaped area and starting from scratch. Engineers and builders advised against it, especially when it came to saving trees within five feet of a foundation. They warned that I would spend a fortune removing dead trees near buildings, but as I write this book those trees are now past the first decade of when the land was disturbed, and only 3 percent have been lost. Again, the key was to step back and ask questions.

- **Using an omega-shaped layout for the first three hamlets.** Traditional development has designed toward grids. But when you consider the geometry of nature, how often do you find grids?

Very rarely. Grids lead to gridlock, not flow. I'd challenge you to find your shape in nature.

If you look at a map of Serenbe, you'll see that each of our first three hamlets is organized around a main street with an omega shape. (If it's been a while since you studied the Greek alphabet, omega is the final letter and resembles a horseshoe.) When compared to a traditional street grid pattern, Serenbe's omega-shaped organization requires minimal land disturbances and allows the community to reserve larger areas of undeveloped green space. Since omegas consist of curves, this layout enabled our clustered development to follow naturally with the topography. This would not have been possible if we had committed ourselves to developing in straight lines, which would have required us to destroy natural features to make way for roads and buildings.

What's more, omegas have an interior space that naturally forms each hamlet's "nucleated center." (You can think of the nucleated center as a modern version of an old English village green.) The nucleated center of each hamlet is occupied by some type of green space, which differs for each neighborhood. For instance, a lake occupies the inner curve of our Grange neighborhood. Mado is centered around a wetland and stormwater pond, while Selborne features a stream and forest. Each hamlet's central green space serves as a gathering place for its residents and visitors, as well as a beautiful natural setting for the footpaths that crisscross our community.

Clearing the Air, Naturally

Arborguard Tree Specialists determined that the saved trees at Serenbe remove 1,484.01 tons of pollution a year from the air. This documentation helps explain why, among Serenbe's more than three hundred children, there is not one report of asthma—practically unheard of in an American community this size. I have also spoken to seniors who have relocated to Serenbe because of our improved air quality.

Ditch Your Lawn

For many people, landscaping is the most commonly encountered type of green space. Grass lawns are one of the "given" features in American residential areas—but perhaps they shouldn't be. They aren't good for the environment or our health, and they are an outdated concept. Here are a few reasons why:

- **Grass lawns are harmful to the environment** . . . Decorative grass itself isn't a native plant and often requires fertilizer, herbicides, and pesticides (not to mention weekly lawnmowing) to thrive and look its "best." Unfortunately, these chemicals also harm wildlife, any remaining native vegetation, and the overall ecosystem.

- **. . . And to our health.** All the chemicals we use for beautiful lawns can't be good for us if the landscaper is legally required to put up a sign warning you and your pet not to walk on the grass for twenty-four hours. But even if you stay off the grass, how much of those chemicals get into the air? The groundwater? What if, despite your efforts, your dog walks across that lawn, comes into your house, and lies on your couch? According to the EPA, "several types of cancer, immuno-response deficiencies, neurological diseases, and birth defects have been associated with exposure to lawn chemicals."[10] Is a manicured green lawn really worth it?

- **They are surprisingly wasteful.** Lawns often take a large amount of potable water to irrigate. According to the EPA, "nationwide, landscape irrigation is estimated to account for nearly one-third of all residential water use, totaling nearly 9 billion gallons per day."[11] This is a tremendous waste, especially in drought-prone areas. The EPA also estimates that in 2018, for example, yard trimmings totaling 35.4 million tons accounted for 12.1 percent of all municipal solid waste.[12]

- **Grass lawns push out native perennials, pollinator-friendly plants, and edible landscaping.** This deprives native species of habitats and food sources and drives away natural predators of pesty bugs (like mosquitos).

• **Grass lawns don't exactly enhance our quality of life.** Anyone who has ever had to block out half a Saturday for some "quality" time with a mower, weed trimmer, and leaf blower knows: Maintaining lawns is time consuming, often uncomfortable, and the work never really ends. What's more, lawn-maintenance equipment (especially the dirty gas-powered vehicles and tools) create noise and air pollution in the neighborhood.

Given all these downsides to grass lawns, Serenbe has taken a different approach. The landscaping, thoughtfully designed with native perennials, pollinator-friendly plants, and edible greenery, blends seamlessly into the streetscape. In fact, visitors often need a few moments to pinpoint what is different about our community. The natural integration is so harmonious that the traditional green lawn around a house would feel out of place.

This saves our community money because less water is used to irrigate, and since native species have evolved to thrive here, there is no need to spray with pesticides. Residents appreciate that with no grass to mow, they spend relatively little time maintaining their yards (which, as I mentioned earlier, are fairly small due to Serenbe's clustered development). Plus, our neighborhoods are more peaceful due to the lack of lawnmower and leaf blower noise pollution.

What Communities Can Do to Increase Green Space and Bring People Closer to Nature

Please don't think that you need to develop a community from scratch to integrate green spaces (and their many benefits) into everyday living. Any existing community can begin to greenify itself, as Serenbe has done from the start, with some small starting steps.

Landscape with Native Perennials and Edible Plants

To build a greener community, always start in your own yard. If you currently have a grass lawn, think about how you can start transforming it to be healthier and more ecofriendly. Add in some native plants and edible plants—especially those that are pollinator friendly. If HOA regulations restrict such changes, think about starting a conversation to educate and raise awareness around the risks of traditional landscape practices. Remember, talking is the best way to share ideas and change minds. One voice, addressing one issue at a time, can make a difference.

"Daylight" Your Stormwater to Restore Nature

Imagine for a moment how the raindrop that falls on your roof finds its way to the local tributary and river. Few can visualize this network within our developed areas because watercourses are often buried below ground. We often don't see or think about them. Daylighting is the process of bringing these buried streams back to life by physically uncovering and restoring them. Many communities are taking this action to revitalize their urban waterways. By incorporating innovative stormwater management solutions that serve both functional and recreational purposes—for instance, creating a public park that features a stormwater retention pond or building a greenway trail that runs alongside a stream—these communities are connecting people with the land and the water.

If you're developing a new community, plan to incorporate existing waterways and stormwater management into the design. For example, at Serenbe we ask for each landscape plan to create bioswales that retain as much stormwater as possible on site. (We'll look more closely at Serenbe's stormwater management system and at how communities can begin the daylighting process in chapter 5.)

Create Pro-Nature City Codes

Most cities prioritize regulations for automobile traffic and parking, but few focus on creating spaces that prioritize pedestrians and integrate natural ecosystems. Ask your municipal representatives to consider creating new pro-nature city codes that can apply to all future development. Point out the physical, mental, ecological, and financial benefits of developing with nature top-of-mind, which are listed in this chapter and throughout the book. Here are two types of codes to consider:

1. **Form-based codes (FBCs)** regulate the physical form of the built environment rather than solely focusing on land use. These codes foster vibrant, walkable communities by encouraging mixed-use development, which reduces the need for driving and promotes pedestrian activity. The fewer roads, parking lots, and other features of sprawl that are necessary, the more nature can be preserved—and the closer connection citizens will have with it.

2. **Street connectivity standards** further support pedestrian-friendly neighborhoods by requiring interconnected streets, pathways, and walkways. These features create accessible and walkable environments that encourage exploration, reduce travel distances, and enhance community interaction. Adding pocket parks, greenways, and urban trails that link homes, businesses, and public spaces transforms neighborhoods into inviting, natural spaces for people rather than vehicles. Additionally, minimizing dead-end streets and cul-de-sacs improves movement and connectivity and—once again—reduces development's incursion into nature.

Beautify Your Neighborhood with Edible Plants

Ask your local governments to start landscaping the community with edible plants rather than ornamental plants. Blueberry bushes, fig trees, and even perennial herbs are wonderful examples of edible landscaping that help create community as people come to understand growing seasons, anticipate harvests, and graze while visiting with neighbors.

"Greenify" Your Schoolyards

Find ways to make the front yard of your school greener and more engaging to the public by planting (you guessed it!) native perennials, or even a food forest full of edible plants and herbs for the community. This can be done during the summer and during non-school hours to minimize disruption. A few other kid-friendly ideas include:

- Create a butterfly or pollinator garden that students can plant and maintain. Native flowering plants can attract bees, butter-flies, and other pollinators while teaching students about bio-diversity. Even if a school doesn't have space for an in-ground garden bed, you can create a "pocket" pollinator garden with raised beds, or even large planters.
- Create a "forest corner" in your playground. Depending on the space you have to work with, you might include logs, tree stumps, and large rocks of various sizes for kids to climb on. (Talk to your local power company to source some of these materials; they are always cutting trees!) If possible, plant some living trees in your forest corner, too.

Start a Campaign for Dark Sky Regulations

Okay, so it's not exactly green, but looking up at the night sky is still a fantastic way to feel more connected to the natural world. There's something awe-inspiring about gazing at the stars and thinking about our place in the universe. On a less philosophical level, cutting down on light pollution can improve our sleep quality, is beneficial to wildlife, and can reduce energy consumption. Enacting dark sky regulations—which restrict the amount of light that is directed upwards at night—is something that entire neighborhoods and cities can commit to, but even individual homeowners can make beneficial changes like selecting outdoor fixtures that direct light downward, using dimmer bulbs, and utilizing timers or motion sensors.

Preserving green space is a crucial component of creating a biophilic community (or even a more biophilic backyard). As I shared at the beginning of this chapter, watching beloved fields, forests, and other natural features be overtaken by manmade construction can be a disheartening, unpleasant experience.

That said, we humans will always have a need to build homes, commercial centers, gathering places, and more. In this chapter, we looked at how to protect and prioritize nature as new and existing communities are developed. In the next two chapters, we'll look more closely at how to approach the built environment—both systems and structures—in a way that's sensitive to the natural world.

Chapter 4 QR Codes

**Master Plan
QR Code 4.1**

5

Commonsense Energy and Water Usage

We all know our planet only has so many resources to offer. Once they are gone, there's no getting them back. But too often, people view conservation as a "cause" that exists separately from our day-to-day lives. They think of it as a political issue, a news story on a global conservation summit, an Earth Day celebration, or a yearly check written to a nonprofit organization.

But what if the 8.2 billion people on Earth, or even just the 350 million or so people in the United States, shifted our mindset? What if we started looking at conserving through the lens of the choices we make in our own backyard in the same way we balance our monthly spending? The cumulative impact of our choices around energy and water usage would make an immense impact on our efforts to preserve the gifts of Earth—and give us more monthly spending money. Younger people understand the personal and global value of reducing our energy demand and will be looking for these features in their future homes, so this effort is also about creating and preserving home value.

What I'm saying is this: Communities need to lead the way. As better options arise, we should aggressively use them so that we and future generations can live in health and comfort.

I'm not pretending that Serenbe is perfect. However, we are trying to get better every day. We continue to use and seek commonsense solutions to help preserve our natural resources. We are moving away from fossil fuels, identifying ways to offset our carbon footprint, and building toward a net-zero community. Before we get to the solutions, let's look at some of the problems we see around our planet's limited resources and many communities' unsustainable methods of managing them:

- **Traditional energy sources harm and pollute the environment.** The burning of fossil fuels releases dangerous greenhouse gas emissions into the atmosphere. Clean energy solutions keep air cleaner and support human life and wildlife.

- **We have a finite amount of fossil fuels.** We carelessly use resources like oil and natural gas to fuel our lives as if we had an unlimited supply. Once they are gone, they cannot be replenished. We can do better.

- **There is only so much water to support life on our planet.** As climate change continues to impact the Earth, water may become scarce (or scarcer) in a growing number of regions. Many parts of the world already lack a consistent, adequate supply.

- **Traditional stormwater systems wreak havoc on our streams, tributaries, and topsoil.** The traditional way of managing stormwater has been to remove it from an improved site by locating drains around the property and funneling the water to hard-surface pipes. This allows the water to flow to fenced retention ponds or directly to tributaries within urban and suburban areas. This management system is highly destructive to our urban and suburban streams. As dirty water builds speed in the pipes, it crashes forcefully into natural water systems leading to both erosion and pollution. Instead of adding to the beauty of the area, these polluted streams become eyesores and dumping grounds for tires, old batteries, and trash. It costs cities millions to clean up these areas.

- **Traditional waste management systems are harmful, too.** Conventional waste management involves digging trenches throughout the landscape for large tunnels to carry human waste great distances. It is then processed with chemicals in a fashion that further pollutes our waterways. In addition to harming the environment, these systems are also visually unappealing. Finally, traditional wastewater contributes to sprawl; miles and miles of pipe systems enable people to live farther away from the urban center.

Clearly there is much room for improvement—and the good news is that many of us are up to the task. More and more people are beginning to understand that poor resource management is creating terrible consequences for us and for the generations to come. That said, why is there not an overwhelming demand for (or at least significant interest in) reducing energy usage and conserving our water supply nationwide?

The answer lies in our human tendency to thoughtlessly adhere to the status quo. At one point in time we had logical reasons to use fossil fuels; they were an efficient, cheap, and plentiful resource. This is no longer the case. Today fossil fuels are more expensive than alternative sources of energy and we now know that burning them releases many pollutants that threaten our environment and our health.

We're at an inflection point. Will we course-correct, or will we continue down a road that leads to the planet's destruction? I feel encouraged, not only due to what we have accomplished at Serenbe, but because of what I see and hear from others around our country who are working toward positive change.

Over the past few decades, the demand for energy efficiency and green building has been on the rise. While Serenbe was at the forefront of this sustainability movement since its inception in the early 2000s, the Great Recession of 2008 kickstarted a national trend toward building smaller, more energy-efficient homes. Home buyers began to look for smarter designs that made better use of space, reflecting both the economic restraints of the time and people's changing lifestyle preferences. Developers and homeowners alike began focusing on environmentally friendly buildings, and during this time LEED certification and other green building standards became increasingly popular.

The movement is gaining even more momentum today, as younger buyers and decision makers are increasingly requesting energy efficiency and certification. At the same time, most national commercial real estate companies—who are now all aware of the benefits of LEED certification—are divesting from or devaluing buildings on their balance sheets that are not green certified in some form.

The choice is ours. We can maintain the status quo or start changing how we design and build. There is no time like the present to do what's best for our communities and planet. Let's take a look at the choices Serenbe is making.

How Serenbe Supports Conservation

Serenbe is doing its part to support conservation while setting a great example for other communities to follow. In addition to making our homes and our buildings as energy efficient as possible, we have found ways to collect and use stormwater and to rethink wastewater management, and have taken other steps to reduce our environmental footprint. Here are some of our approaches.

Constructed Wetlands Treat Wastewater Without Chemicals

Back when I was exploring how conventional methods of wastewater treatment would impact the Chattahoochee Hill Country, I realized that once these tunnels for human waste were created, new development could lay claim to a connection anywhere along the corridors. This would compromise the clustered villages I envisioned for the Chattahoochee Hill Country and Serenbe. Fulton County, our local county government, had already designed a complete grid system of these pipes so that they would be ready to develop this 40,000-acre area—and they had even sold bonds to pay for it! Just this one choice would create massive sprawl. To defend against this, we developed our own wastewater management system.

Fast-forward to today: Serenbe now employs a cutting-edge decentralized wastewater collection, natural treatment, and reuse system that supports our commitment to water conservation and stewardship. Designed by Biohabitats, a conservation planning and ecological restoration firm based out of New Mexico, the system uses constructed wetlands to move wastewater through various cells into sand filters without any chemicals. Once the water has been processed this way, we reuse it for irrigation in the community. This system is the first of its kind in the eight Southern states that make up the EPA's Region 4. (Side note: Serenbe's wastewater system is far from the only choice. Look back at chapter 3 for more biophilic wastewater management options that communities can use.)

Beyond building for function, we decided to make a statement about what wastewater management can look like. It doesn't have to be ugly and industrial. On the contrary, it can be *beautiful*. Serenbe shared the engineering plans with Reed Hilderbrand landscape architectural firm to develop a visual plan for the treatment plant area. Some treatment cells contain specified plant material. There are also sand and gravel pits that remain bare. The firm engineered a boardwalk to pass across the middle of the treatment center. Today, this area is one of the most highly photographed locations in Serenbe, creating a stunning backdrop for wedding, prom, and family photoshoots alike.

However, Serenbe's beloved boardwalk wouldn't be here today if we hadn't questioned the status quo. When the system was first built, we were told we would need a six-foot chain-link fence surrounding the treatment site. I asked why. After all, I pointed out, there was no standing water and no dangerous chemicals posing a threat to people or wildlife. Eventually we were able to get the fence requirement removed, allowing people to fully enjoy the picturesque area. When we take a step back to consider "how we've always done it" we can make life better for everyone.

Boardwalk across constructed wetland of the environmental wastewater treatment center at Serenbe. *Photo by Mia Yakel.*

Leveraging Natural Stormwater Management Infrastructure

Natural landscapes retain water on their own. However, when we disturb the land and add manmade surfaces, the ground's ability to retain water is greatly compromised. Unless retention methods are re-created, the water builds up force and causes damage as it flows to lower levels.

Therefore, the goal with stormwater management is to slow the water down in a more natural way. At Serenbe, we have designed mechanisms that allow us to collect our stormwater in bioretention swales throughout the community. Pipes run through these swales at different angles, so the water seeps out slowly through the earth and the plant matter. By the time it reaches the streams and waterways, it has been cleaned and slowed down to prevent damage and erosion.

Here are alternative ways Serenbe manages rainwater:

- **Rain gardens:** These appear to be landscape islands separating parking areas on the street, but they serve an important function beyond aesthetics: to capture and filter stormwater in underground pits.

- **Bioswales:** Rainwater that has not flowed into the rain garden tanks travels through engineered bioswales that continue to slow the water down for filtration and cleansing on the way to the nearby tributaries. These bioswales can be found in the woods and along the paths in Selborne. In Grange, the bioretention swales are planted with a variety of edible plants, including blueberry bushes, apple trees, fig bushes, and muscadine grape vines.
- **Engineered wetlands:** From the bioswales, rainwater flows into engineered wetlands situated along Serenbe's trail system. The natural landscape of these wetlands creates an amenity for residents to enjoy.
- **Pervious pavers:** Serenbe uses pervious pavers along many of its sidewalks and in its courtyards to channel stormwater into the root systems of the nearby plants.

Improving stormwater management infrastructure is one of the easiest things cities can change as they seek to become more environmentally responsible—especially as existing infrastructure breaks down in older cities and needs to be replaced.

Scan QR code 5.1 at the end of this chapter to see examples of stormwater management.

Build a Watershed Oasis in Your Community

Many watershed departments own great amounts of land simply to handle stormwater. Often, these aging plants are outdated, fenced from public use, and not environmentally friendly. But some communities are coordinating efforts between their stormwater and parks departments to convert watersheds to beautiful parks that are amenities for the community. These innovative approaches manage runoff more effectively than underground pipes while also creating enhanced recreational opportunities that connect people to nature and each other. Here are a few success stories:

- In Atlanta, the Historic Fourth Ward Park's two-acre stormwater pond is surrounded by rain gardens, bioswales, and permeable surfaces that are designed to enhance the park's beauty. It serves as a focal point for recreational activities, walking paths, and scenic views, blending infrastructure with public use.
- Also in Atlanta, the Beltline incorporates stormwater features like bioswales and retention ponds in a trail network that connects neighborhoods and parks.
- For the past several years, Los Angeles has transformed the concrete ditch that channels the Los Angeles River into a linear bioretention park. It is becoming an urban oasis of free-flowing water, wildlife, bridges, pocket parks, and walking and bike paths.
- The 11th Street Bridge Park in Washington, DC, combines stormwater management with public green spaces, walking trails, and educational opportunities along the Anacostia River.
- Mill River Park in Stamford, Connecticut, daylighted a section of the Mill River, transforming it into a vibrant park with walking trails, restored habitats, and improved flood control.

Plus, many college campuses are daylighting their stormwater routes. Ask your city parks and watershed departments to work together to daylight your forgotten or neglected waterways. It may help to remind municipal representatives that these initiatives improve mental health, enhance quality of life, and cultivate a stronger sense of place. Plus, turning an eyesore into a green oasis can attract new residents to the area. The improved tax base can help pay for these upgrades!

Structures Built According to EarthCraft Standards

Serenbe is an EarthCraft-certified community, which means that every home and building has earned a certification. As with all communities that embrace green building, our residents enjoy environmental, health, and economic benefits through reduced energy and water use, improved indoor air quality, and lower utility bills.

In 1999, Southface and the Greater Atlanta Home Builders Association developed the EarthCraft high-performance building certification program to address the energy, water, and climate conditions of the Southeast. EarthCraft standards provide a practical blueprint for green building and sustainable development. They maximize indoor air quality, reduce moisture and the potential of mold, maintain comfortable temperatures, and help homeowners or renters save money on utility bills. On average, EarthCraft homes are 30 percent more energy efficient than other homes. They also help conserve water through highly efficient fixtures.

How to Protect Your Home from Energy Loss

Energy-efficient homes save money in the short term and over time. Here are two steps you can take to get started.

Seal your home to prevent energy loss. To conserve energy and lower your power bill, make sure your house is not a leaky sieve. To reduce the amount of air that seeps in and out of your home, insulate your windows, attics, floorboards, and so on. Otherwise you'll be paying to heat or cool the air space around your house.

Try solar or geothermal power. Once you have a tight seal for your house, geothermal energy (which is most efficient for new construction) and solar power are energy savers you might consider. While there may be an initial added cost to install geothermal or solar, it tends to be offset by projected energy savings. When geothermal and solar power systems are financed, monthly savings (as compared to a traditional energy system) are often greater than the interest and principal payments. This means that the energy-efficient system is cash flow positive in month one of homeownership. Plus any local, state, or federal tax rebates make this a logical, commonsense decision.

Side note: If you live in an older home and determine that geothermal is cost-prohibitive or undesirable for another reason, consider installing a heat pump when it is time to replace your HVAC system. Heat pumps tend to be the more energy-efficient choice. If you're not ready or able to switch from an HVAC system to a heat pump, there are also grant programs to help improve (and create quieter) HVAC systems that communities can take advantage of. These programs, which can offer local and national tax incentives to help lower the costs of HVAC systems, are ever changing. Always check with your power company and your income tax advisers for the most current information.

While EarthCraft certification is only available in the southeast region of the United States, there are many other certifications, including LEED, Energy Star, and more. To learn about some of the other certification options in the States and abroad, scan QR code 5.2 at the end of this chapter.

Electric Vehicle–Friendly Homes and Electric Landscaping

Every house is designed to make it easy to install EV chargers in the garage or carport, on parking pads, or along the curb in front of the house. EV charging stations are also located throughout each neighborhood. Additionally, Serenbe has transitioned from gas-powered landscaping maintenance equipment to electric maintenance equipment.

Geothermal Heating and Cooling in All Homes and Structures

Geothermal is a renewable energy system that takes advantage of reservoirs of water found a few hundred feet below the Earth's surface. These reservoirs remain at a relatively constant temperature of around 50°–60°F (10°–16°C) year-round. I was initially interested in geothermal energy due to its lack of noise and visual pollution when compared to large, loud air compressors. But soon I discovered that there are many other benefits. The most obvious are the financial savings (which I mentioned earlier in this chapter) and environmental impact: geothermal can yield a 50 percent or more reduction in energy usage and utility bill savings, while also reducing carbon emissions.

The other important benefit of geothermal energy is that it is one way to get us much closer to self-sufficiency. In the United States, our energy grid is divided into three interrelated systems. If an event—whether caused by an act of nature, vandalism, or cybersecurity hack—impacts a section of the grid, it can short out the entire network, leaving us all vulnerable. Geothermal energy puts us one step closer to energy independence and the security that comes with it by significantly reducing energy consumption. The next step in that chain is to combine alternative energy sources like solar with battery storage, enabling true independence from the grid in regional failures.

Despite geothermal's benefits, we encountered multiple roadblocks and general resistance when trying to move Serenbe toward using 100 percent geothermal energy. (For example, we could not get banks to fund spec buildings that included geothermal because appraisers do not tend to recognize geothermal as a feature that increases the value of the house, despite its benefits.) We soon realized that the only way to make geothermal mandatory was to form and fund our own utility company to install and support all of the community's geothermal HVAC systems.

To learn about many of the obstacles communities face when trying to move to geothermal energy, scan QR code 5.3 at the end of this chapter.

Solar Power Capability

Once a home is EarthCraft certified and uses geothermal, the resident has reduced their demand for energy by about 65 to 70 percent. At this point, it makes good fiscal sense to consider adding alternative energy, like wind or solar, to get closer to net zero. For example, a 2,300-square-foot house with EarthCraft and geothermal might only need one-third of the solar panels required for a "typical" home. Most roofs for houses that size have the space to accommodate a solar array.

Dr. Phillip J. Tabb did sun studies at Serenbe to help optimize our solar capabilities. Based on the studies, we ultimately planned neighborhood layouts in such a way that when trees were cleared for foundations along the omega formations throughout the community, it also opened clear paths to southern sun exposure. (Southern sun exposure is necessary for optimum solar energy generation.) Incorporating additional renewable energy sources into the community is Serenbe's next step. Serenbe's future neighborhoods have the capability to be 100 percent solar, with homes designed and optimized for solar panels that can be added by buyers.

While geothermal and solar power are two major energy sources in Serenbe, they are far from the only sustainable and ecofriendly options. Look back at chapter 3 for a breakdown of biophilic energy solutions that may work for different geographical locations.

Scan QR code 5.4 at the end of this chapter to see How We Build charts comparing Serenbe to traditional development.

* * *

No matter your political beliefs or your stance on climate wars, we can all agree that it makes good economic sense to preserve and conserve our resources, explore innovative alternatives, and make community-wide changes to protect our planet. A greener future benefits us all and helps ensure that the generations ahead of us will have clean air, ample green spaces, and plentiful water. Plus, all practices to reduce demand on our natural resources result in dollars in our personal pockets due to less money spent on energy to maintain our homes, yards, or cars. The time to act is now, and the power is in our hands.

Chapter 5 QR Codes

**Stormwater
QR Code 5.1**

**Certification
QR Code 5.2**

**Geothermal
QR Code 5.3**

**How We Build
QR Code 5.4**

**Chapter 5
Image Gallery**

6

The Power of Inspired Architecture

Architecture is a crucial part of placemaking because it shapes our physical environment and gives the places we live, work, and play their character, identity, and function. When we think of engaging and memorable architecture, we usually think of older buildings from a bygone era. In the United States, that might be charmingly weathered Cape Cods, refined Federal-style buildings, ornate Victorian rowhouses, or eye-catching Art Deco–inspired skyscrapers.

Contrary to widespread opinion, inspired (and inspiring!) architecture *wasn't* left behind in a previous century—but you do need to look past today's bland, cookie-cutter neighborhoods and utilitarian commercial centers to find it. When today's architecture is thoughtfully developed and integrated with the surrounding natural world, it creates spaces with an authentic charm that can be felt as well as seen.

Creating a pleasing balance between nature and the built environment has always been top-of-mind in developing Serenbe. This chapter will explore our approach to marrying manmade architecture with nature's beauty to create an elevated yet comfortable environment. First, though, let's explore some insights explaining why architecture matters in placemaking and community building, along with some of the common pitfalls we sometimes encounter in modern development.

Humans Are Naturally Drawn to Beautiful Places

Throughout most of history, a primary goal of architects and designers has been to create picturesque settings made from landscapes and building designs that are pleasing to the eye.

Pleasing Architecture Promotes Wellness

Medical research has identified a link between beautiful places and well-being. Observing nature, art, and pleasing architecture increases serotonin levels and sends blood flow to the parts of the brain associated with pleasure.[1] Serotonin levels influence learning, memory, and happiness, and regulate body temperature, sleep, sexual behavior, and hunger.[2]

Zoning Has Removed the Vitality from the Places Where We Live

Zoning ordinances dictate what kind of structures can exist in a given location, and often these laws disallow the mixing of residential, industrial, and commercial buildings. It may also disallow the building of certain types of residences (like apartment buildings) amid or alongside single-family homes.

Not only do these segregated-use laws result in a boring uniformity of structures, but they also don't take into consideration the common-sense way people would like to live. For example, they make it impossible for a corner market to be built steps from a block of single-family homes—forcing people to drive, not walk, to pick up a gallon of milk. Further, zoning regulations focus on automobiles—where they park and the efficiency of moving them through various areas. Little focus, if any, is given to the pedestrian experience.

Placement and Massing Are More Important Than Style and Details When Creating Buildings or Homes People Are Drawn To

In many communities, emphasis is placed on architectural style and details. Most design guideline books (an essential element of community development today) limit the style variety of structures, yet at the same time there is often a desire by the architect and homeowner for each house to stand out. These guidelines do not always yield the desired results. Communities fare better when developments focus instead on placement and massing. Places that have maintained their vitality through decades and even centuries have taken into consideration how forms relate to one another along a street scene. Even if the architectural style varies due to its evolution over time, good placement and massing ensure that the overall effect is pleasing to the eye.

It's Not (Always) About Age

Many historic towns in Europe and even in America were built over centuries, resulting in a larger variety of architecture. Even in places where older buildings and homes were replaced with newer structures, the "younger" buildings were generally constructed with a massing and placement mimicking their predecessors, and their presence created moments of interesting punctuation accenting the streetscape.

Here's an example: If the ridge caps along a row of houses mirror the flow of the street, they provide a pleasing sense of calm. But when placement and massing are not considered in development, it can create the opposite effect. When no guidelines are mandated and each home is designed without regard to the neighboring residences, the result is often a zigzag appearance that resembles a mouth with missing or broken teeth. As you might imagine, the overall effect is *not* pleasing to view, but few understand why the street has less appeal than others.

"Nature Forward" Is the Future of Design

Increased awareness around LEED certification has educated the development industry about the financial benefits of environmental design. This has helped increase the popularity of biophilia in design nationwide. But in recent years, society has also begun to recognize the many ways in which our environment shapes our well-being. In the post-COVID-19 era we now have even more awareness around how our environment impacts our mental health—and more of a drive to do all we can to enhance our wellness. It's no surprise that in this post-pandemic period, two of the most popular development terms are "nature forward" and "biophilic design."

Putting It All Together to Build a Town (Not Just Another Development)

When I was considering becoming a developer, I visited many developed communities and started paying attention to what I liked as well as what I might do differently. I observed that the developments, with their detailed design guidelines, all tended to lock the architecture into a specific time period or style.

Eventually I realized that what truly inspired me were towns, not developments. Most towns have varied architecture, some by plan and some simply from decades of change. On the other hand, developments tend to have variations of one architectural style.

This realization prompted me to start studying small-town America predating the urban sprawl that began in the 1950s. My goal was to identify and understand the specific differences between the older housing clusters that I found so inviting, and the ho-hum housing developed during the last few decades. I didn't want to build just another cookie-cutter development. I wanted to build a town that had heart and soul.

Serenbe's Approach to Inspired Architecture

When it was time to break ground at Serenbe, we did a study of the Southern vernacular architectural styles that had stood the test of time and remain popular a hundred years later. I decided that the first phase of Serenbe's development, Selborne, and much of the second phase, Grange, would be based on the Southern rural vernacular of the late 1800s and early 1900s.

This graceful, simple Southern style is characterized by wide-open porches that reflect the region's history and environment. Using it as the foundation for the streetscapes, then mixing in varied architecture from other periods and regions, gives the village the appearance of a town designed in another era.

Around the same time, Dr. Phillip J. Tabb (who at the time was head of the architecture department at Texas A&M University while also serving as Serenbe's land planner) assigned one of his semester studios Serenbe's first live-work compound with twelve units, located in the center of Selborne. While the student designers focused on contemporary architecture instead of Southern rural vernacular, they expertly captured the desired massing I had envisioned for these units. Viewing the student model, I was delighted with how the units flowed together beautifully. Their rooflines complemented one another, and the tallest building of the group aligned with the adjacent hillside. We kept the wonderful massing but used more historic architecture from the 1920s for all but one live-work, which gives interest to the street with its contemporary lines.

We were off and running, and I was brimming with ideas to infuse future buildings with characteristics that attract people into homes and structures. Here are some of the main elements that helped us not only design and build beautiful, desirable, and sustainably constructed homes, but create a community where people *want* to live.

Element 1: Individualized Placement and Massing of Every House

At Serenbe, much effort is made to ensure that the streetscapes flow and fit together. One way we achieve this is by individually surveying each lot to determine how any structures built there will fit into the streetscape. After civil engineers stake and grade a new street inside Serenbe, Dr. Tabb and I walk through the lots one by one and decide how far each house will sit from the curb and how tall that house should be to ensure that the rooflines flow together and that no home overshadows the others along the street.

Massing and placement of homes, along with a mix of varied architecture among the Southern vernacular homes in the Selborne hamlet.

Element 2: Organized Transects That Seamlessly Merge Urban and Rural Areas

Another way we manage the flow and feel of Serenbe's streetscapes is by applying the transect model, which gradually and organically informs the transition from rural to urban. A transect is a conceptual framework used to organize different types of land use and human activity along a continuum that ranges from natural, undeveloped environments to urban, highly developed areas. It is a pattern that coordinates diverse zones to ensure a balanced, sustainable integration of natural and built environments. Well-planned transects encourage walkability, reduce sprawl, and integrate nature into urban design. Serenbe's architecture and landscape vary intentionally from transect to transect and differ in each hamlet.

Within the first half mile of entering Serenbe there are six transects that gradually flow from rural residences to an urban mixed-use core:

- Transect One consists of the rural pastures and forest where we have a few homes.
- In Transect Two, homes begin to appear with low density and include a required twenty-foot buffer of undisturbed nature along the street.
- Transect Three has a higher density of homes, and along the street we introduce curbs, crosswalks, and streetlights. The homes in this transect start to form an urban wall, with those on one side stepping down from a hill while those on the other side step up from a streambed.
- In Transect Four there is higher density (in the form of smaller lots). The front porches of each house are the same distance from the curb of the sidewalk, forming a more organized line. In fact, as you travel down the street, the porches begin to feel like a nearly continuous outside room.
- Transect Five has three- and four-story townhouses and live-work buildings with retail, restaurants, and residences all mixed together.
- The final transect, Transect Six, is the highest-density commercial district. This is only found in two of Serenbe's hamlets, with a five-story hotel currently planned for the center of Selborne and mixed-used buildings planned for the center of Mado.

Scan QR code 6.1 at the end of this chapter to see transect diagrams.

Element 3: Vitality Due to Variety of Use

As I just mentioned, Serenbe residents can live, work, eat, shop, and more all in the same place. (This is an unusual feature for American communities built since the mid-twentieth century.) For example, on the corner of Selborne Lane and Flynn Ridge in the Selborne hamlet, there are single-family homes, attached homes, live-work, and commercial spaces all converging at one intersection. This would not be allowed even in the most progressive cities because of zoning laws today, although it was common in pre-1930 communities. (See photos on page 83.)

To circumvent "the way things are usually done," the Chattahoochee Hill Country overlay was established to allow mixed used throughout its 40,000 acres. We developed zoning regulations that modeled land plans from Europe and the United States in the 1800s. Then, when the area became a city, named Chattahoochee Hills, the overlay regulations became the city's zoning regulations that still govern our development today. (For clarity, Serenbe is a 2,000-acre collection of neighborhoods within the greater 40,000-acre city of Chattahoochee Hills.)

Element 4: An Emphasis on Distinct and Varied Architecture

Unlike other communities that limit the style of architecture allowed, at Serenbe we encourage a variety of different architectural styles. Some of these are Antebellum, American Craftsman, American Colonial, Art Deco, Arts and Crafts, Contemporary, Dutch Colonial Revival, Edwardian, Elizabethan, Federal, Georgian, Mission Revival, Modern, Northwest Regional, Saltbox, Storybook, and Tudor, plus others. If the architectural style is appropriate for a particular lot's massing require-ments and the architect understands the details of the style, almost any type of architecture can fit in the visual landscape of our streets.

For example, amid one row of homes whose form and color are inspired by the Southern vernacular, there sits a single stark contemporary home that differs greatly in style. This contrast works, however, because the placement of the contemporary home lines up with its neighbors and

Streetscape in Selborne with a mix of architectural styles and uses that blend well due to organized massing. *Photos by Robert Rausch.*

the massing aligns with the ridge cap height of the neighboring houses. Taken as a whole, the street has an uninterrupted and pleasing flow.

Complementary contrasts like these continue throughout Serenbe. At one pedestrian intersection in Grange there are four distinct architectural styles that visually complement each other due to the placement and massing of each. I cannot think of another twenty-first-century development that has a Queen Anne Victorian next to a modern brutalist across the street from a Scandinavian cottage, which is next door to a mid-century modern ranch. At Serenbe, this blending of architectural styles gives our community a sense of authenticity and permanence because it is reminiscent of the mix of homes found in older cities that have developed and grown over many decades. (See photos on page 85.)

Element 5: A Requirement of Only One Architectural Style Per Lot

Because Serenbe is intended to be a town rather than a cookie-cutter-style development, we encourage and allow varied architectural styles within the community. However, we do require that designers stick to only one architectural style per house lot with a reasonable amount of restraint in designing the overall blueprint. Classic, enduring architecture does not mix styles—the result is often too confusing to the brain.

Serenbe uses a design review process, overseen by a design review board (DRB), to approve all architectural designs before any structures are built. Each homeowner or architect must declare the architectural style for the buildings on their lot and then adhere to that one style. (This stands in contrast to the many types of mixed-style homes that have become popular in America during recent decades.) So, for example, a house's window cornice must be in the same architectural style as its eaves. Furthermore, the architect must be able to defend the style of the house and its details by explaining his or her design choices. (If you're wondering what the design committee tends to consider "good" architecture, one of the most common words used in design review meetings is *restraint*.)

Massing facilitates a blend of architectural styles—from Victorian to Brutalist Contemporary—that enhances the streetscape. *Photos by J. Ashley.*

Element 6: Homes of All Sizes

Because Serenbe has homes of every size, there is something to suit everyone's needs. You'll see everything from 900-square-foot cottages to charming single-family homes to sleek townhomes to rambling estate houses. There are apartments and condo buildings, live-works with housing units above commercial spaces, and multi-resident aging-in-place housing.

We also have a selection of 900- to 1,200-square-foot homes that are always in high demand. We began selling these smaller homes during the Great Recession (then priced around $265,000), when larger, more costly homes were not selling. This pivot came a little ahead of the nationwide tiny home phenomenon. Then and now, as people assess what they really need, many are drawn to Serenbe by these smaller and more streamlined residences.

Finally, the Chattahoochee Hills zoning regulations allow and even encourage adding additional living spaces onto residents' properties (such as carriage houses or mother-in-law suites). Accessory dwelling units (ADUs) and detached accessory dwelling units (DADUs) are an excellent way to add affordable rental properties into the housing mix while bringing in extra income for homeowners.

The blending of different types of residences in Serenbe mirrors the many sizes and styles of homes found in historical villages of the past, long before zoning laws dictated a more homogeneous style and look in communities. Our varied home sizes, configurations, and styles create an interesting tapestry of streetscapes, and contribute to the vibrant neighborhood feel that many people desire.

Element 7: A "No Visual Pollution" Approach to the Street Scene

Serenbe's overarching approach to architecture and design minimizes visual pollution. This is why you won't find residents' garbage receptacles lining the street. Instead, each home is equipped with an in-ground receptacle for their garbage, recycling, and compost. These "hidden trashcans" keep the community free of eyesores that most people prefer *not* to look at (or smell!) when appreciating a beautiful street scene.

Serenbe takes a similar approach to mail delivery. Instead of punctuating the street with a clunky mailbox at the end of each driveway, residents visit the centralized mail houses situated throughout the community.

Breaking Ground at Serenbe:
The First Four Buildings

The year was 2004. We had passed an overlay for the 40,000-acre Chattahoochee Hill Country in 2002, which allowed for a mix of housing in a pattern reminiscent of communities from a century ago. During a four-day charette we developed a land plan with Dr. Phillip J. Tabb. I also had a stack of conceptual house plans and designs for the first street of forty houses, developed with the help of a host of architects, including Lew Oliver, Randy Miller, and Peter Block. Now it was time to face the questions I had been wondering about from the beginning: "How can I fund this, and will anyone buy a house in the middle of the woods?"

In an effort to fund the infrastructure, I worked with Robert Rausch and Ryan Gainey to create an ornate wooden box to share the concept of Serenbe with potential investors. It featured a bronze cast of an acorn from our woods and this tag line: "A community of people living in a community of trees." Inside the box was a book of hand-drawn images of Serenbe and the original maps of the hamlets. No one signed up to help me fund the project.

The resistance I was encountering from the financial and real estate community gave me pause, but I believed that Serenbe's biophilic ethos would eventually become more widely accepted. I felt I had to move forward despite the initial lack of enthusiasm and financial support. My new plan for growth could be boiled down to a familiar phrase: "If you build it, they will come." Once the buying public saw the vision of Serenbe come to life, I was confident they would begin to purchase homes. The buildings I purchased in Midtown Atlanta in the 1970s had nicely escalated in value by 2004, allowing me to secure the funds needed for the infrastructure.

I decided that the first building in Serenbe would be a townhouse for my wife and me to live in. That's right, a townhouse in the middle of the woods! Up to this point, people could not comprehend the idea of a townhouse surrounded by wild forests, so I decided to show them what it would look like.

The first people to come aboard were friends and family. My sister-in-law reserved a home, and then a good friend who enthusiastically embraced my vision for Serenbe committed to building an estate house. As a hospitality guy, I knew we had to have a cafe to gather in. My reasoning was that these four buildings would give us the start we needed.

It was now time to let the public know we were ready to sell. I sent out a flyer showing availability of twenty of the forty lots that were being developed—a mix of townhomes, estate houses, cottages, and live-works. Forty-eight hours later, all twenty homes were spoken for. Serenbe was finally on its way! (Incidentally, our story proves that while consumer trends can't be identified for a product that doesn't yet exist, that doesn't mean demand won't be there when the item hits the market!)

The Hamlets at Serenbe and Their Architectural Focuses

As Serenbe grew and we planned new hamlets, I decided that each one should have its own distinct architectural style and a different commercial focus. This would help each neighborhood establish its own identity and sense of place. Here's a brief introduction to each of our hamlets.

Selborne

Selborne, Serenbe's first hamlet, was built to highlight the Southern vernacular and features many homes constructed in the architectural style of the 1920s and '30s. Selborne's commercial area is inspired by the

Romanesque Revival period as applied in the rural United States, and Selborne's commercial and lifestyle focus is "art," which dovetails nicely with the hamlet's 1930s-inspired architecture. The 1930s produced several influential movements in the United States, notably:

- Art Deco, which influenced visual arts, fashion, interior design, and architecture
- The Harlem Renaissance, which celebrated African American literature, music, and visual arts
- Social realism and regionalism, which was a response to the Great Depression
- The WPA Federal Art Project, a part of the New Deal that provided funding for artists and resulted in an explosion of the arts in America

Grange

Serenbe's Grange hamlet is focused on agriculture and the agrarian lifestyle (complete with an organic farm and horse stables), and features architecture from the rural 1890s. Many of its residences were designed in the Southern vernacular style, while the hamlet's commercial area is built in a style known as Boomtown architecture. This refers to the storefronts' false facades and parapets found in new towns of the late 1800s.

Mado

The houses and structures in Mado, our hamlet focused on health and wellness, are inspired by the minimalist design popular in Scandinavian countries like Denmark and Sweden. The architecture—which includes both historic and contemporary structures—focuses on simple design. What it lacks in ornamentation, it makes up for in its striking use of color and shape.

In Mado, the architecture draws inspiration from both contemporary and historic Scandinavian design.

Spela

Spela is Serenbe's newest hamlet and focuses on play at all ages. As I write this book, it is currently under development. It will consist of 380 homes in a mix of Victorian Cottage and Arts and Crafts Cottage architectural styles. Spela's homes will be centered around a stunning Victorian four-acre park that cascades down the hillside. Walled in red brick, the park will include meditation gardens and play structures for all ages. A commercial district in the Italianate style will be located at each of the park's two main entrances.

Transition Clusters: Crossroads and Overlook

Serenbe has two "transition clusters." These are smaller, primarily residential neighborhoods that connect two or more larger hamlets (which feature larger commercial centers). The first transition cluster, Crossroads, connects Selborne, Grange, and Mado. It features sixteen cottages, four townhouses, and two live-works that each have two apartments on upper floors. Crossroads' architecture is mid-1800s Southern vernacular, and all homes are painted white. (During that period, due to the cost of paint pigment, buildings tended to be unpainted or painted white.) The second transition cluster, Overlook, connects Mado and Spela. Its thirty-two Victorian homes and eight contemporary town-houses are also all painted white.

In Conclusion

In building Serenbe from the ground up, I experienced both the challenge and the great joy of building an authentic community that feels like it has been here "forever." By welcoming all types of architecture (always designed and built tastefully), Serenbe has been able to create a town that people really connect with and feel comfortable living in.

If you live in an older town or city, then you likely already enjoy a vibrant mix of homes and buildings of varied structures and styles. As your community continues evolving, make sure that any newer construction is guided by the tenets covered in this chapter—especially the use of placement and massing to create a coherent and inviting cityscape. Remember, modern architectural styles can project an image of the future while still blending with the existing fiber of the city. Best of all, your community will stand the test of time and remain a place where people want to be.

Chapter 6 QR Codes

**Transects
QR Code 6.1**

**Chapter 6
Image Gallery**

7

A Fit Community

itness and wellness are multi-trillion-dollar global industries. Social media trends, must-have products, gyms and spas, specialty grocery stores, wearable tech, supplements, dietary plans *du jour*, self-help materials, and so much more form the background noise to our daily lives. It's practically impossible *not* to be aware that physical and mental wellness *should* be goals we all strive to achieve (or at least get closer to). What's more, thanks to the aforementioned commercial bombardment, most of us also know how—at least in theory—to start pursuing increased wellness. So why don't more of us do it?

The short answer is that, despite all the messaging pushing us to get fit, eat healthier, manage our stress, and generally improve ourselves, modern life doesn't make it easy to achieve those goals. Often, we have to actively work *against* widespread norms and systems to pursue our physical and mental health. Given the challenges we're facing, it's no wonder many of us struggle to achieve the whole-person wellness we desire.

Working toward greater well-being is a core component of a bio-philic lifestyle. But before we talk about individual and community-wide changes that can boost holistic health, let's look at some of the main factors that prevent many people from achieving the fitness and wellness levels they'd like.

Unpacking Our Unwell Nation

We Often Don't Get Enough Movement

An inactive (and stress-filled) lifestyle increases our risk for weight gain and illness. Most of us know this. And yet many people find it difficult (or even nearly impossible!) to get enough daily movement and exercise. According to the Office of Disease Prevention and Health Promotion, "about 2 in 5 adults and 1 in 5 children and adolescents in the United States have obesity."[1] Being obese is also linked to other health issues such as type 2 diabetes, heart disease, stroke, and some cancers.[2]

The reason why we generally don't move our bodies as much as we should isn't as simple as a lack of motivation or misplaced priorities. Nearly everything about the way our lives are organized works to keep us stuck (literally) in a sedentary lifestyle:

- **We spend long hours sitting at a desk.** From school children to working adults, many people are required to sit at a desk for eight hours a day or more.
- **It's the highway, or no way.** Thanks to urban sprawl, communities are designed primarily for car travel. Spread-out neighborhoods are connected to far-flung commercial centers by miles of highway. In this automobile-centric landscape, there may be little or no infrastructure for pedestrians or cyclists (like sidewalks, crosswalks, and walking paths). This makes it difficult to get from place to place on foot. When people want to walk for exercise or relaxation, they often have to drive to a park, trail, or greenway. And if it's too difficult to find a safe, inviting place to walk, people usually won't do it.

Our Diets Aren't Always Healthy

Our lack of motion isn't the sole culprit, obviously. Our fuel has become increasingly suspect. We eat foods of convenience that are overly processed and full of preservatives. We'll take a much closer look at our culture's problematic relationship with food in the next chapter. For now, here's a snapshot of how our diets impact our wellness.

Instead of consuming fresh, whole foods, our diets are often full of low-quality foods and beverages that ravage our health. These choices tend to be highly processed, full of sugar or sodium, high in unhealthy fats, and low in fiber. This type of diet, sometimes referred to as the Standard American Diet, or SAD, is associated with weight gain, cardiovascular disease, and type 2 diabetes.

If we know that eating unhealthy foods leads to poor health outcomes, why do we do it?

- Convenience foods can be eaten immediately without any prep time or energy expenditure.
- They're cheaper than healthier food options.
- Many communities lack healthier options. Especially in so-called "food deserts," there may be few or no supermarkets and/or farmers markets with fresh food choices.

The "Diet" Myth

Many people purposely buy foods and beverages branded "diet," "low fat," or "sugar free," believing that these choices are healthier and will help them achieve fitness or weight-loss goals. Unfortunately, that's often not the case. For instance, diet soda has been linked to mood disorders, fatty liver development, autoimmune diseases, cancer, heart issues, diabetes risk, weight gain, and more.[3]

Our Built Environments Are Divorced from the Natural World

Finally, the way we have designed our backyards and community has increased our stress levels by divorcing us from the natural world.

While they may have grass lawns, manicured landscaping, and carefully designed parks, cookie-cutter suburban neighborhoods are often devoid of the untamed natural green spaces that we are instinctually drawn to, like forests, meadows, creeks, and hills. Other neighborhoods have very limited access even to manmade green spaces. For instance, lower-income and non-white neighborhoods are more likely to be located in "park deserts," where public parks are smaller and serve more people than parks in majority high-income and majority-white neighborhoods.[4] Especially in areas where these parks are difficult to access or seen as less safe, many people may not use them—and as a result, may not regularly encounter the natural world.

As a result:

- We are more likely to stay inside, isolated from the company of other people.
- Indoors, we breathe stale air and live under artificial lights (versus the fresh air and sunlight exposure we might get outdoors).
- With no green spaces nearby, we don't seek out opportunities to interact with nature.
- Separated from nature, our mental health suffers. While frequent contact with nature supports mental health and wellness, a lower connection to nature has a negative impact.[5]

It's Easy to Become Disconnected from Our Spirituality

With its endless demands and responsibilities, modern life has a way of separating us from the spiritual aspects of the human experience—and that in turn can have a detrimental effect on our health as well. Spirituality (which may or may not be connected to organized religion) has been shown to relieve stress, decrease negative emotions, and boost confidence and self-esteem.[6] One Harvard study even concludes, "Spirituality should be incorporated into care for both serious illness and overall health," noting that "spiritual community participation" is associated with increased longevity and decreased depression, suicide, and substance abuse.[7]

Urban Sprawl Leads to Isolation

As I discussed at the beginning of this book, urban sprawl has disconnected us from nature and from each other, which contributes to isolation and has negative effects on our mental and physical health. For instance, for more than one-third of Americans, there isn't a park within a ten-minute walk of home.[8] When people lack a public gathering place (such as a park or playground), this limits their ability to meet and interact with others organically. Over time, this can lead to social segregation and overall disengagement from the community.[9]

As I watch Serenbe's "free-range kids" (about whom you'll read in chapter 10) run around our community, I'm reminded that the social consequences of sprawl hit youngsters and their social lives particularly hard. In the more physically clustered and socially connected communities of the past, children could easily walk to one another's homes and gather in an outdoor public space for a game of tag, hide-and-seek, baseball, or other activity. In most modern neighborhoods, though, pickup ballgames and the like are things of the past. Many kids can't walk to a friend's house or playground because it's too far away or because there aren't trusted, engaged "eyes on the street" to watch over them—or both. Our spread-out, car-centric infrastructure disconnects kids from nature and from each other.

Here are some reasons why a strong spiritual life is elusive for many:

- **We are busier than ever.** Between work, child raising, and our social calendars, there's often little time for looking inward or spiritual exploration.

- **We are enmeshed in the material world.** A preoccupation with earning money, as well as a focus on material pursuits and personal achievement, can distract us from connecting with our souls.
- **We don't take time to experience the awe of nature.** Witnessing the beauty, serenity, and grandeur of nature and its mysterious rhythms is itself a sacred, awe-inspiring, and spiritual experience that every human needs. But we don't get enough exposure to it when we exist primarily in the built environment.

In short, the way most people live runs counter to what we need to be holistically healthy and happy. It's no wonder so many of us feel lonely, sluggish, disconnected, and less fit than we'd like to be. The good news is that a biophilic approach to placemaking can help people live healthier lives and avoid unnecessary illness.

Healthcare Studies Reveal the Healing Power of Nature

An often-quoted 1984 study took advantage of an inadvertent architectural experiment. On the surgical floors of a two-hundred-bed suburban Pennsylvania hospital, some rooms faced a stand of deciduous trees, while others faced a brown brick wall. Patients were randomly assigned to one of these two types of rooms after their surgeries. Individuals in rooms with tree views had shorter hospitalizations, less need for pain medications, and fewer negative comments in the nurses' notes, compared to patients with brick views.[10]

In another study, patients undergoing bronchoscopy (a procedure that involves inserting a fiber-optic tube into the lungs) were randomly assigned to receive either sedation, or sedation plus nature contact—in this case, a mural of a mountain stream in a spring meadow, and a continuous tape of complementary nature sounds (e.g., water in a stream or birds chirping). The patients with nature contact had substantially better pain control.[11]

What Biophilic Design Does Differently

Life at Serenbe naturally results in whole-person wellness. That being said, I didn't initially set out to address the many health and wellness problems associated with modern life. My goal was to build a community underpinned by respect for the natural world, as well as for all living beings and systems within it. The result has been a village that fosters mental and emotional well-being, along with physical fitness and a deepened sense of spirituality.

Because Serenbe differs from traditional developments in numerous significant ways, it really highlights how our built environment encourages a lifestyle that supports optimum health (as opposed to being a root cause of poor health).

Serenbe Is Highly Walkable

One factor that makes Serenbe unique is that its grid is primarily designed for ease of use by pedestrians, not automobiles. While residents are welcome to own and drive cars, the most direct route between two points is often via our large network of footpaths. Sidewalks provide convenient shortcuts through residential and commercial areas, and more than twenty miles of rambling nature trails connect our neighborhood hamlets to each other.

This network of sidewalks and trails makes it easy to walk between shops and homes while providing residents with daily doses of exercise. People also appreciate that Serenbe's footpaths keep them connected to nature and to each other. It's rare to walk around our community and not encounter a friend or neighbor!

Scan QR code 7.1 at the end of this chapter to see Serenbe circulation maps and the Serenbe community master plan.

Walkable Communities: The Future of Real Estate?

The 2008 financial crisis profoundly impacted the real estate industry, leading to several significant changes that have reshaped the market. One of those was a shift from car-dependent suburban sprawl to walkable, mixed-use neighborhoods with easy access to amenities. This trend was driven by both financial necessity and a growing consumer preference for sustainable, community-oriented lifestyles. Perhaps not surprisingly, walkable communities proved to be more resilient during the recession and came out of it faster.

That was certainly our experience at Serenbe. Planning for our community began in 2001, and we broke ground in 2004—putting us on the leading edge of the "walkable environmental community" trend. When our fledgling real estate market bounced back from the recession faster than traditional developments around us, we began to receive serious attention (for the first time) from the traditional finance and development sectors.

Serenbe's walkable layout continued to be an asset during the COVID-19 pandemic. With ample outdoor gathering spaces and porches pulled close to the street, people were able to interact regularly and at a safe physical distance. Numerous individuals who moved to Serenbe during the pandemic shutdowns cited these things as top reasons why they chose our community for relocation.

Serenbe continues to be called out as a national model for biophilic, wellness-focused, walkable, mixed-use communities—but it isn't the only one. Other planned walkable communities around the country include The Waters (Pike Road, Alabama), Seaside (Walton County, Florida), and Daybreak (South Jordan, Utah). Good examples of refurbished neighborhoods that are now mixed-use and walkable are Pearl District (Portland, Oregon), Over-the-Rhine (Cincinnati, Ohio), The Gulch (Nashville, Tennessee), and LoDo (Lower Downtown, Denver, Colorado).

Some cities are even creating new walkable developments within "forgotten" districts. For instance, the High Line (New York City) converted an old elevated rail line into a linear park. It connects neighborhoods and promotes pedestrian activity while integrating green space into the urban fabric. The Beltline (Atlanta, Georgia) is a comprehensive redevelopment project integrating trails, parks, and transit along an old and mostly abandoned twenty-two-mile rail line. The Beltline connects inner-city neighborhoods with walking and bike paths and has led to the addition of mixed-use hospitality and residential development.

Serenbe Was Designed to Promote Balance

Serenbe was designed using the principles of sacred geometry, which promote a sense of wellness by seamlessly blending nature with the built environment. Geometry is a common universal language that resonates with all of us—in part because geometric balance is found throughout nature. Sacred geometry in particular is the ancient art and study of energy patterns that unify all things in a state of balance.

When we use sacred geometry in land planning and town building, we are working with the truth that any given space affects our energy field, and thus our general well-being. Building in harmony with the natural flow of the land and bringing out sacred geometric shapes and patterns in our placemaking efforts can potentially produce a sense of both calm and awe. It can connect us more strongly to our own creativity, insight, spirituality, and intuition.

Compare this with traditional "asphalt jungles" that deprive our minds, bodies, and spirits of something essential. We are all part of a natural global ecosystem that can enhance our lives in so many ways, but it's easy to shut out that connection when we are surrounded by noise, busyness, buildings, and clutter.

If you haven't encountered the concept of sacred geometry before, I know the theory of it might feel a bit foreign. To help you understand how sacred geometry plays out in practice, I'll share three examples of how sacred geometry's principles shaped Serenbe's design.

1. We worked with the land to evoke a nurturing, healing energy.

Besides creating functional spaces where people want to be, placemaking can also involve the needs of the spirit. So, from the beginning of Serenbe's development, I knew that I did not want to proceed according to the norms of traditional design, which does not consider natural elements or how the built environment might clash with them. I consulted with Dr. Phillip J. Tabb, a sacred geometry expert.

As Dr. Tabb and I walked the acreage that would soon become Serenbe, we observed the various ridges, hillsides, valleys, and pastures, and considered how we could best introduce housing and commercial structures into the existing pattern. We had both recently been to Italy and initially talked about drawing inspiration from the hill towns that seem to seamlessly blend into Italy's natural vistas. As beautiful as these hill towns are, we came to the conclusion that building on Serenbe's elevated areas wasn't right for our vision.

We wanted this place to have a nurturing, peaceful energy. We both agreed that would mean locating our hamlets in Serenbe's valleys, where they would feel enfolded and protected. This location would also place hamlets near streams and other bodies of water, which, in sacred geometry, are associated with healing energy. Our ultimate goal was to work with the land to build structures that harmonized with the landscape and enhanced the well-being of residents—and I believe we achieved that aim!

2. We settled on the omega shape as a layout for the first three hamlets.

As Dr. Tabb and I observed the topography and characteristics of the future building sites scattered throughout Serenbe, it became obvious that we should organize each hamlet around main streets shaped like omegas. (In sacred geometry, "omega"—which is the final letter of the Greek alphabet—represents completion, perfection, and infinity.) There were several advantages to this layout:

- As I shared in chapter 4, Serenbe's omega-shaped hamlets allow us to disturb the land as little as possible while surrounding residents with green space. This immersion in nature has a direct impact on residents' physical and mental well-being.
- Crossing an omega's central green space via a footpath is a great example of how it's often quicker and more convenient for Serenbe's residents to walk instead of drive. Using a footpath that directly connects one side of the omega to the other takes much less time than getting into a car, driving up one side of the omega, around the curved apex, back down the other side, and then parking.
- Serenbe's overall land plan is designed so that the outer curve of each omega-shaped hamlet backs up to an open expanse of natural space, whether that's forest, a meadow, or our organic farm. Since all buildings are clustered around the main road that forms the omega, each residential and commercial lot is in close proximity to the natural world. Many of Serenbe's residents say that they reap the numerous fitness and wellness benefits offered by our trails and outdoor spaces primarily because they are so easy to access. (In other words, many people might not go on a hike, for instance, if they were required to drive to the trailhead.)

In Serenbe's fourth hamlet, Spela, the omega shape did not enhance the existing conditions of the land. Thus, its central green space is a four-acre square-shaped park. In sacred geometry, the square represents stability, strong foundations, and order—all of which symbolize Serenbe's aspiration to be a post-pandemic model for human and environmental health. The biophilic approach is to find a pattern that is compatible with the land—not to impose a desired pattern on the landscape.

Further Reading on Sacred Geometry

Dr. Phillip J. Tabb's book *The Sacred Geometry of Nature* explains the principles of sacred geometry and explores its relationship to nature and design. In particular, Dr. Tabb shines a light on how sacred geometry dovetails with biophilic design and the integration of natural principles into community planning. Dr. Tabb discusses how these concepts can enhance wellness and create harmonious environments, which aligns closely with the vision of Serenbe. (In fact, the book uses Serenbe as an example.)

3. Serenbe's labyrinth provides a "sacred" space where residents can focus on spirituality.

Next to the Inn Lake near Serenbe's Selborne hamlet is something you might not expect to find in a Georgia forest: a labyrinth made of stones that were sourced from the surrounding woodland. During visits to France, my family and I drew inspiration from the labyrinth in Chartres Cathedral. Like the Chartres labyrinth, ours is characterized by a single path made from eleven concentric circuits that lead to the center. Once a person reaches the center, after pausing to reflect, they should retrace the path back to the exit. This design represents the inward journey of the soul toward a place of spiritual centering, self-reflection, and contemplation, followed by a gradual return to the outside world.

Walking the labyrinth can be used as a meditative or prayerful exercise, and many people who have done it report that their journey has enhanced their mindfulness and decreased their stress. The labyrinth was built early in Serenbe's development by my family and friends from around the United States, and it's located in a spot where I regularly meditated before the labyrinth's construction. Serenbe's residents and visitors alike are invited to walk the labyrinth at their leisure and enjoy the awe, peace, healing, and enlightenment it provides.

An interesting side note: On the evening of the labyrinth's completion, Dr. Tabb (Serenbe's land planner, who is trained in sacred geometry) plotted its location on a map and discovered that the labyrinth, Selborne's commercial green, and our planned fire pavilion site formed a perfect equal-sided triangle. I don't believe this placement is coincidental. It reminds us that when humans choose sites to gather, interact, and even retreat for contemplation, we are often feeling the unseen energy of the earth—and basing our decisions on that innate intuition.

Aerial view of Serenbe's stone labyrinth, which is 80 feet across. The space is used for private meditation or collective services for healing or celebration. *Photo by Robert Rausch.*

We Provide Opportunities for Staying Active While Having Fun

In addition to our ever-growing network of footpaths that encourage residents to get in their daily steps (and then some), Serenbe offers numerous amenities, activities, and events that allow people to stay fit and active while sticking close to home. (Again, if someone has to get in a car and drive twenty minutes to a gym or athletic facility before they can start exercising, they're less likely to do it.) Here's a snapshot of how Serenbe's residents stay on the move:

- There are several bocce ball courts throughout the community, tennis courts in the Selbourne neighborhood (which residents also use for pickleball), basketball courts, a baseball diamond, a soccer field, and several swimming pools, including a heated four-lane lap pool.

- We also offer a robust slate of formal and informal events that promote staying active, including our fun and quirky Fast Bananas Trail Race (if you've ever wanted to run a 5k in a banana costume, here's your chance!) and our post-Thanksgiving game of flag football, fondly known as the "Serenbe Turkey Bowl."

- Serenbe has several community sports leagues that allow residents to join a team for a structured "season" of soccer, kickball, or softball. For the more casual athlete, there are plenty of chances to join an afternoon pickup game of basketball, tennis, pickleball, or bocce ball.

- At Serenbe we believe people of any age should have opportunities for fun and fitness, so we installed in-ground trampolines at Grange Green, the mound at Sunset Point, and on the Serenbe Inn grounds. Since they are situated at ground level, these trampolines are safe for children and adults of all ages. Everyone enjoys them, from toddlers to teens to grandparents.

One Neighborhood Was Developed with Wellness in Mind

It's rare to find a neighborhood development built specifically for wellness, but part of my vision for a biophilic community included a neighborhood based around health, fitness, and well-being. Since its development, Mado has become a hub for health practitioners of all kinds—not just traditional doctors. It was created to treat and nurture the whole person, and to help people stay healthy at every stage of life.

Scan QR code 7.2 at the end of this chapter for a listing of Serenbe's health and wellness businesses—many of which are located in Mado.

In particular, the One Mado building, which is anchored by the Scandinavian-inspired, health-focused restaurant Halsa, was built to serve as a central hub for health and wellness services at Serenbe. While new businesses are frequently being added, some of the current offerings

Designing varied gathering spaces throughout the community encourages both spontaneous interactions and organized events. *Photos by J. Ashley.*

include a holistic mental healthcare center, a dental office, a pediatric practice, a physical therapy practice, a general family medicine practice, an acupuncture and traditional Chinese medicine practice, a 24-hour gym and cycling studio, a yoga studio, and a full-service spa.

Clustered around the One Mado building, you'll find sixteen live-work buildings with residential upper floors and a street-level commercial space. Many of these feature health-oriented businesses: a chiropractor, an organic cold-pressed juice bar, a Pilates center, a martial arts school, a small animal vet (pet health is important too!), and more.

How Communities Can Incorporate Biophilic Infrastructure

Many, if not most, of the problems I overviewed at the beginning of this chapter come down to the design of our built environments, which are often planned around our culture's notions of convenience and status (as opposed to true quality of life). Sticking to the status quo will only lead to more of the widespread health problems we see today.

As Serenbe has shown, embracing a biophilic approach is a great way to help people achieve their best health and well-being. Here are some ways to grow your own community's biophilic infrastructure, thereby boosting residents' fitness and wellness by starting in your own backyard:

- **Encourage foot (and pedal) traffic.** When people are able to walk and bike easily around their neighborhoods and towns, it reduces their risk for diabetes, heart disease, hypertension, and obesity. As much as you are able, connect different areas of your community with sidewalks, walking paths, trails (with lighting so people can also walk at night), and bike lanes. We'll look more closely at overhauling layout to maximize connection in more depth in chapter 9. When pedestrian and bike routes intersect with roads, be sure to install traffic signals that give people plenty of time to cross the street.

- **Provide public gathering places.** When people can sponta-neously meet, chat, and spend quality time together, it does wonders for their mental well-being. "Gathering spaces" could be anything from parks to benches to restaurants, bars, coffee shops, and more. Again, in chapter 9 I'll share more about how Serenbe has created natural gathering places for residents and visitors alike.

- **Design your built environment with plenty of green spaces.** Green spaces like parks, gardens, and undisturbed natural areas reduce stress and promote mental wellness. They also encour-age people to get outdoors and move their bodies. Again, as resources allow, integrate these spaces into your community. If you are building new infrastructure, leave as much land as possi-ble undeveloped so that people will have access to nature. In par-ticular, work with developers and established residents to leave trees and native flora in place around the built environment. (Look back at chapter 4 for more information on this topic.)

- **Offer healthy food options.** Every community should have access to fresh, healthy food options. This certainly includes conveniently located neighborhood markets and grocery stores (bonus points if they are within walking distance of residen-tial neighborhoods). Community gardens, farmers markets, and locally owned restaurants that serve in-season foods from local farms also fit the bill. You might even consider plant-ing (or replanting) public areas with edible landscaping like berry bushes, fruit trees, and herbs. Chapter 8 will share more in-depth information about how to integrate a healthful food landscape into your community.

- **Get the community involved in creating a shared "spiritual space."** Invite community members to collaborate in the cre-ation of a public space that can be used to enhance spiritual and emotional well-being. Like at Serenbe, you might create a laby-rinth; other options include meditation trails, healing gardens, outdoor secular "chapels," and the like. The idea is to set aside a quiet space—ideally a green space—where people can find peaceful refuge, meditate, engage in self-reflection, and so on.

Chapter 7 QR Codes

Maps
QR Code 7.1

Wellness
QR Code 7.2

Chapter 7
Image Gallery

8

Access to Healthful Foods

We are what we eat. It's an oft-repeated mantra for a reason. Our nutritional practices are directly and inextricably linked to our health, vitality, and happiness. When we regularly choose fresh, wholesome, colorful, locally grown fruits and veggies—especially when we nurture, prepare, and consume them in community with those we love—we thrive. We're more likely to be fit and energetic. And healthful food, mindfully savored, is a prime ingredient of joy.

At Serenbe, we know that good food is pivotal to a good life. That's why it's one of the cornerstones of our community—and a big reason why, relatively speaking, our citizens are physically and mentally healthy.

Unfortunately, many Americans can't relate to Serenbe's approach to food. As a nation, we simply don't have the healthy relationship with food that humans crave. Countless communities face food insecurity. The Standard American Diet (aptly abbreviated "SAD") is making us sick. We don't know where our food comes from, and our lives are simply not conducive to making healthier food choices. This is a tough problem to untangle because it is a multipronged issue.

Following are some of the factors at play.

The Stress and Busyness of Modern American Life Make It Hard to Focus on Eating Healthy

Most people don't have a lot of time to think about their food—where it comes from, its quality, and the daily choices they make around food consumption. Between work, juggling busy schedules, raising kids, and more, thinking about our diets takes a back seat. Even though we might like to, we don't prioritize sourcing, growing, and eating healthy food.

We've Lost Touch with Where Our Food Comes From

In the World War II era, the government asked its citizens to grow their own food, and Victory Gardens soon sprang up in homes across the country. Eventually, Americans were growing nearly 40 percent of all produce consumed in the United States in their own backyards, on rooftops, and in city parks.[1] But today we are so removed from our food that most people—children and adults alike—don't know how to grow it . . . and a startling number of people don't know how to cook it either.

It's not hard to see why. With modern conveniences like grocery stores, big-box stores, food delivery services, and restaurants, we no longer need to think very much about where our next meal comes from or how far it travels to get to us. And because today's adults are so far removed from the food growing process, future generations will also miss out on this knowledge, as well as the benefits of growing their own food.

Unless we do something about it, that is.

Connecting Americans with Our Agricultural Systems

While the disconnect between Americans and our food has grown over the generations, many communities are seeking to reverse this momentum by educating citizens of all ages about agriculture and the value of fresh, locally grown food. Programs like the Georgia Ag Experience are leading the way in agricultural education. This high-tech, mobile classroom was created by the Georgia Foundation for Agriculture and partners and is housed in a state-of-the-art trailer that travels to schools, events, and festivals statewide. Inside, interactive exhibits cover topics such as crop production, livestock, farming technology, and sustainability, helping students connect with the vital work that sustains us and encouraging them to explore careers in the field.

Across the United States and beyond, other programs are also bridging the gap between communities and agriculture. For example, Ag in the Classroom (AITC) operates nationwide with state-specific branches, including mobile units in states like Illinois, California, and Wisconsin. Similarly, Seed Survivor Mobile Units, run by Nutrien Ltd., travel across the United States and Canada, offering interactive lessons about agriculture, sustainability, and food origins. No matter where you live, there are programs highlighting the unique crops, livestock, and agricultural industries of your region. Many of these initiatives tie agricultural education to STEM subjects, promoting agricultural literacy and showcasing exciting career pathways.

As a former chairman of the board for Children & Nature Network (C&NN), I've seen firsthand the growth of C&NN's initiatives like Green Schoolyards and Urban Farming Youth Programs. They provide invaluable opportunities for young people to engage with gardening, food systems, and the natural world. I am also a longtime supporter of a standout nonprofit, the Captain Planet Foundation, which has collaborated with Alice Waters, founder of the Edible Schoolyard Project, to promote garden-based learning and sustainable agriculture in schools. Through these programs, we can empower future generations to understand and appreciate the agricultural systems that sustain us, while cultivating skills and awareness that will benefit their lives and communities.

Many Americans Lack Access to Healthy Food

Across America, communities struggle to find or afford healthy foods, and therefore they must rely on refined or processed foods packed with sugar, preservatives, and empty calories. Unfortunately, these are the very foods that lead to weight gain and illness.

In many urban areas known as "food deserts," fresh fruits, vegetables, whole grains, and healthy proteins are expensive and hard to source. Often these communities also lack the space to grow their own food. People must drive a longer distance to big-box stores (or else rely on local convenience stores) to get their groceries, or they must eat at food chains that serve processed, unhealthy food. It's not just cities facing these problems. Rural areas also experience shortages of healthy food. Like urban areas, they are impacted by our loss of the agrarian economy.

Increasing Access to Healthy Food with Traveling Markets and More

A practical idea we can adopt from European cities is the concept of traveling food markets. Organized by cities, religious groups, or farm collectives, these markets could help address food deserts in American cities while fostering community connections. I particularly enjoyed experiencing this tradition while visiting Italy and France, where these markets—known as *mercati ambulanti* in Italy and *marchés itinérants* in France—are a cherished part of local culture and daily life.

Traveling food markets operate on a rotating schedule, setting up in different towns or villages on specific days. For example, one village might host a market every Tuesday, while a neighboring town welcomes it on Thursday. These markets offer fresh produce, cheeses, meats, seafood, baked goods, flowers, and regional specialties, often sourced from nearby farms and artisans. Beyond providing high-quality goods, they serve as vibrant social hubs where residents gather, enjoy street performances, taste local delicacies, and connect with producers. While rooted in tradition, modern adaptations include food trucks, prepared meals, and sustainable practices like reusable bags and organic products. These markets meet practical needs in areas without large supermarkets, provide fresh and seasonal goods, and celebrate culinary and cultural heritage.

Introducing traveling food markets to American cities not only could address food insecurity but could also create immersive cultural experiences that strengthen the connection between communities and their local food systems.

For a more permanent (e.g., nontraveling) option, cities might use Atlanta as an example. In its ongoing efforts to increase food accessibility, Atlanta has approved over $8 million to help local franchise Savi Provisions open two new shops in food deserts. While Savi Provisions is typically known for offering higher-end groceries, these locations will aim for a lower profit margin while offering foods community members need—including local produce and meats—at affordable prices.[2]

Big Agriculture Has Replaced the Agrarian Economy That Once Fed America's Communities

Until recently, our country's food supply was grown and distributed locally. Outside of large cities, most communities were based on an agrarian economy—one where much of the area's income was earned through agriculture. But today, food production is no longer carried out at the regional level. There are fewer local farms providing food to their neighbors. Instead, food is grown, processed, and packaged by corporations that focus on large-scale production. A significant portion of our country's food supply is also imported from other nations.

As big agriculture has taken over, it has stripped small-town America of the key product that fueled most local economies. As economist Austin Frerick writes in an article for Civil Eats, "Economic power is more concentrated today than at any other point in American history and nowhere is this power more apparent than in agriculture. The

American food supply chain—from the seeds we plant to the peanut butter in our neighborhood grocery stores—is concentrated in the hands of a few multinational corporations."[3]

This concentration of agriculture poses serious risks to our supply chain in several ways. The past provides a window into the threats ahead if we do not adjust US farming habits: During the 1930s, intensive farming practices in the Great Plains, combined with drought, led first to severe soil erosion and then to food shortages resulting from poor soil management. History refers to this period as the Dust Bowl. We do not want a modern version of this crisis, yet without intervention we could be heading in that direction.

Here are some of the conditions threatening US agriculture today:

- Monoculture farming vastly depletes soil nutrients, leading to erosion and reduced fertility. Once it has been compromised, restoring soil health takes decades.
- Pesticides and herbicides (which are used in many nonorganic farming practices) harm ecosystems and pose health risks to humans. Pesticide drift can affect nearby communities, and pesticide residues are often found in food and water. Rodale Institute, which we will learn more about later in this chapter, is a leading source on solutions to producing food without the use of these chemicals.
- There are also major risks to importing much of our food supply. If another country that has agreed to ship us food cannot or will not fulfill its promise, it becomes a matter of national security.

To learn about many other problems stemming from the rise of Big Agriculture in America, scan QR code 8.1 at the end of this chapter.

Our SAD Diets Are Making Us Sick

The Standard American Diet that so many people in our country eat is SAD indeed. Instead of reaching for fresh, organic fruits and vegetables, lean proteins, beans, nuts, seeds, and whole grains, too many people choose processed foods and drinks full of sodium, sugar, and chemicals. They top it off with a high intake of processed meat, red meat, fried foods, and saturated and trans fats. This has led to a sharp rise in obesity, diabetes, heart disease, and other health conditions in many of our citizens.

A perfect storm of factors led us to this perfectly destructive eating pattern. It's faster and easier to reach for "convenience foods" than to cook healthy meals from scratch (and when your day is jam-packed with obligations, "fast and easy" takes precedence). Many of the items on the SAD diet are also cheaper than healthier alternatives. For a variety of reasons, many families—and not just those who might be considered "food insecure"—may not be able to spend the money required to buy high-quality foods at the farmers market or supermarket. Furthermore, they may not have the time, knowledge, "bandwidth," or other resources to provide or teach their children about healthy food. This lack of resources and education trickles down to negatively impact the next generation, perpetuating food insecurity for years to come.

Alarmingly, our SAD diets have created a new paradox that we touched on in chapter 1: for the first time in civilization, we have obesity and malnutrition in the same body.[4] The State of Food Security and Nutrition in the World 2021 report provides data on global food insecurity, malnutrition, and obesity. It highlights that poor-quality diets leads to multiple forms of malnutrition, with the coexistence of obesity and nutrient deficiencies in many populations.[5]

We Waste a Shameful Amount of Food

Americans have a fascination with "perfect" and "pretty" food. Sadly, this means a lot of produce in our fields and orchards never makes it to the store. Instead, "ugly" produce is left in the field to rot. Additionally, the mechanical harvesting processes used in big agriculture leave behind a lot of perfectly good produce that goes bad. The US Department of Agriculture estimates that 30 to 40 percent of the US food supply goes to waste.[6] This is yet another problem with Big Agriculture: Efficient production has yielded an excess amount of food. Moving forward, we should all be asking what we might do with this food instead of letting it rot. We'll look at a few options to utilize so-called ugly produce later in this chapter.

Food and Medical Expenditures Paint an Alarming Picture

A comparison of Americans' expenditures on medical care and food over the past decades drives home the point that we are spending less on commodities to feed us at a high cost to our personal health. Adjusted for inflation, health spending was $2,072 per capita in 1970. In 2022, that amount had risen to $13,493.[7] Meanwhile, the amount Americans have spent on food has significantly decreased. In 1963, US consumers spent around 17 percent of their disposable personal income on food. In 2023, that number had dropped to around 11 percent.[8]

To explore some statistics on diet-related disease in the United States, scan QR code 8.2 at the end of this chapter.

Why We Need Lifestyle Changes Around Food

As we've seen, our country's current relationship to food is unsustainable. Of all the things we *shouldn't* outsource, food is at the top of the list! When we are too far separated from how and where our food is grown, we make unhealthy choices that make us sick. Eventually, we pass along those bad habits to our children. Meanwhile, without a local food-based economy, communities are losing their vitality and stability. And in the background of it all, big agriculture continues its wasteful and harmful practices while making it harder for small independent farmers to survive.

Here are some benefits of bringing food back to the center of our lives and livelihoods:

- **Local foods are healthier (and taste better).** After just twenty-four hours of being harvested, foods begin to lose their nutrients.

An apple picked at peak ripeness from a nearby orchard is far more nutritious and flavorful than one picked ahead of its ripeness that ripens on a 1,000-mile cross-country truck ride. Local foods enable us to eat with the seasons while lowering our carbon footprint.

- **Local food systems keep the economy strong and restore the vitality of forgotten rural villages.** Eating locally grown produce allows us to meet and build relationships with local farmers. And when you buy from local farmers, your dollars stay in your community. Additionally, farms and farmers markets can be magnets for other community businesses, which further supports the economy. This revitalization attracts people who may be looking to "come back home" or move to a more rural area. New residents will invest in the community as well.

- **Connecting with others over food is a strong community builder.** People have gathered around food since time immemorial. Sharing meals feeds our bodies as well as our souls because it supports our social well-being.

Implementing changes that will bring back local food economies requires an integrated approach. Food can't be just another siloed industry. To be optimally healthy and well fed, communities need to come together and work together as they find ways to grow and consume more local whole foods. It is my hope that by sharing Serenbe's own "food" story we can inspire others to move in a healthier direction that makes common sense.

A Focus on Farming

At the edge of the Grange hamlet is Serenbe Farms, a certified organic farm bringing fresh food to Serenbe residents and the surrounding community. It has produced more than three hundred varieties of heirloom and hybrid vegetables, and harvests more than sixty thousand pounds of produce a year. Serenbe Farms is proud to be one of the first of only 145 certified organic farms in Georgia.

Serenbe Farms also serves the community at large:

- We have a community-supported agriculture (CSA) farm share program that anyone in our region (not just Serenbe residents) can join. For thirty weeks out of the year, members can pick up a weekly share of fresh, in-season produce grown at Serenbe Farms.
- Serenbe hosts a farmers market on Saturdays where local farmers, fishmongers, and butchers from the region can sell their produce and meats. During the winter season we host a Friday farm pop-up where visitors can shop.
- Besides growing farm-fresh fruits and vegetables, Serenbe offers a selection of other locally grown and locally sourced products visitors can purchase.

Welcome to Our "Agrihood"!

In building Serenbe Farms directly adjacent to Grange, our community started the "agrihoods" movement. ("Agrihood" is a term coined by a *New York Times* editor covering Serenbe.)

Farms are a great attribute to any community, but often they operate on the outskirts of villages and towns—they aren't truly integrated *into* them. Serenbe was one of the first modern developments to purposely build homes directly adjacent to a farm. For many residents of our Grange hamlet, fields and pastures are literally in their backyard!

Building homes next to a farm was one of the many things traditional developers thought I was crazy for doing. However, I recognized that there were plenty of undiscovered benefits. Serenbe's residents build an intimate relationship with the farmers, the farm itself, and all the people who visit it. Plus, healthy, fresh produce is never far away.

Healthy Food Outside the House

Hospitality is the center of placemaking.
—**Steve Nygren**

If you think our diets are bad at home, take a look at the quality of food served at many restaurants. Preservative-laden fare freshened up and delivered to our tables has become the norm at many eateries—but it wasn't always this way.

Over the course of my career as a restaurateur and placemaker, I've had a front-row seat to the evolution of "eating out"—a journey that began in the 1960s with a part-time college job at Stouffer's Top of the Rockies in Denver. It was during this transformative decade that dining outside the home began to revolutionize American culture. For instance, TGI Friday's pioneered the casual dining concept, creating a laid-back atmosphere with a full-service bar and a menu tailored to young professionals. The decade also saw the explosive growth of fast-food chains like McDonald's, Burger King, and Wendy's, and the emergence of ethnic cuisine chains like Taco Bell and Benihana.

In the home kitchen, Julia Child had a profound impact on America's culinary landscape. Her 1961 publication of *Mastering the Art of French Cooking* and her TV show, *The French Chef* (1963), introduced French haute cuisine to a wide audience and inspired restaurants—including my own—to explore international trends and flavors.

After nearly a decade working for Stouffer's Restaurants and Hotels, I opened my first restaurant in Atlanta in 1973. The Pleasant Peasant was a country French bistro, and the first Atlanta restaurant to serve farm-to-table cuisine, even though no one called it that at the time. Soon, lines were forming out the door for our style of food. And before long, with a group of talented team members, I began opening more restaurants around the country.

It was around this point that I became acutely aware of how the rapid growth of the 1960s had transformed the restaurant industry. Fresh, locally grown foods were increasingly difficult to source as fast food and casual dining chains demanded consistent supply chains to ensure uniformity across locations. To meet this demand, large-scale food distribution networks emerged. Sysco, short for "Systems and Services Company," was founded in 1969, becoming one of the first companies to offer a comprehensive network combining local suppliers with national reach. Today, Sysco is the largest foodservice distributor in the world, delivering products globally.

Not surprisingly, the shift toward industrialized food distribution came with trade-offs. As the gap between harvest and consumption grew, preservatives became essential for maintaining shelf life and food safety. However, we are only now beginning to understand their health implications. Research highlights the potential health risks of some of these additives, which have been linked to developmental and reproductive harm, DNA damage, behavioral difficulties in children, heart disease, hormone disruption, an increased risk of asthma, an increased risk of cancer, and more. Worryingly, these chemicals are found in commonly consumed foods and drinks like packaged baked goods, processed meats, cereals, salad dressing, beverages that are carbonated, fermented, or decaffeinated . . . and the list goes on.[9]

While preservatives have been instrumental in reducing waste and enhancing food safety, their widespread use underscores the need to rethink our food system. A return to regional food networks, where we prioritize locally grown, seasonal produce, offers a sustainable path forward. Such a system not only could minimize reliance on preservatives but also could revive biodiversity. According to a report by the Food and Agriculture Organization of the United Nations, 75 percent of crop genetic diversity was lost during the twentieth century as heirloom varieties were replaced by hybrids bred for commercial agriculture.[10]

Serenbe Farms is fully woven into the community, offering educational insights, volunteer opportunities, and a bounty of fresh fruits and vegetables available through our CSA (community-supported agriculture) program, Saturday farmers market, and local restaurant menus. *Photo by Robert Rausch.*

I believe that a true biophilic success story is one that brings whole foods into all the places we eat, so I took what I had learned in hospitality and applied it at Serenbe to offer a range of amazing dining experiences that are fostering a healthy relationship between our community members and the food they eat. Our restaurants—and the farms where we source our ingredients—are helping to develop a market for people who appreciate fresh, flavorful, in-season food. Our chefs work directly with Serenbe Farms farmers to plan their menus a season ahead. They have the luxury of deciding what they would like the farmer to grow, rather than picking from what the farmer has already harvested. Today, Serenbe's culinary landscape includes award-winning restaurants, casual eateries and cafes, bars and cocktaileries, grab-and-go options, and more. Scan QR code 8.3 at the end of this chapter for Serenbe's current food lineup.

Many events are centered around the local food system.

Creating Connections Through Food

While Serenbe's farms are typically confined within a fence, we wanted to give our community members open access to seasonal foods right in their own neighborhood. I recalled that the Atlanta History Center re-created a farm from the early 1800s and that there were edible plants in the front yard and along the paths. I thought this would be a great way to bring edible plants into the community so that fresh food was not *just* about having a farm. Hence, we planted blueberry bushes beside the crosswalks in Grange, our agriculture neighborhood. Since Serenbe doesn't allow grass lawns, it seemed only natural to use edible plants for our common areas in this hamlet.

To my surprise, "berry season" has proven to be quite the community builder. When the blueberries are in for about six weeks each year, it does wonders for community engagement. Everybody is out on the street talking about the pies they're making, sharing recipes with one another, walking, and picking and eating fruit.

In addition to the blueberry bushes, Serenbe has also added other edible plants to our landscaping lineup. First the serviceberries bloom, then the blueberries, then the figs, then the apple trees and plums, and finally the pecans. Over the course of the year, Serenbe's children learn all about the seasonality of food. They understand that blueberries come from a bush and not the refrigerator.

Think about your community, your own backyard. Are there opportunities to organize produce-picking expeditions with family, friends, and neighbors? If berry bushes aren't abundant, what about fruit orchards? Could you coordinate group trips to pick apples, peaches, and more?

Beyond the world of cultivated fruit, our natural world provides ample places for us to find food together. For instance, there is a strong culture of foraging among Serenbe's residents, who search our natural spaces for mushrooms, blackberries, muscadines, persimmons, and other wild staples. Foraging for wild edible plants is a rewarding way to connect with nature and learn about local ecosystems.

Find a Foraging Group Near You

In the United States, numerous organizations and groups offer foraging classes, tours, and community events. For instance:

- **Eat the Planet** (eattheplanet.org/foraging-tours-classes-and -groups-near-you) provides a state-by-state listing of foraging tours, walks, and classes across the United States.
- **FindAForager.com** (robingreenfield.org/findaforager) provides a database to help you locate foragers and foraging instructors in your area.
- Search **Meetup** (meetup.com) for foraging events, educational sessions, and organizations in your area.

Serenbe has taken foraging one step farther and made it more accessible to all by establishing Anders Garden, a medicinal food forest developed by Professor Alfred Vick from the University of Georgia. A food forest is an intentional food-producing landscape that mimics the structure of a native forest. The food forest features canopy trees, understory trees, shrubs, ground layer species, herbaceous perennials, vines, and root crops.

With very few exceptions, our food forest consists of all native plants. It is a microcosm of our Piedmont forest found in this region of Georgia. If you explored some of the 1,400 acres of natural areas around Serenbe, you would find the same species growing wild. Scan QR code 8.4 at the end of this chapter to see a list of edible and medicinal plants located in Serenbe's food forest and throughout our Mado hamlet.

Of the thousands of plant species around the world, we rely only on a small number of them for our plant-based foods. While not every plant in our food forest is edible (some are used for medicinal purposes), the very presence of a food forest empowers people to learn about and use many of our native plants that might otherwise never cross their plates. People visiting the food forest are free to take what they need. Scan QR code 8.5 at the end of this chapter to read a master's thesis by Melanie J. Bowerman on food forests and how they can be integrated into public urban spaces.

Finally, taking all this food we've gathered together and sharing it with one another taps into the strong culture around food and hospitality that can be found in Serenbe and throughout the surrounding region. People understand that community is built around shared meals. Food is an integral part of connecting and nurturing people mentally, emotionally, physically, and spiritually—and Serenbe's tradition of hosting potlucks throughout the year helps the community connect in a magical way.

Our potluck tradition started organically when Serenbe was small, consisting of only six to eight houses. Conversations between neighbors often began with "What's everybody doing for dinner?" Then we brought the food out to the street and spent the evening dining and chatting. That rich culture of hospitality continues today. Residents sometimes set outdoor tables with linens, place settings, and home-cooked food, then sit down to break bread with their neighbors. There are also more organized supper clubs, cooking groups, and spontaneous back porch gatherings. These meals are always healthy, beautiful, delicious, and, most importantly, soul-filling.

Potlucks are something that just about any neighborhood or community can tap into. I encourage you to start this fulfilling tradition in your own backyard!

Soil Health Now, for Good Food in the Future

In many ways, the quality of life we experience in our backyards comes right down to the quality of the dirt we're nestled atop. Regenerative farming practices and a strong commitment to composting are easy-to-implement actions that you can take immediately, further develop, and use to help your soil (and your food system) flourish.

The Rodale Institute is a nonprofit organization dedicated to uncovering and sharing regenerative organic farming practices that restore soil health, fight climate change, and fix the food system. Rodale also provides education and support for the newest generation of young people choosing agriculture careers. Through various events and meetings, a mutual respect developed between the leadership of Rodale and Serenbe. When they shared plans of establishing a Southeastern Research Center in a Southern state, I hosted a cocktail party to introduce the Rodale leadership and their dream for this center to Georgia friends and neighbors. As a result of that evening, the center is on a neighbor's farm. Since its arrival, Rodale has been an educational resource center for Serenbe Farms and other farms throughout the Southeast. Its presence in the region, along with other state and national organizations, is establishing Serenbe as a think tank for the regenerative agriculture movement.

Serenbe has also built a thriving culture of composting. Composting is a way to turn food waste trash into valuable treasure for our soil. When we allow organic matter to decompose, it eventually breaks down into a nutrient-rich fertilizer, all the while reducing the massive amount of waste that goes to our landfills. In rerouting our food waste, we reduce dangerous methane emissions, cut down on erosion, and conserve water.

Serenbe residents and the restaurants at Serenbe give their compost to Serenbe Farms, where it is processed in the farm's state-of-the-art community composting facility. Of course, people can also do casual composting individually; every effort, no matter how small, counts. But a community-wide program, like the one we have at Serenbe, can make a bigger impact.

At-Home Composting 101

Composting is a lot easier than it might seem. These EPA-recommended guidelines will guide you in starting a compost pile in your own backyard:

Select a space in your yard for a compost pile or purchase or build a compost bin. Make sure the area you choose is close to a water source.

Chop the compost. Your compost will consist of both nitrogen-rich "greens," such as fruit and vegetable scraps, lawn clippings, and eggshells, and carbon-rich "browns" like dry leaves, shredded cardboard and paper, and (untreated) wood chips. Try to break them down into smaller pieces to help them decompose more quickly.

Start your compost pile with browns. To build your compost pile, start with a four- to six-inch layer of browns to help absorb extra liquids and keep your pile elevated for air circulation. Layer your greens and browns and add a small amount of water if needed to dampen the compost.

Maintaining the correct ratio of browns and greens is important. When adding to the pile, be sure to add two to three times the number of browns as the number of greens. To ensure air circulation, occasionally turn the compost pile and make sure that the moisture level is such that your compost has the consistency of a wrung-out sponge.

Turn, wet, repeat (and more). Turn and mix your compost from time to time to help air circulate and to encourage decomposition. If the compost is too dry, add water. If it has an odor, it could be too wet; add more dry browns and turn the pile. A well-maintained compost pile will rise to temperatures of 130 to 160 degrees Fahrenheit. If your compost pile is not heating up, add extra greens and continue to turn it.

Add your finished compost to any soil. Once your compost pile no longer heats after mixing, and when all visible food scraps have decomposed, it is time to cure it. Wait at least four weeks while the pile shrinks to a third of its original size. Remove any pieces that have not broken down and add them back into a new pile. Add the finished compost to your garden beds and potting soil.

To learn more about composting, please visit the EPA's composting website at www.epa.gov/recycle/composting-home.

Best Practices for Bringing Healthful Food to Communities Everywhere

Building a closer relationship with your food improves your individual health, contributes to a healthier planet, and brings you and the community a step closer to self-sufficiency. Here are some tips for communities and individuals.

Educate the Community About Food and Where It Comes From

People are healthier when they have access to better-quality food. Atlanta is a good model illustrating how to connect people with healthy options. It is the first major city to appoint an urban agriculture director who reports directly to the mayor. The city is actively working to eradicate food deserts by putting community gardens and farms into low-income communities and teaching people how to grow their own fruits and vegetables.

This education should occur nationwide. We need to teach people how to grow their own foods in their own neighborhoods and yards. Schools should teach gardening classes so that every graduate knows not only where food comes from, but also how to grow it. School boards can join the efforts to make these changes. Over the last ten years, the Georgia Department of Education has improved its Family and Consumer Sciences (FACS) program, which now teaches nutrition and food sciences, among other topics.

Concerned chefs are another way to empower communities and effect change in their food landscapes. Celebrity chef Hugh Acheson is a prime example. His Seed Life Skills program is a living curriculum dedicated to empowering youth to be sustainable stewards of food and financial resources. The program focuses on providing low-cost or no-cost resources for teachers with topics including hands-on culinary instruction, conscious consumer economics, and DIY design principles.

Take Advantage of Programs That Put Healthy Food on Tables

Educate your community on any local or federal programs that support families in providing healthy food. For example, Wholesome Wave is a national program in partnership with the Department of Agriculture that aims to get fresh food into homes using SNAP (Supplemental Nutrition Assistance Program). It allows participants in federal nutrition assistance programs like SNAP to double the value of their benefits when purchasing fresh fruits and vegetables at participating farmers markets and grocery stores. For example, if a SNAP recipient spends $10, they receive an additional $10 to spend on fresh produce grown by a local farmer. By increasing access to healthy food options, Wholesome Wave's programs help reduce diet-related diseases, support local agriculture, and strengthen community ties.

Educate and Urge Residents to Take Ownership of Their Food Supply

For example, individuals and families can:

- **Plant their own victory garden.** On an individual level, this is a great way to make a difference for a family. Even a relatively small front yard or backyard (or even a porch) can grow an abundance of produce. Plant some organic seasonal vegetables and enjoy a harvest of delicious food that promotes health and wellness.

- **Buy and use the "ugly" produce.** Far too much of the food produced in this country goes to waste (about 30 to 40 percent, according to the USDA).[11] We need to develop a network of systems that allow us to use 100 percent of what's being produced on our farms. This can happen at the community level. For example, religious communities and other groups that are trying to address health and hunger might organize programs that divert cosmetically imperfect produce to food banks or charitable organizations so less food goes to waste. Additionally, consumers can help reduce waste by subscribing to food delivery services like Imperfect Foods and Misfits Market that offer cosmetically imperfect (but perfectly good) produce.

- **Support local farmers. (Hint: Don't get too hung up on the "organic" label.)** Support local farms and support your own health by buying their meat and produce whenever possible. This may mean seeking out farmers markets, buying directly from a farm, or shopping at a supermarket that sources local produce. Some of these may be organic farms, and if so, great. Just remember that while many local farms aren't certified organic, they may still implement all or many of the practices that organic farmers do. Talk to your local farmers and ask how they grow their food. Often, local farms can be just as healthy and high quality as those bearing the organic seal.

Make the Most of Compost

Every community member can compost. Unused food scraps can become a powerful fertilizer for your local farmer, or for your own garden. Use a compostable bag or a compost bin to collect food scraps, egg shells, and coffee grounds along with biodegradable materials such as tea bags, newspaper, toilet paper rolls, hair from hairbrushes, and wood chips. Avoid adding citrus peels (these are too acidic), dairy products, meat, fish, and bones.

Many cities are now starting compost programs, whether they are government-led or helmed by community organizations. For example, Compost Now is a local Atlanta biweekly compost pickup service. If your neighborhood does not already participate in a community composting program, find or start one in your community.

Scan QR code 8.6 at the end of this chapter to learn more about the type of community composting center we have installed at Serenbe.

Chapter 8 QR Codes

Big Ag
QR Code 8.1

Diet Statistics
QR Code 8.2

Food Lineup
QR Code 8.3

Food Forest
QR Code 8.4

Food Thesis
QR Code 8.5

Composting
QR Code 8.6

Chapter 8
Image Gallery

9

Better Together

In the past, "connectedness" was built into the fabric of our lives. The cliché of older gentlemen talking politics around a potbelly stove or hanging out on the porch of the general store exists for a reason. And it was not just elderly men! Younger men had their hunting buddies. Women had their quilting circles and coffee klatches. Most people had strong ties to their churches. Yes, life was harder in many ways (it's not my intention to glorify the past with all its flaws), but there was a bright spot: It was normal for people to have a rich social network.

Over the past fifty years or so, something has shifted. As our built environment changed, we disconnected ourselves from others. The clubs and community groups that provided a natural mechanism to download our frustrations about, say, our spouses and kids fell away. Now, many of us aren't sure who to turn to when we need to vent or seek advice. While mental health professionals provide an important service, they occupy a different role than friends and neighbors who have been part of the fabric of our lives for years or even decades.

Today, people are more isolated than ever. Many of us live far from extended family. We don't know our neighbors. We lose close touch with friends and instead superficially "keep up" with everyone through social media. Our children, too, lack connection. Instead of playing outside with friends, they hole up in their rooms over their screens.

In fact, the national threat of loneliness is deadly serious. In 2023 Surgeon General Dr. Vivek Murthy raised the alarm about a public health crisis of loneliness, isolation, and lack of connection in our country. He warned that that this epidemic poses a threat to our individual well-being and could even splinter our national unity.[1] Unfortunately, loneliness is more than just a feeling. It can actually kill you. Researchers have found that social isolation and loneliness may increase our risk of premature death.[2]

The message is clear. To safeguard our health and well-being, we must create positive social connections centered around strong relationships. Even though it's historically done a lot of harm to connection, as we'll see soon, the built environment can actually help with this.

People were never meant to "do life" in isolation. We are social beings wired to crave connection. When we have a strong network of support spanning family, friends, acquaintances, and neighbors, it enhances our well-being and gives us a sense of belonging.

Why Is Human Connection Missing from Our Lives Today?

It's no wonder that many of us are lonely and anxious, and that mental health issues continue to rise.

Before we talk about solutions to these problems, let's look at some of the factors that brought us to this point of disconnection.

We're Busier Than Ever Before

We spend a huge amount of our time working and commuting. (In addition to spending many of our waking hours at the office, we Americans spend about 6 percent of our time in a vehicle!)[3] Once we add in time devoted to childcare and the pursuit of our personal goals, we barely have time for a quick cup of coffee with friends, let alone time to build and maintain strong relationships.

Technology Has Changed How We Communicate

Thanks to the internet and social media, many people now do most of their communication online. While these technologies make it easier to "connect" than ever before, they tend to foster interactions that lack substance and intimacy. Too often, online vitriol foments anger and outrage, while the images of glossy perfection projected by many on social media cause envy, unhealthy comparison, sadness, and exclusion. It's no surprise that digital communication and social networking sites are linked to feelings of loneliness and isolation.

Zoning and Building Patterns Have Sanitized and Segregated the Places We Live

As discussed earlier in this book, suburban sprawl took hold of the country after World War II. Developers are rarely allowed to place commercial buildings next to residential areas. Instead, we've moved all our commercial buildings into one section of town (complete with lots of parking). Unable to depend on public transport in suburban areas, most people must drive private automobiles to get from place to place. This insulates and prevents them from having chance encounters with neighbors and community members on the sidewalk or on public transit.

Zoning also segregates people by income level. For example, zoning regulations often put townhouses and apartments in a different section of the community than single-family homes. Occasionally developers instigate these divisions by dividing their acreage and allowing different levels of builders to build on different streets. In effect, this means that all the million-dollar homes will be one street while the $500,000-to-million-dollar homes will be on another street, and all these homes are separated from the townhomes and live-work units. When people are divided by their income levels, it's tough to feel plugged into the larger community. Harmful economic and social divisions are perpetuated. Instead of seeing, learning about, supporting, and celebrating each other, people are more likely to be ignorant of their neighbor's lives—and to feel that others' problems don't concern them.

Lastly, have you ever noticed how subdivisions often don't connect to each other, with each existing in their own little isolated pocket? Modern zoning laws don't usually require connection, so developers have no incentive to go the extra mile when planning roads and other infrastructure. I noticed this problem one day while using my car's map feature in a community close to Serenbe. Two large subdivisions backed up to each other and came within four hundred feet of contact. But because there was a wetland in between, each subdivision connected to a different main road. The children in each of these subdivisions are part of the same school district. If there were a bridge or boardwalk between the neighborhoods, they could easily walk to one another's homes. But because no bridge exists, it's seventeen miles, or about a twenty-minute drive, from one subdivision to the other when it could be a five-minute walk.

Is Kids' Obsession with Technology a Problem of Our Own Making?

We complain about "kids being glued to their phones." But it is a problem of our own making (at least partially), born out of our built environments. Before we can expect children to get off their phones or laptops, we must provide an alternative that meets their need for connection.

It's likely that many of these kids end up talking to one another after school on their computers or phones. But would they meet up in person (or perhaps even explore the woods and wetlands together!) if they could? Based on what I've observed in Serenbe, I think so. And while adults' schedules might not feature as much free time as kids', the same principle applies. Personally, I'd be much more likely to go on a walk with a friend or meet up for a drink if I didn't have to drive twenty minutes (or get in my car at all) to do so.

The Curse of Living on Top of Each Other

Paradoxically, those living in large cities can feel the loneliest and most isolated. Just because we have neighbors and community members close by doesn't mean we have (or make) opportunities to know them.

While many people prize the experience of living in bustling cities because of the myriad options, activities, and entertainments they offer, this environment can also take its toll. For instance, too much noise causes us to turn away from others. In crowded commercial and residential areas, loud sounds like rushing traffic, whirring HVAC units, and nightlife noise grate on us. We turn inward and "cocoon" ourselves to keep our nervous systems from becoming dysregulated. We don't make eye contact with others on the street. We seldom say hello. We don't slow down to notice each other or have a conversation.

Weren't suburbs supposed to be the answer?

Perhaps. But as people have left the anonymity and distraction of the city, they have increasingly found themselves surrounded by . . . a *lack* of others. Many people have turned their homes into fenced-in "compounds" (and never need to leave).

As humans spread out in the suburbs, we started to view amenities such as swimming pools and swing sets as the trappings of success. Then we fenced in our properties to protect our hard-earned material items. In many areas, sidewalks were eliminated. Since people weren't leaving their homes as often (and there were no services, amenities, or nature to walk to), the social fabric of these communities slowly began to break down.

Simultaneously, so did front porch culture. Before air conditioning, people flocked to their front porches to cool off in hot weather. The front porch also gave them a way to socialize with friends, neighbors, and passersby. But, coinciding with the rise of the fenced-in "compound," the front porch has been supplanted by the back deck, which affords more privacy. Unfortunately, we now have fewer spontaneous conversations and therefore are less likely to form the organic connections that help create a strong community.

Of course, there are other factors that further the deterioration of human connection. The ongoing rise in mental health disorders can cause people to withdraw and disconnect. So can chronic health conditions, old age, and retirement. People regularly move away to new cities for jobs, leaving friends and family behind. And while families once lived in multigenerational homes, grown children now move out and start new homes with their own partners and children.

All of these factors have left many American communities in a sad state, literally.

Urban Planning Can Be an Antidote to Disconnection

In a Bloomberg article titled "City Life Is Too Lonely. Urban Planning Can Help," author Linda Poon shares how we can feel alone even in a sea of people. As the article explains, casual encounters do not need to generate deep connections to be beneficial. Communities can encourage more of these interactions using simple design fixes such as providing shaded seating areas, using art installations to encourage conversations, and converting the common areas inside multifamily building (such as stairways and hallways) into "social corridors" where people can socially interact.[4] The best thing is that fixes like these are relatively inexpensive and easy to implement. And the payoff for the community is immense.

Serenbe Is a Canvas for Human Connection

Serenbe has been mindfully designed and geared to support connection, civility, and community in its residents. First, it's highly walkable, creating plenty of opportunities for spontaneous interactions. It's sprinkled with spaces for people to gather, interact, and get to know each other. And with its focus on total wellness, residents have the bandwidth to see each other and form lasting relationships that strengthen the social fabric of the community.

Following are some of the features that make human connection possible.

Hamlets Are Designed to Encourage Neighborly Togetherness and Friendships

Through mixed-use zoning, Serenbe neighborhoods offer residents everything they need to live an active, connected life. They don't need to stay inside their homes when a few steps away they can shop, eat, socialize, exercise, and experience the beauty of nature.

Front Porches Are Everywhere

Country Living magazine named Serenbe "the porch capital of America," with good reason.[5] Serenbe requires each of its homes to have a front porch or stoop large enough for at least two chairs, and the porches are all pulled very close to the sidewalks and street. This allows friends and neighbors walking through the neighborhood to enjoy plenty of impromptu chats or to sit down and visit over a glass of iced tea.

Practically all American houses built before 1930 had porches so people could cool off and socialize with friends and neighbors. But with the advent of air conditioning, porches became less necessary. Fewer and fewer homes have them, and their disappearance has disconnected us from our communities. Neighborly conversations just don't happen as much when you're not outside your home. But I've seen firsthand that if there *is* a large porch on a house, people will use it. In the evenings and early mornings, you will see Serenbe residents enjoying the fresh air and sunshine on their porches. You see neighbors stopping by to chat with one another.

During the pandemic, front porches were crucial for everyone in Serenbe. Because we all had them, we didn't lose our connections during the lockdown period. Kids could stay in touch with their classmates (and stay socially distanced!) by simply walking down the streets. Residents could check in on one another and make sure everyone had whatever they needed to get through that difficult time. And everyone enjoyed having a safe space to interact and enjoy some small sense of normalcy.

Mailboxes Are Placed at Common Gathering Places

You'll find them strategically located where people already gather for other reasons (for example, close to a restaurant, coffee shop, park, or play area). The running joke at Serenbe is that it takes hours to get your mail because on that walk to get mail, people catch up with neighbors and meet new ones.

Plenty of Paths, Sidewalks, and Trails Make It Easy to Navigate

Serenbe was designed for people, not cars. It has lots of direct paths that make it easy to walk between hamlets as well as to shops, restaurants, and other amenities. Whether you're using sidewalks, walking paths, or nature trails, you're sure to connect with other travelers as you go about your day.

The abundance of paths also makes it easy to get around by golf cart or bike, which many residents choose to do.

To view a color version of this map of Serenbe's trail system, scan QR code 9.1 at the end of this chapter.

There Are Plenty of "Third Places" to Gather, Socialize, and Eat

When we first started building Serenbe, I realized we needed a hub, or a "third place." This concept was coined by sociologist Ray Oldenburg and refers to spaces outside of home and work where people can gather, relax, and build community. So when the community was still a forest with only a few houses, I decided to put a bakeshop/coffee shop in the middle of the woods. Everyone thought I was crazy. But we opened the Blue Eyed Daisy by the time the fourth resident had moved in.

As Serenbe has grown, we've added plenty of other places for residents to gather and be social. For example:

- **Steps and public stairways that invite gathering:** These include the Mado Hillside, the steps in front of the Lofts, the steps in front of 9110 retail, and the steps at the Spela park.
- **Benches everywhere:** Benches are placed along the streets, in front of retails shops, in the green spaces, and in openings on the nature paths.
- **Cafes and restaurants:** Serenbe prides itself on offering plenty of restaurants and other refreshment stops where people can socialize and connect. Residents can meet for a morning coffee and chat at the Blue Eyed Daisy, an expertly mixed cocktail at Austin's, a pizza or burger at the Hill, or a celebratory dinner at the Farmhouse. Friends can catch up over a bagel from Radical Dough, an ice cream from Nigel's, or a cold-pressed juice at Bamboo Juices. They might even enjoy a custom coffee and fresh pastry at Minro while taking a pottery class or participate in a redefined happy hour at Soberish, a premier nonalcoholic bottle shop and cannabis boutique.
- **Edible crosswalks:** Anyone can pick and snack on seasonal fruits and nuts while striking up a conversation with other passersby.

The Beauty of an Open Community

Having plenty of opportunities and locations for connections is healthy for residents and makes the community strong in so many ways.

To start, there's less anonymity. People at Serenbe know who each other are. They run into each other again and again. Also, they get to know the shopkeepers, the farmers, the landscapers, the restaurant employees, and more.

Throughout the community, inviting spaces foster intergenerational play and interaction, sparking bonds among neighbors and inspiring spontaneous encounters with new friends.

With a practiced focus on connection, versus isolation or suspicion, the community has become eager to draw in newcomers. A foundation of happiness is evident among residents, who eagerly talk to everybody they meet. They wave at you as you pass through and look you in the eye, even if the encounter is rushed. Many people have lost touch with this way of living alongside others, but it's a fundamental part of being in a community. We naturally crave true civility and connection. We want to be seen and welcomed.

It takes some visitors and new residents a while to get used to the warm welcome they receive, but eventually they come to delight in Serenbe's spontaneous conversations and friendly hellos. To read a humorous *Men's Health* article that further discusses Serenbe's focus on human interaction, scan QR code 9.2 at the end of this chapter.

A path in the woods can lead to spontaneous joy and
connections to nature, as well as others experiencing joy.

While it's difficult to identify any one "type" of Serenbe resident
because our population is made up of many different ages, races, income
levels, sexual orientations, and political leanings, our community has
become rich with unexpected friendships. You'll meet people you may

not otherwise have encountered, and they'll help you grow and evolve in amazing ways. It's not uncommon to develop strong bonds with people twenty years older—or younger—than you. One thing people do have in common is their global outlook on life. Most residents have a passport, and even more are curious about the world, other people, and other cultures. Everyone has a hunger to learn and be a good citizen of our planet.

When you build your environment to prioritize connection, you never know what the day will bring. Life at Serenbe has continually proved this truth. Accidental encounters with neighbors create tight bonds that become lasting friendships. You might leave your home to grab a coffee or walk the dog, but after a chance meeting with a neighbor you could end up sharing an impromptu dinner or playing a game of pickup basketball.

In addition to casual encounters, Serenbe's walkable design and natural opportunities for connection foster a social framework that meets people's psychological and social needs in organic ways. Often, this takes the form of simple friendship. One man, initially concerned about his mother-in-law moving to the same neighborhood, now jokes that she's so socially active that he and his wife have to schedule babysitting nights in advance—a far cry from the spontaneous help they'd expected!

Other Serenbe residents have "formalized" the bonds that drew them together by forming clubs, discussion groups, and other types of organized gatherings. The retired men's morning coffee group, affectionately called the "Circle of Knowledge," is one example. There's also the group of adopted adults who meet regularly, the quilting and knitting circles, a network of authors who share resources, the local AA support group, a robotics club, and an artificial intelligence information hour.

Our community is entertained by the retired men's band called Neuroplasticity, where the only rule is that members must play an instrument they've never tried before. Inspired by Neuroplasticity, a group of women formed the Ukeladies. Serenbe also boasts the Serenbe Singers, a community theater, a children's theater club, and more.

Serenbe residents are also eager to share their expertise and help each other. Mentoring groups have sprung up throughout the community. For example, there is now a mentoring group for young dads. The older dads who have been through all the stages—newborn and toddler, tween and teen—informally gather and spend time with the newer fathers who are in the thick of raising young kids. Their support and advice help the new generation of fathers on the rewarding yet often difficult journey of childrearing. For those transitioning into parenthood or the end of life, we have support groups led by birth doulas and death doulas.

The list of community relationships goes on—and I'm sure there are connections I've yet to discover. That, to me, is perfection—and it stands in stark contrast to more typical examples of modern life. You can go through your day in most urban spaces without colliding with anyone. (But if you do, one is bound to give the other a look of aggravation!) Online shopping enables you to get everything delivered without having to talk to a single soul. I believe this separation from one another is one of the reasons we are more divided as a society. Without the reminder to smile at a cute dog or a baby, or have a quick chat with someone in the post office queue, what's holding us together? Connections simply can't be underestimated. They do too much for us collectively to leave them behind.

Community Connectedness Is a Pressure Valve for Relationships

Modern life's fast pace and emphasis on productivity (not to mention the societal expectations placed on parents in particular) often leave little time for romantic partners to nurture social connections. Plus, many people don't live near an external support system, such as family or long-term friends. In this type of environment, partners are likely to lean heavily on each other for emotional support and practical needs.

But it's not healthy to depend on our romantic partners to be our "everything." Psychotherapist Esther Perel (www.estherperel.com) challenges the modern idea that romantic relationships can meet every need—intimacy, passion, companionship, adventure, emotional support, and even purpose.

I tend to agree. In my experience, fostering strong, interconnected communities can naturally redefine the role of romantic relationships in our lives, leading to a more holistic and fulfilling approach to love and support. Here are a few examples of what I mean.

One woman shared with me that her husband, long considered an introvert, has undergone a transformation since moving to Serenbe. For over thirty years, she had taken on the role of managing their social connections, often coaxing him into events he attended reluctantly. There was always a subtle tension: He wanted to leave early, while she cherished every moment and preferred to be among the last to leave. Since they typically drove together, they had to compromise on departure times.

After moving to Serenbe, that tension dissolved. Because most events were within walking distance—or a short golf cart ride away—home was always just around the corner, allowing each of them more flexibility. Her husband began joining men's coffee groups and attending events independently, discovering social engagements not even on her radar. She was amazed by how much the "Serenbe lifestyle" improved her marriage. She and her husband both became more autonomous and less codependent, which led to each of them developing a stronger sense of self and a renewed appreciation for one another.

A few years ago, a very anxious mother stopped me after recently moving to Serenbe. She had countless questions about which school to choose, where to find sports teams, and how to organize the perfect playgroups for her children. After listening to her litany of concerns, I simply told her, "The best thing you can do for your family is relax. None of those decisions really matter."

She looked puzzled and disappointed as she walked away, but the advice must have resonated. Six months later, her husband stopped me to share how moving to Serenbe had saved their marriage. Curious, I asked him to explain.

"In our old neighborhood, we were just chauffeurs for our kids' activities. With conflicting schedules, we rarely had dinner together. But here, we've relaxed. Our kids play with the neighbors and walk to school. We have dinner as a family almost every night. Their behavior has improved, and our marriage is better than ever."

These two simple stories illustrate how embracing a community-driven lifestyle not only strengthens families but also reduces the pressure we place on ourselves and our relationships. By focusing on walkability, connection, and simplicity, we can create a natural balance in our lives that benefits everyone.

How Communities Can Strengthen Their Human Connections

By now you understand that humans aren't meant to be islands. We need each other to keep us all healthy and happy. And yet many built environments deny us the basic necessity of human interaction. This innate desire for interconnectedness explains the tag line for Serenbe: The best reason to live here is the life here.

What can you do right now in your own backyard to start prioritizing connectedness? Here are some ways to help your community rekindle the power of connection.

Start Redesigning the Community Around People, Not the Automobile

In most communities, rules and regulations (and even the way we think about living) are centered on the automobile: where they park, where they turn, efficiency, radiuses, speed, and so on. Think of your community. Chances are, it's been designed around automobile travel, not the people living there.

You will likely need to redesign the built environment so that the streets, walkways, parks, and amenities are geared more toward people. Once people feel safe and comfortable walking and biking places, the likelihood for social interactions increases. Here are a few examples of what communities can do:

- **Convert main streets to greenway activity centers.** In many towns and cities, main streets are being converted to greenway activity centers. We don't need all the asphalt thoroughfares! Serenbe isn't alone in taking streets "back" from cars. New York City has been putting in more pedestrian plazas and expanded public spaces, and similarly both Denver and Boulder, Colorado, have removed some of their streets and replaced them with a pedestrian mall full of fountains, sculptures, and public art.[6] This is a trend we are starting to see across the United States.

- **Make it safer for pedestrians to cross the street.** A lot of city streets have two lanes of traffic going one way and two lanes going another. On the sides of these streets, there may be rows of parking spaces. Dividing the four lanes of traffic by placing landscape islands with planting beds and trees in the middle makes people feel safer crossing these roads. Not only is this setup more human-scaled, but the extra landscaping slows down traffic.

- **Add bike lanes.** Protected bike lanes make it far safer to travel by bicycle, and more bicycles on the streets means fewer cars.

- **Create places for benches.** This is a simple and inexpensive way to design your community to human scale rather than vehicle scale. People who are walking may need to stop for a break or opportunity to connect with others, and a well-placed bench will be much appreciated for these encounters.

- **Plant shade trees along bright sidewalks.** This will eventually provide cover for pedestrians on sunny days. (Consider placing them beside your benches!)

"Unfence" Your Schoolyards

While regulations do not allow communities to literally remove fences, some communities are "unfencing" their schoolyards by reimagining their use beyond just play periods. They are now being converted into parks and gardens for community use during summers and after school. This is one way to "uncage" our children: Instead of barricading them behind fencing with only a manmade play structure, they can enjoy time together in a natural area while learning about where their food comes from.

Transform Common Spaces and Front Yards into Food Forests

As we've seen at Serenbe, people love to congregate around a food source. Consider utilizing berry bushes, figs, grapevines, fruit and nut trees, native ground covers, and swaths of herb gardens in residential and common space landscaping. Not only do edible plants provide nourishment while educating communities around food and growing seasons, but they also draw people together (perhaps luring them out of their homes in the first place!) and spark conversation.

Update Walking Paths in Natural Areas with Seating and Educational Signs

Place markers identifying the vegetation, tree species, and bird and insect life along nature trails. Signage might also feature information about the historical aspects of your area. Not only do these signs educate the community, but they also provide great conversation starters. Provide benches along the way so people can stop, rest, or enjoy a snack together.

Embrace the "Pocket Park" Model

Even if you don't have space or resources for a large park, you can create a mini oasis for locals to enjoy. Not only does this give people a place to play and relax, but it can also help revitalize a neighborhood. Any city can build pocket parks to create more gathering spaces for the community. Mike Bloomberg, former mayor of New York City, vastly expanded the city's parkland. Under his administration, NYC added more than 850 acres of new parkland—400 acres of which were waterfront land. He also opened new recreational facilities in all five boroughs of New York. By 2013, which was the end of Mayor Bloomberg's term, 76 percent of New Yorkers lived within a ten-minute walk of a park or playground.[7]

Use Your Front Porch

If your home has a front porch or even a roomy stoop, make full use of it. Put a couple of chairs and a small table out there and, if you're so inclined, a few lamps, an outdoor rug, and some throw cushions as well. Then, make good use of it. Your porch is a great place to enjoy your morning cup of tea or coffee or to unwind with a book.

If you don't have a front porch, consider adding an outdoor sitting area situated toward the front of your house—think Adirondack chairs, a firepit, and/or a picnic table. You'll be surprised by how much use you will get out of this addition to your home, and the social interactions it will inspire with your neighbors. If you're a developer, consider the positive impact that front porches will have on the community you are creating.

I know I've spent a lot of time extolling the virtues of porches, but let me add one more point. It benefits all communities when adults can have more "eyes on the street" to watch over their young people. Porches provide a vantage point for those eyes. Adding more porches in areas where parents feel the need to keep their children "caged" inside their homes for their own safety would go a long way toward keeping neighborhoods (and vulnerable children) safer.

Help "Silence" Become Your Community's Default Setting

Even if you don't live in a bustling big city, the background noise of everyday life can still drive people indoors, cause us to feel dysregulated, and keep us from noticing and engaging with our surroundings outside the home. All of these things keep us from encountering and connecting with each other. As we've done at Serenbe, there are several ways you can protect against the harmful effects of noise pollution in your own backyard:

- If you are considering new construction, whether that's a single home or an entire neighborhood, consider using geothermal energy. Aside from its reduced energy demand benefits (which results in lower power bills), a big benefit of geothermal is that it's silent. Without a whirring, roaring air compressor attached to every home, it's possible to hear the pleasing and organic sounds of nature, such as birds and insects. Look back at chapter 5 for more information on geothermal.
- In residential areas, use golf carts, rather than garbage and recycling trucks, to collect rubbish, recycling, and compost. This is what we do at Serenbe, and no one is jarred awake at 6 a.m. by crashing garbage cans. Well-rested residents are more likely than tired, grumpy ones to have pleasant interactions!
- Disallow traditional grass lawns. By requiring homes to have more natural landscaping, there's no need to use noisy lawnmowers. Plus, when people aren't forced to spend hours each week maintaining their lawns, they'll have more time to spend with each other.

Many visitors are amazed by how quiet Serenbe is—and by how much that silence allows them to tune in to other people. When they go back to their neighborhoods, they suddenly "hear" the ambient noise that they had been mentally blocking. (It's important to note, though, that even when people aren't consciously aware of environmental noise, their nervous systems are still absorbing the disruption!)

> ## Want a Good Night's Sleep? Seek More Silence
>
> Studies show that environmental noise, particularly at night, can disrupt sleep. For instance, so-called "background noise" from aircraft, automobiles, and trains has been associated with annoyance, stress, sleep disturbance, and impaired cognitive function. Traffic noise has even been linked to increased risk for cardiovascular and metabolic diseases.[8]

When you visit Serenbe, it's immediately clear that the people here care about each other. You see it in their engagement. In the eye contact, the smiles, the waves. Serenbe is a part of the modern world, but it displays the tight-knit closeness of the communities of the past. This connection doesn't have to be rare. It can flourish anywhere, including in your town.

Chapter 9 QR Codes

**Trail System
QR Code 9.1**

*Men's Health
QR Code 9.2*

**Chapter 9
Image Gallery**

10

A Place for People of All Ages

We've just finished talking about the amazing benefits of human connection. If this calls to mind an image of thirty-something moms hanging out at the local coffee shop or day spa, or retirees bonding over a round of golf, well, you're missing a big part of the picture. Human connection *also* means eighty-year-olds reading to eight-year-olds on the porch . . . or gathering herbs and preparing meals together . . . or simply strolling side by side along a woodland path.

Children and elders are the bookends of communities. When we create and perpetuate artificial divisions between these groups—keeping kids confined indoors and "managed" via structured activities and keeping older people "caged" in senior living facilities—we all lose out.

Humans at all ages and stages have great value, and so much to give each other. We are all meant to mingle and interact, to learn together and play together, to share laughter and joy and wisdom.

Serenbe is intentionally designed to encourage and reward genuine connections between members of every generation. Read on to see how our village nurtures, nourishes, and builds bridges between humans of all ages . . . and why we've created a place where everyone can thrive.

Bringing Back Free-Range Kids

One of my goals in building Serenbe was to create a community where children can roam freely and safely. This isn't the norm for most kids today. Many children suffer from nature-deficit disorder, a concept we talked about earlier that was introduced by journalist and author Richard Louv in his bestselling book *Last Child in the Woods: Saving Our Children from Nature-Deficit Disorder*. Shut away inside their homes or school buildings, with little access to nature, our young people lack the exposure to fresh air and sunlight that benefited children in past generations. This makes their lives less healthy and vibrant.

Let's take a look at why this is happening.

Children Are Spending Most of Their Time Indoors

In America, we try to keep our children safe by "locking them up" at home. For example, if they live beside a busy highway, or in a neighborhood parents deem unsafe, kids stay perpetually inside. This is especially true in urban settings. Even if kids *do* live in nature-connected communities, they're still often glued to devices that make them less likely to venture outdoors for play.

In fact, according to the American Academy of Child and Adolescent Psychiatry (AACAP), "on average, children ages 8–12 in the United States spend 4–6 hours a day watching or using screens, and teens spend up to 9 hours."[1] The AACAP warns that too much screen time can lead to issues with mood, sleep, weight, relationships, school, and more.

When they aren't sitting at home, children are sequestered inside their schools for "optimal" learning. Many school systems place a great emphasis on academic learning, in particular on STEAM education (science, technology, engineering, the arts, and mathematics), which usually occurs indoors. With little or no regard for outdoor learning, students rarely see the light of day.

Estimates of how much time children spend indoors versus outdoors each day vary, but the one thing they have in common is that time in nature—especially time spent in unstructured play—is losing out. For instance, the National Wildlife Federation says that "the average American child spends as few as thirty minutes in unstructured outdoor play each day."[2] The National Recreation and Park Association's estimate is even more meager: just four to seven minutes of unstructured outdoor play per day![3]

Meanwhile, parents become full-time chauffeurs—sometimes as a safety measure and sometimes because they live in unwalkable areas. This is not good for anyone!

Communities Have Unequal Access to Nature

Often a child's zip code, race, and ability level impacts whether they get any exposure to nature. Many youngsters stay indoors because they have limited to no access to green spaces and natural environments. It shouldn't be this way. All communities, urban or otherwise, need natural areas so that children can experience the benefits of the outdoors.

Past generations felt "at home" in nature. People today—kids included—are afraid of it. With the rise of cities, we've intentionally created communities that disconnect us from nature and from each other. But the human longing to be immersed in the natural world and in community with one another hasn't changed. We still need the trees, the fresh air, and the night skies to nourish our bodies and souls, and to bring us together with our neighbors.

Our children would benefit greatly if we "rewilded" our cities and communities by integrating nature into the built environment. Elements of nature can and should be incorporated into our cities' housing developments and in pockets throughout urban centers. When children have opportunities to play and relax outdoors, they can be their best selves no matter where they live. What's more, these outdoor areas naturally create community as adults gather to watch the children.

Next, let's learn about the many benefits that nature provides.

Why Exposure to Nature Is Good for Our Children

A study of 253 urban schoolchildren in Barcelona, Spain, explored the association between exposure to green space and brain structure. Results from the study showed that "lifelong exposure to greenness was positively associated with gray matter volume in the left and right prefrontal cortex and in the left premotor cortex and with white matter volume in the right prefrontal region, in the left premotor region, and in both cerebellar hemispheres. Some of these regions partly overlapped with regions associated with cognitive test scores (prefrontal cortex and cerebellar and premotor white matter), and peak volumes in these regions predicted better working memory and reduced inattentiveness." The conclusion we can draw from this is that growing up in greener communities supports our kids' brain development and cognitive functioning.[4]

"Nature-Deficit Disorder" Has a Huge Impact on Children

As previously mentioned, Richard Louv describes "nature-deficit disorder" as the growing disconnection between children and nature, and its negative impacts. In *Last Child in the Woods*, Louv documents studies on the improved mental health and cognitive development in children when spending time in nature. He points to research by Dr. Frances Kuo and Dr. Andrea Faber Taylor from the University of Illinois. These researchers found that children with attention deficit hyperactivity disorder can benefit from spending time in natural settings.[5]

Louv also refers to Robin Moore's research on outdoor play in naturalized settings, such as in "The Need for Nature: A Childhood Right," which emphasizes the importance of unstructured play in natural settings for cognitive and social development.[6]

Scan QR code 10.1 at the end of this chapter to read "Growing Outdoors," an article Richard Louv wrote for the National Wildlife Federation. It provides a fascinating overview of the many health, social, and educational benefits children (and the rest of us) stand to gain from being in nature.

"Though nature isn't a panacea for everything that ails us," Louv writes, "it's one of the few prescriptions that act as *both* prevention and therapy."

Louv's Children and Nature Network (www.childrenandnature .org) also provides a wealth of research showing how nature benefits children.

Nature's benefits go well beyond the brain, though—they also have a positive impact on kids' health and well-being. For instance, having access to green spaces like parks and forests may foster an increase in physical activity and a reduced risk of obesity.[7] Additionally, when children live near trees and other greenery, they are better able to cope with stress.[8] Outdoor play in girls specifically increases the likelihood that they will remain active into adolescence.[9]

Finally, I've personally noticed that unstructured time in nature bolsters youngsters' confidence, judgment, resilience, and problem-solving skills. When children are free to explore trees, trails, and waterfalls, it imparts valuable wisdom and life lessons that require a certain level of independence. Your mom can tell you not to climb too high up a tree all day long, but you'll never learn the lesson until you lose your footing on the rickety limb you chose as your next step. Children need room to test the proverbial waters (or real ones), fail or fall, then find solutions on their own.

For all these reasons and more, it makes perfect sense that we are meant to be outdoors—yes, often unsupervised—from the time we are young. After all, our ancestors spent most of their lives outdoors, and it's only in recent generations that the pendulum has swung far in the other direction. Getting our kids outdoors is a commonsense strategy to help them live their best lives.

Raising Free-Range Kids: The Serenbe Approach to Parenting

One of the first things people notice when they visit Serenbe is that children are roaming the neighborhood without obvious adult supervision. The sense of joy in the air is palpable as kids run and play together. Many parents move their families to Serenbe because they want this kind of unfettered environment for their children. Even so, they find the transition terrifying at first, because even if we agree that a free-range childhood makes common sense, we just aren't accustomed to letting our kids run free. It usually takes parents a few weeks after they move to Serenbe to adjust to the new normal and get over the panic of not having eyes on their children at all times. But once they do, they cannot imagine living any differently.

The truth is, allowing kids to roam freely without adult supervision is not a new concept. It's a throwback to a simpler time. In fact, Serenbe re-creates the neighborhood experience that many of us adults had growing up—and even long before that. Children can have a wide range of life-enhancing experiences when they are free to explore the wooded nature trails, or ride bikes, or play outdoors with their friends. This creates a whole new level of fun and well-being that is hard to match with indoor play. Serenbe's kids are thriving (more on that later)!

All that said, it's understandable that parents in many communities are afraid to adopt this approach to parenting. When windows and doors are closed, all adults are inside their respective homes, and people don't know their neighbors, it's hard to feel confident that your kids are safe. It's the "connectedness" factor that makes free-range parenting work in Serenbe.

In her famous book *The Death and Life of Great American Cities*, urbanist Jane Jacobs talks about the benefits of having "eyes on the street." Plenty of people milling about on city sidewalks (or in this case, Serenbe sidewalks), means that all people—including kids—are safer.

What's Fueling Our Free-Range Fears?

Many parents perceive the world as more dangerous for children today, driven largely by sensationalized media coverage of rare but tragic crimes. This creates an inflated sense of danger, even though actual risks remain low. Statistics show that crimes against children, particularly stranger abductions, have not increased, and in many cases have declined over the past few decades. Most incidents involving children involve someone they know, not strangers.

Additionally today's cultural norms favor intensive parenting, where constant supervision is seen as essential. This need for parents to be constantly engaged has been exacerbated by the erosion of close-knit community networks.

Serenbe demonstrates how the physical layout of a community with dense housing, front porches pulled close to the street, and services within walking distance (which are all reminiscent of the way communities were laid out fifty-plus years ago) can enhance safety. Neighbors are always looking out for one another, not in a "nosy neighbor" way, but simply because they care and are connected. People who are sitting on their front porch, walking to get their mail, riding a bike, or driving a golf cart to a restaurant or store all notice where children are and what they're doing. They can step in or call a parent if a situation seems concerning or unsafe. And as mentioned, after a few weeks of living in Serenbe, parents begin to trust their neighbors to do so.

As the children roam freely, parents seem to relax as well. Instead of hovering like helicopter parents, many revert back to the relaxed rules of their own childhoods. I've heard many moms and dads tell their kids something like "Have fun playing with your friends—just make sure you stay in our neighborhood! If you want to go on the trails, please tell me first. See you when the streetlights come on!" Meanwhile, adults gather on front porches, in pocket parks, or at sidewalk cafes, keeping a collective eye on the community while connecting with one another.

And what about the kids themselves? Well, one of the best parts of "free-ranging" your kids is how readily they take to the outdoors. Once they start spending time in nature, they don't want to go back inside! They're simply having too much fun. They don't realize how much they're growing and developing—but others do. Educators and medical professionals visiting Serenbe often remark that there is something unique about the children here. When asked what they mean, they frequently mention the laughter, energy, and strong sense of teamwork and confidence they observe.

One weekend, a couple—both college professors specializing in childhood development—approached me during their visit to celebrate an anniversary. Shortly after their arrival, they said, an encounter with two young girls running a lemonade stand sparked their curiosity. They spent the rest of the weekend observing the children of Serenbe. The professors noted a striking sense of optimism, enthusiasm, and maturity in the children's interactions. For instance, the five- and seven-year-old girls at the stand confidently managed their tasks without an adult in sight. They eloquently explained that they were raising money to start a girls' soccer team and buy uniforms, sharing why they believed it was important. The professors described this as an uncommon level of maturity and grounding for children of that age.

Currently, we are seeking a third party to professionally assess the vitality and health of Serenbe's children, with the goal of documenting how our community design significantly contributes to their well-being.

Best Practices for Raising Free-Range Kids

Create Central Play Areas Where Kids Can Congregate

Most suburban areas in the United States feature fenced backyards. If you live in one of these communities, consider removing the fences to create open, free-range spaces. Rather than each family having play equipment in their own fenced yards, create central play areas in your community. You might include playground equipment like swings, jungle gyms, sandboxes, or even tree houses or wading pools.

While certain fences may still be necessary, such as for pool safety, pet containment fences can be replaced with electric dog containment systems, commonly known as invisible fences. This approach not only creates convenient gathering spots for children to play but also fosters connections among parents in the neighborhood.

"Greenify" Your Schoolyards

As suggested in chapter 4, you can help kids develop a love of nature by planting schoolyards with pollinator gardens or seasonal produce. Not only will a greener schoolyard be more engaging; it will teach children about biodiversity, the growing cycle, and perhaps even provide them with snack or lunch food that they grew themselves!

Use Libraries to Foster a Deeper Connection to the Outdoors

Local libraries can help teach kids all about the great outdoors. Start a program at your branch in which children can check out backpacks with educational tools and supplies to get them excited about nature. They can be filled with items such as a local plants guide, a wildlife book, binoculars, a magnifying glass, and a notebook for recording observations.

Another option is to start a seed-sharing program at your library. This is a great way to improve food security and expose people of all ages to gardening.

Reclaim Underutilized Urban Areas by Letting Them Grow Wild

Most towns and cities have abandoned lots, scraggly common areas, and even desolate rooftops that people tend to avoid. Why not turn them into vibrant green spaces by reintroducing native plants and trees that can either be tended by people or left to grow wild with minimal human intervention? Encouraging the return of displaced species and establishing wildlife corridors to connect fragmented green spaces can help restore balance to the environment while providing children and families with pockets of nature in their neighborhoods to enjoy and explore.

Parks Provide Nature Rx

Investing in community parks (whether in conjunction with your stormwater management department or separately) comes with many potential benefits. One study suggests that "park prescriptions" (e.g., "prescribing" park visits) can be a valuable community health resource. The authors write, "Park visits are one environmental factor, we hypothesize, that can serve as a resource to pediatricians to alleviate toxic stress and bolster pediatric resilience." The authors also point out that for many children, parks are the most accessible point of contact with nature.[10]

Team Up Your Parks and Stormwater Management Departments to Build New Kid-Friendly Public Amenities

Collaboration between stormwater departments and parks departments is becoming increasingly common in urban planning and infrastructure development. This type of partnership maximizes the use of limited urban space and offers both environmental and community benefits. As you'll see referenced elsewhere in this book, Atlanta's Historic Fourth Ward Park is a great example. Rather than simply installing stormwater management infrastructure underground to address flooding problems in the area, the city opted for a solution that could serve both functional and recreational purposes by integrating stormwater management with a beautiful public park that children of any age can safely navigate and enjoy.

Rethinking Education: Learning in (and from) the Great Outdoors

Because our children spend so much time in school, there is no way to create nature-centric lives for them without taking education into account. Most schools are about as disconnected from nature as an institution can get. There is nothing inherently "bad" about indoor learning, but it simply doesn't provide the same benefits we see when we take students outside.

As we will discuss shortly, the Serenbe community has turned the education model on its head by literally moving the classroom outdoors. While the schools in and around the Serenbe community are currently outliers, my dream is that other communities can learn from our model and give children across the country the opportunity to learn from all nature has to offer.

But before we talk about Serenbe's approach to education, let's learn about some of the problems with traditional schools in America:

- **There is no emphasis on nature.** In traditional school settings, children focus on STEAM education as the core curriculum. There is certainly a place for STEAM in the classroom, but the lack of emphasis on our relationship with nature, along with biophilia and agriculture, is a serious oversight.
- **Classes are held in a factory-like setting.** Traditional education operates as if it were a factory environment rather than a learning environment. Unsurprisingly, this model came about during the industrial revolution. Students work in cramped, enclosed

classrooms as they follow schedules dictated by bells and listen to a teacher. It's a good system for creating compliance and for supporting rote learning, but it isn't the best way to teach collaboration, critical thinking, autonomy, and creativity—all the skills people need to thrive in today's world.

- **Children can't easily learn at their own pace.** Traditional education takes a one-size-fits-all approach. Children aren't treated as individuals with their own unique strengths and capabilities.

Why a Biophilic Approach to Education Benefits Students

Connecting students to the outdoors gives them what they truly need to learn. The Children and Nature Network has compiled compelling evidence that natural environments support and improve academic achievement and help children focus and better control their mood. Scan QR code 10.2 at the end of this chapter for a helpful infographic that sums up their findings.

Consider these benefits as well:

- Learning in a natural environment can boost performance in reading, writing, math, science, and social studies.[11]
- Spending time in nature can help increase children's focus and attention.[12]
- Nature-based learning is associated with children showing more impulse control and less disruptive behavior.[13]

It's no secret that K–12 learning today is not an "easy street" for students, who must deal with unprecedented levels of pressure and stress—not to mention the struggles many children face due to learning, behavioral, or attention disorders. Nature exposure has been proven to help children achieve better outcomes; we should give them every possible tool to support them along their educational journey.

A good first step is to move class time outside! Classwork typically happens inside a school building at a desk, but that doesn't have to be the case. Lessons can happen outside, too. As you'll soon read, the classrooms for the Chattahoochee Hills Charter School are cottages in the woods, and one-third of the day is spent outside using elements in nature to teach advanced math and science. The Terra School at Serenbe has two large garage-style doors in each room allowing one wall to open to an outside teaching space. Even if you don't have facilities like these, you might be able to bring classes into the schoolyard when weather permits. Especially if you are "greenifying" your schoolyard with edible plants or a pollinator garden, for instance, this option will come with even more educational applications.

Serenbe's Approach to Learning: Engaged Citizens Make All the Difference

Twenty-five years ago, the area where Serenbe now thrives was considered an educational desert. By the 1980s, the local schools had been consolidated into a larger, more distant school district, leading to a decline in education quality. As a result, families who had lived on this land for generations began relocating once their children reached school age. Serenbe's model has transformed this dynamic. Over the past twenty years, Serenbe's residents and the surrounding community have created access to a range of high-quality, biophilia-infused schooling options, demonstrating the power of intentional community design to foster educational excellence. It has all been driven by grassroots efforts! If we can do this, others can as well.

Before I get into what we did and how we did it, I would like to make an important point about Serenbe's citizens: When there is a need, they step up to fill it.

Like everyone in the community, Serenbe's parents are deeply engaged—and it shows. In particular, they don't drop their kids off at kindergarten and hope for the best. Like most of our residents, parents don't believe in outsourcing important things—and education definitely falls into that category. Just as our society outsources our food supply, elder care, and other critical functions, it can be said that we outsource our kids' education when we aren't engaged in it—and the consequences are often negative. But when parents and people from the community are actively engaged, they make a tremendous difference.

Strong relationships are key to making Serenbe's educational approach work. Because our citizens live in a community that fosters human connections, they know and trust each other, and assume good intent of their neighbors. Our residents see education as a shared value, and most operate on the understanding that it's everyone's job. Having the whole community understand that we're all in this together is a game changer because there is widespread support for education.

Ultimately, education in Serenbe doesn't just take place within the four walls of a classroom. The whole Serenbe community is a place to learn. What and how you learn may vary based on who you are, your age, and your interests, but the emphasis on education is there to support you no matter what. This only works when the whole community is engaged. And as you will see throughout this chapter, Serenbe provides many opportunities for people to do just that.

Chattahoochee Hills Charter School

As Serenbe grew and attracted more residents, we began to recognize the need to create a school for our children. The south section of Fulton County, Georgia (where Serenbe is located), has some of the lowest-scored schools in the Atlanta region. So in 2009, we formed a committee to look at the various education models available.

The committee determined that a charter school could best address the needs of the community. They agreed that the campus would need to support the research from the Children and Nature Network and be built under biophilic principles. First things first: We needed to get the right team in place to spearhead the project.

A group of talented Serenbe residents came together to lead the effort for charter school approval, to design the campus, and to fundraise. We tapped several community members with relevant experience to get these efforts underway. At the outset, we had no idea that we would be able to connect with so much talent, but once we set the intent and got to work, the right people with just the expertise we needed showed up.

Soon, Chattahoochee Hills Charter School, affectionately nick-named Chatt Hills, was up and running. The school takes a hands-on, thematic instructional approach that uses the school's unique rural sur-roundings as a framework. It positions agricultural, environmental, and artistic themes as lenses through which the Georgia state performance standards are achieved and exceeded. Today, Chatt Hills is so popular that five hundred students come from all over Fulton County to attend it, and they have a long waiting list.

Chatt Hills believes that getting children outside is good for learn-ing and for their mental health. Their campus design is modeled off of Richard Louv's work, including *Last Child in the Woods* and *The Nature Principle* (which has a chapter featuring Serenbe). As I've pointed out before, Louv describes how a lack of exposure to nature negatively impacts children's physical and mental health, leading to attention prob-lems, obesity, and increased stress. Louv claims that exposure to nature can improve attention spans, lower stress levels, and improve well-being, creativity, and problem-solving skills.

Thus, the school features greenhouses, nature trails, and a vibrant farm. There are no hallways, and each classroom has patio doors that provide easy access to nature. Chatt Hills also has outdoor classrooms. Further, students frequently visit nearby Serenbe Farms to learn how an organic farm operates.

Chatt Hills has been such a success because of the aforementioned engagement level of Serenbe's citizens. Their willingness to step up explains how the school board was able to attract representatives from the education, legal, communication, and technology sectors. The board's collective talent and expertise has given it plenty of credibility in the community. When board members make a request or recommendation, people listen and believe them. This high level of engagement is a function of living in a community where people feel inspired and believe they can make a real difference.

Exterior view of the Toddler Building of the Terra School at Serenbe featuring an innovative roof design where water flows into a rainwater bioswale. *Photo by J. Ashley.*

Terra School

Serenbe is home to Terra School, an onsite school that nurtures and educates children six weeks old through twelfth grade: "from cradle to cap." The school was started in a basement when a group of Serenbe residents banded together to form a preschool. Over the years it has grown into a campus for 450 learners. Today the community-based

STEAM school resides in the Mado hamlet across from Serenbe's Aging in Place campus.

In Terra School's educational philosophy, the natural environment assumes a unique and foundational role and acts as a nurturing element in students' lives. One wall in each classroom opens to an adjacent outdoor classroom. The school also features a library built into a hillside, trips to the farm, and plenty of opportunities to learn and play. The tree house is a student favorite!

Terra School serves not just Serenbe families, but also children of local employees and nearby farmers. In fact, the board established a multimillion-dollar scholarship fund, and 25 percent of the student body receives financial aid. This also engages families from a wider geographic and economic landscape into the parent community of connectedness.

Serenbe's Children Have Other Schooling Options as Well

As Serenbe has grown, our acreage has expanded over the county line into Coweta County, giving some residents access to that district's public schools—including a top-scoring elementary school four miles away—and bus system. Additionally, for parents who prefer more traditional education structures, two private schools now send buses to Serenbe to transport students to their campuses, which offer athletic programs and traditional enrichment programs in the arts.

Other Educational Opportunities Around Serenbe

Serenbe's children have the opportunity to access a great deal of education that occurs outside of traditional learning environments. In many cases, residents themselves lead the learning. Here are some other ways Serenbe's kids—and other students of *all* ages—learn.

Camp Serenbe

Camp Serenbe was created in 2007 by our daughter Kara as an outdoor haven for kids to be kids. Imagine a world of green pastures, hiking trails, animals, and nature at its best. Campers spend their time out in the woods, splashing on canoes, building campsites, and going on hayrides. The goal of Camp Serenbe is to make sure every kid has the time of their life among nature and friends.

Enrichment Programs

There are plenty of other opportunities for enrichment that do not fall into any specific category. Serenbe offers programs through the Art Farm centered around art and environmental studies, as well as through the organic farm and the nearby Rodale Institute campus. We also offer cooking classes with a focus on local foods and nutrition. Finally, the Inn at Serenbe regularly hosts groups who book the facilities for their own programs—and these presentations, seminars, and workshops are often open to the public.

Semester Away Program with the Biophilic Institute

www.biophilicinstitute.com/semester-away

Serenbe and the Biophilic Institute are developing facilities to offer semester away programs in which college students (and their professors) come to Georgia to learn all about what constitutes biophilic life. Serenbe, Chattahoochee Hills, and various other locations throughout the Atlanta area serve as living laboratories for research. In the past, for example, students from Texas A&M have come to stay at Serenbe for thirteen weeks. Serenbe is currently planning a campus with onsite classrooms and enough housing to serve several hundred students and professors.

Uncaged Elders: What Aging Can— and Should—Look Like

On the other end of the spectrum from young people are Serenbe's senior adults. One of our goals is to help elders age with dignity and maintain their rightful place in their community. Our elders have so much to contribute to our society, yet they are often shut away, to their detriment and to ours.

The fact is, America is growing older every day. The birth rate has slowed down, and a massive cohort of aging baby boomers, who make up a significant portion of the US population, are entering their golden years. This massive demographic shift will have all kinds of implications for our nation, impacting everything from how long people work to how they approach healthcare to where (and how) they live. Plus, boomers have far different expectations for their golden years than previous generations held. Rather than viewing "retirement age" as a time to slow down and rest, many of them want to continue working or at least stay active and engaged in life.

Despite our growing elder population, there's still an ugly and harmful stigma around aging, which is perpetuated by a number of negative stereotypes. Many of them center around the false assumption that older people are "less than": less energetic, less healthy, less vital and robust, less cognitively sharp, and generally less able to navigate and contribute to our modern world. I hope and believe this attitude will change as the graying of America truly takes hold! In the meantime, though, incorrect stereotypes about aging often lead to elders feeling excluded from society. They may internalize a negative view of themselves, struggle with self-esteem, and retreat from their communities.

Too often in America, we force our elders to retreat even if that's not what they want for themselves. We wrongly believe we need to lock up our older community members in so-called "eldercare" facilities, so they are "safe." Think of the walls, locked doors, and gates common to these places. It paints a desolate picture, as seen during the pandemic. I call them cruise ships to death.

All this so-called "safety" really does is isolate our elders and remove them from their support systems, even though isolation is known to be extremely unhealthy for people of any age. When older adults are shut away from family and friends, they miss out on the daily interactions and activities that would otherwise keep them healthy, vibrant, and "in touch" with the world. Plus, being socially and physically isolated can lead to depression and loneliness, which often leads to cognitive or physical decline—this is the last thing our elders need!

Why Elders Belong at the Center of Their Communities

The commonsense solution, of course, is to keep elderly people as an active part of their communities, rather than shutting them away in assisted living facilities. Back in the 1950s, there were a few compounds for senior living. But generally, as people aged, they simply lived in the community with family members and remained engaged in daily activities with their neighbors.

Serenbe's Aging in Place campus (as well as our general approach to living) empowers seniors to grow older with more independence by reflecting the bygone atmosphere and attitude that was common before we started segregating people by age. When we enable older citizens to go on living independently, they are able to interact with all other age groups, and everyone thrives.

This is the way it is meant to be for several reasons:

- **Elders are integral to society.** They are an essential part of our social fabric. When elders are able to stay active and independent, they foster strong connections with all younger generations, provide essential support to their families, maintain relationships with friends, and remain pillars of their communities.
- **They have plenty of wisdom to impart.** We have a lot to learn from older adults, but they can't share their knowledge and wisdom if they never interact with their younger counterparts.

- **They are volunteers, mentors, and contributors in their communities.** When elders are supported and able to maintain their vitality, they are a force for the betterment of society. They often spend time with children, are caregivers for their families, stay active in their communities, work part-time or full-time jobs, and volunteer for causes they believe in.

How Serenbe Is Freeing Its Elders

As I write these words, Serenbe is redefining senior living by building an Aging in Place campus in our Mado neighborhood. The campus will be very different from what we typically see in America. Our vision has been influenced by the design of Hoegweyk, the famed "dementia village" in the Netherlands. But rather than focusing on dementia, the campus will focus on decoupling the stigma surrounding aging from the aging-in-place community.

Here are a few of our strategies.

Promoting Intergenerational Living

Hearing the laughter of children from your front porch puts a smile on your face at any age. Yet we've been building places in America for years that separate us from the younger and older generations. It's almost as if we've been putting our kids and our elders in prisons. The Aging in Place campus is located across the street from the Terra School, ensuring that our seniors have plenty of opportunities to interact with the community's children (more on the benefits of intergenerational living a little later).

No Gates

While some residents may receive higher levels of supervision from caregivers through wearable monitoring, the campus itself will not be enclosed, gated, or locked. We do not want to keep residents in—we want the campus to fit seamlessly into the wider fabric of Serenbe.

Eliminating Age Restrictions for Campus Residents

Age restrictions are removed because people need various services (which I'll describe in the next section) at many stages throughout their lives. Instead, residency within this campus will be need- or lifestyle-based.

Providing Personalized Amenities

The rising generation of older adults expects and deserves personalization. Bundled models where senior housing and medical care amenities are combined do not appeal to them. Serenbe's seniors will be able to choose the retailers, restaurants, and healthcare they prefer.

Specifically, the Aging in Place facility will provide a health and social concierge to help residents of all ages schedule a wide range of services and activities to enhance their daily lives. This can include:

- Scheduling medical and alternative health treatments
- Booking tables at on-site restaurants
- Arranging shuttles, car share programs, or private drivers
- Organizing tours and experiences
- Securing tickets for events, such as Art Farm performances, concerts, games, or shows
- Booking massages, treatments, or other wellness services with a variety of providers in the village
- Organizing special occasions like birthdays, anniversaries, or romantic experiences

In short, the concierge will act as a personal assistant, making recommendations and handling arrangements to ensure residents have a seamless and enjoyable experience as they age. Because of the campus's location in the Mado hamlet, residents will live in close proximity to many of these amenities. (See chapter 7 for an overview of what Mado has to offer.)

The Aging in Place campus will also feature a wellness club and an onsite health-focused medical team with practicing privileges at major area hospitals.

Connecting to Nature

Older people, like everyone else, need to be connected to nature throughout their lives. We're stronger, happier, and healthier when we understand that connection. As I describe throughout this book, Serenbe's biophilic elements enhance quality of life for people of all ages. Our community celebrates and focuses on all living systems: humans, animals, and everything else that is alive. Serenbe's walkability, coupled with its intermingling of the community and the natural world, makes it a place where people can thrive at any stage of life.

Thoughtful Design

The Aging in Place Campus will feature an anchor building with street-level commercial spaces and forty-four one- and two-bedroom apartments on the upper two floors. The campus will also include twenty-four scattered independent houses as well as twenty-four cottages that all face a single courtyard to create a subcommunity within the larger network of homes.

Best Aging-in-Place Practices for Communities

With a large baby boomer generation entering elderhood, municipalities should prepare now to incorporate the needs of seniors into their urban planning. Ensuring that neighborhoods, transportation systems, and recreational spaces are designed for active aging benefits everyone. Policies should encourage mixed-use, walkable communities that support active, connected lifestyles for all ages.

Additionally, it's time that we rethink the way we build our senior housing. In the United States, housing for elders often prioritizes safety and comfort but tends to result in environments that encourage a more sedentary lifestyle. To promote healthier, more active aging, the United States can take inspiration from Blue Zones—regions of the world where people live significantly longer and healthier lives. (To learn more about Blue Zones, visit www.bluezones.com.)

Inspired by ways of life within Blue Zones, here are some tips for helping community elders age in place and thrive.

Build Senior Housing in Walkable Neighborhoods

Senior housing should be integrated into neighborhoods where amenities like grocery stores, parks, cafes, and cultural centers are within a short walking distance. This reduces reliance on cars and promotes regular movement.

Give Seniors Active Transportation Options

Encourage biking or walking with bike lanes, pedestrian pathways, and shuttle services that take seniors to key community hubs, making it easier to choose active transportation over passive options like cars.

Include Senior-Friendly Programming at Your Community Centers

Offer fitness classes, art workshops, and group activities in which seniors can participate and socialize with people of all ages.

Build More Thoughtful Senior Housing

The next time your community develops (or renovates) a senior housing neighborhood or complex, keep these tips in mind:

- **Use biophilic design to ensure access to nature, even indoors.** Build indoor spaces in a way that connects seniors with nature. Consider large windows, indoor gardens, courtyards, and plenty of indoor plants. These environments improve well-being and invite residents to engage with the outdoors.
- **Provide communal kitchens and dining areas to encourage connection.** This encourages senior residents to cook together and share meals, promoting both movement and connection.
- **Incorporate plenty of quiet spaces.** Provide a place for meditation, yoga, or prayer to support seniors' mental health.

- **Encourage mental stimulation.** Be sure to offer opportunities for seniors to engage in intellectually stimulating activities such as classes, book clubs, or hobby groups. These activities promote mental engagement while often involving light physical movement.

- **Offer programs to promote flexibility and strength.** Programs like yoga, tai chi, or walking groups can help seniors stay active. When held outdoors, these classes can combine physical activity with exposure to nature.

- **Add more stairs!** Elevators and escalators are necessary, but they should not be the most available means to access upper stories. Instead, create attractive and inviting stairways with good handrails and lighting. Stair-climbing has numerous health and wellness benefits, particularly for seniors. To learn more about the benefits of stairs, scan QR code 10.3 at the end of this chapter.

What Has Driven the Generations Apart?

As previously mentioned, in generations past people of all ages lived interconnectedly. But gradually our lives became more separated, until our children and elders became isolated from the rest of us. Intergenerational bonds have eroded greatly in the post–World War II era. Many events and mindsets led to these unintended consequences.

For example, the highway system designed by the Eisenhower administration led to the proliferation of disconnected, subdivided neighborhoods. The road systems surrounding these subdivisions often do not connect, nor do the pedestrian sidewalks. Simultaneously, a shift toward nuclear family living meant that these neighborhoods began to be tailored to specific demographics, which separated the generations. Think of neighborhoods full of "starter homes" for young families, smaller units for empty nesters, and age-restricted fifty-five-and-older communities. Multigenerational households, once a cornerstone of many

Western cultures, have become much less common as families prioritize independence and personal space.

Furthermore, in the post–World War II era, more women began entering the workforce—another leap of progress with unintentional consequences. In the absence of an adult caregiver in the home (typically the men were working outside of the home as well), increasing numbers of elderly family members were moved to senior care facilities. Of course, it is a very good thing that women gained autonomy and earning power, but as is often the case, positive changes came with less-positive trade-offs.

And, of course, an emphasis on single-use zoning segregated residential areas from commercial centers. Many newer communities lack shared spaces, such as town squares or mixed-use developments, that naturally foster connections among people of different ages.

Finally, younger generations frequently move to new areas for jobs or education, leaving behind family-centered communities that once thrived on intergenerational connections. In the post-pandemic era, however, that may be shifting.

Despite growing awareness of the negative effects of generational segregation, these outdated patterns persist. Communities are stuck in what I call "rut thinking," where we repeat past approaches due to a lack of forethought and our reliance on feasibility studies that focus on past data rather than visionary ideas for the future. Children and elders, who are kept "safe" in walled facilities (i.e., schools and elder care facilities) and who may lack the ability to independently navigate their community's infrastructure, are disproportionately affected.

To create vibrant, thriving communities, we must rethink how we design places for people to live—not just as efficient shelters, but as environments that nurture connection and prosperity. Communities that prioritize mixed-use development, walkability, and public spaces can encourage greater interaction across generations. Shared parks, community centers, and diverse housing options can provide opportunities for people of all ages to thrive together. Outside-the-box, commonsense thinking can spark new solutions that don't require us to segregate our youngest and oldest citizens.

For example, what if we created daycares that also included eldercare? Our beloved family members—young and old—could be dropped off, spend the day together, and later be picked up so they could return to the family home for dinner and intergenerational engagement. If the federal government funded solutions like this rather forcing seniors into compounds in order to receive benefits, it would save a great deal of money—not to mention offer older Americans a much more humane option.

How Serenbe Supports Intergenerational Living

At Serenbe, we believe everyone does better when all age groups are able to commingle as they enjoy life together. Our focus on human connection—which the community was physically designed to foster through walkable, mixed-use neighborhoods—means that children, the elderly, and adults of every age in between have opportunities to organically spend time together without artificial age-related barriers. But that's not to say we don't make intentional efforts to connect with one another across generational lines!

As mentioned, the Aging in Place campus is located across from the Terra School, which educates infants to twelfth-grade children. Serenbe's swim club (a favorite hangout for kids) is also nearby. The close proximity of children to elders (and vice versa) gives the bookends of society plenty of opportunities to interact and benefit from one another. As the wisdom bearers of the community, seniors have an important role to play in the lives of our children. Kids have curious minds, and seniors who have the time to explore the world with them can help unleash their creativity and support their learning.

It's common for older residents to adopt neighborhood children as their honorary "grandkids"—especially if their own grandchildren live far away. Our senior citizens sometimes set out boxes of books on their front porches, and local kids will stop by to say hi or read to them. Many of our older residents actively volunteer by reading in elementary classrooms, tutoring students, or leading after-school clubs. These relationships not only enhance children's academic performance but also provide older volunteers with a sense of purpose, boosting their mental and emotional well-being.

Younger adults and middle agers also benefit from relationships with Serenbe's elders. For instance, there's no shortage of older "aunties" eager to throw a baby shower for a mom-to-be. And more mature residents are frequently willing to serve as mentors to their younger counterparts who might need advice and wisdom as they navigate life's challenges. You might recall that in chapter 9, I mentioned a group of older fathers with adult children who mentor newer fathers currently navigating the ups and downs of raising young kids. Additionally, seniors can also be found leading cooking classes, book clubs, nature walks, and more. Adults who are a generation or two behind them appreciate the opportunity to learn about life skills and hobbies from someone who has been there, done that.

On any given day at Serenbe, you might see children, young adults, middles agers, and elders enjoying life together. Everyone interacts on the street, sitting on their porches, or hanging out in the swing park. Seniors and children alike may enjoy fishing in the pond, wading in streams, taking nature walks, and making sand sculptures.

Here's the bottom line: Instead of forming friendships only with peers of a similar age, Serenbe enables residents to foster friendships of all ages. A tween can befriend someone in their thirties or forties. A five-year-old can befriend a fifteen-year-old. A twenty-five-year-old can befriend a seventy-five-year-old. This is how communities used to be, and everyone was richer for it. At Serenbe, we are so excited to bring back this beneficial dynamic.

Organized and spontaneous gatherings attracting
residents from multiple generations.

Connect Seniors and Youth in Your Community

If you'd like to encourage intergenerational relationships in your community beyond those that form naturally, there are many structured programs that foster these connections. For instance, if you're a senior who would like to help out the younger generation, you might be interested in:

- **AARP Foundation Experience Corps** (www.aarp.org /experience-corps/) is a national program that connects adults age fifty and above with elementary schools, where they can serve as tutors and mentors.
- Some communities have developed **Grandfriends** programs, where schools partner with senior living communities or elder organizations to connect students with older adults through activities like storytelling, art, and collaborative learning.
- **AmeriCorps Seniors Foster Grandparent Program** (americorps.gov/serve/americorps-seniors/americorps-seniors -foster-grandparent-program) enables seniors age fifty-five and older to provide one-on-one mentorship, tutoring, and emotional support to at-risk and special-needs children in schools, childcare centers, and other settings.
- **Big Brothers Big Sisters** (www.bbbs.org/programs/) is an established program that allows adults to mentor youth, particularly those in underserved or single-parent households.

These are just a few of the many programs that operate across the country. Your community might also have its own initiatives that connect seniors and youth. Check with your local library or senior center to learn more.

One recurring observation I hear from visitors and residents alike is the profound sense of joy evident in the interactions among Serenbe's children and adults. People often mention the "Serenbe wave"—a simple yet meaningful gesture where people of all ages make eye contact and greet each other with a wave as they pass. While this may seem like common courtesy, it has become rare in many places, making it a powerful expression of community and connection here. To me, the Serenbe wave is anecdotal proof that age-inclusive communities can effectively combat modern social challenges like loneliness, isolation, and generational tension by fostering environments that encourage meaningful connections and shared experiences across all ages.

For other communities that would like to achieve something similar, a foundational approach is the integration of mixed-use designs with communal spaces like parks, cafes, and town centers, which naturally facilitate intergenerational interactions and deeper relationships. While this should be the standard for new community developments, creative retooling of existing neighborhoods can also create this atmosphere. Walkable layouts further ensure that residents of all ages can easily engage in community life, fostering a stronger sense of belonging.

Organized events, mentorship programs, and shared activities further bridge generational gaps, offering older adults and younger residents opportunities to connect, find purpose, and foster understanding. Older adults mentoring youth or collaborating on shared projects can break down stereotypes, build mutual respect, and encourage collaboration. Mixed-age communities create a dynamic web of support where older adults provide wisdom and guidance, while younger residents bring energy and fresh perspectives. This reciprocity benefits all involved, emotionally and psychologically.

It is common sense that by fostering environments where generations coexist and thrive together, we can create healthier, more connected, and resilient communities. I invite you to join our movement of Free Range Kids and Uncaged Elders!

Chapter 10 QR Codes

**Louv Article
QR Code 10.1**

**Infographic
QR Code 10.2**

**Stairs
QR Code 10.3**

**Chapter 10
Image Gallery**

11

Communicating Through
the Heart with Art

*I also have nature and art and poetry, and
if that is not enough, what is enough?*
—Vincent van Gogh[1]

F ood and shelter and neighborliness and even access to the glories
of nature can't, by themselves, comprise a thriving community. We
also need a healthy dose of the creative human force that brings
color and magic and inspiration to our lives. By that I mean *music.*
Dance. Theater. Literature. Poetry. Sculpture. Paint. Art installations
that enhance, celebrate, restore, or make accessible the natural world.

Arts and culture are essential for healthy communities because,
as Serenbe suggests in its Art Farm mission statement, they touch the
deepest wells of the human spirit. They show us new ways to think about
and understand our lives and the world around us. Art is a means of

expression, a uniting force, and a way of communicating ideas and perspectives. It also challenges us when it exposes us to different points of view. Here are a few ways art impacts us.

Art Is Transformative

It finds channels within us that can't be accessed through the conscious mind or through our normal means of communication. When we see an impactful work of art, it really sticks with us. We continue thinking about it throughout the day and weeks ahead. Sometimes, art can even help us process life events or uncover a deeper understanding of ourselves, our feelings, or our experiences.

It Is Personally Rewarding

Creativity and the creative process is for everyone, not just professional artists. Using your hands to make something is deeply therapeutic, whether you are taking an art class, doodling in a notebook, or working on a commissioned piece for a patron. The healing power of art is there for us all.

It Contributes to Well-Being

Study after study shows an association between arts participation and arts education with improved cognitive, social, and behavioral outcomes in children and adults. In a study examining the effects of music training on cognitive and brain development, some preschoolers from low-income backgrounds were introduced to music activities such as listening to, moving to, and making music, as well as singing. Meanwhile, control group students received regular Head Start instruction. Those participating in the music training improved significantly in their numeracy, special cognition, and nonverbal IQs.[2]

Older adults benefit from art as well. In one study, older adults who participated in a chorale program experienced higher overall physical health, fewer falls, fewer health problems, less medication use, and fewer doctor visits.[3]

Art Is Good for the Local Economy

Art events attract visitors who spend money in restaurants, cafes, and other nearby businesses. I noticed their impact in my former life as a restaurateur. The Pleasant Peasant was located within blocks of the Fox Theater and the Civic Center, two venues where many productions were staged. Another restaurant, the Country Place, was across the street from the Woodruff Art Center, home to the Atlanta Symphony Orchestra, the High Museum of Art, and the Alliance Theatre. It became clear that guests who dined with us before and after events extended our peak dinner period and brought in more revenue.

Yet despite the known benefits that art and culture events bring to communities and individuals, in many cases they're underemphasized. Costs of putting on events are high, audiences are shrinking, and because it's hard to quantitatively measure the impact of art, communities don't always see the value of funding it.

A Few Reasons Why the Arts Are Struggling

COVID-19 Hurt the Arts

People got out of the habit of seeing live art during the pandemic, and in the years since, COVID-era government loans that sustained organizations have dried up. Further, many funded programs have been cut from our schools. All of these factors mean that the next generation is not being exposed to art and is missing out on the benefits of participating in and learning about the arts.

Artists Today Lack Funding Previously Provided by Patrons and Endowments

Great places throughout history have had a robust art presence due to patron families, church engagement (think of the art presence in cathedrals and in the Vatican), or government leadership, all of which provided essential funding that enabled artists to create. In contrast, few artists today have access to funders that prioritize public art—visual, performance, or sound. Instead, they are struggling for long-term funding security. Over the years, I have been invited to join arts boards and have seen this problem firsthand.

Most Communities Don't Prioritize New Ways of Funding

With the old ways of funding no longer in place, most communities simply give up on figuring out how to fund art. This is understandable because many budgets are stretched thin and local governments might have their hands full with other issues. However, if we don't find ways to keep the arts alive, they will eventually vanish. The costs of living in a world without methods for self-expression, hand-made creations, and soul-stirring performances to lose oneself in are simply too high.

When I began my work as a developer, I knew that art needed to be a foundational piece of building any community. However, I was not able to be a patron on any scale. And like so many others, our rural area did not have government funding for arts—even basic services were lacking. What could be done?

How Serenbe Supports the Arts and Artists

After years of serving on several arts boards, I had a chance to see first-hand the benefits that the arts bring to a community. And so when I started developing Serenbe, I wanted to honor the arts in a significant way. To do that, though, we needed to set up permanent funding.

Funding the Arts Through Transfer Fees

When planning for Serenbe was underway, I was visiting various communities as part of my research. One community I visited had a 0.25 percent transfer fee for the environment. This means that when anyone bought a home in that community, 0.25 percent of the home's value was paid by the buyer to a fund that supported the environment. I looked further into this methodology and decided, why not add a transfer fee that helps support art and environmental education in the community? There were no regulations preventing a private developer from leveling this fee. So, we added a 1 percent fee for all developed properties and a 3 percent fee for nondeveloped lots as a requirement in Serenbe's original Covenants, Conditions, and Restrictions (CCRs).

This fee is paid by the buyer every time real estate is sold or resold. At closing, the 1 or 3 percent transfer fee is sent directly to a designated nonprofit. Developers have the option annually to designate which non-profit receives that year's transfer fees, but they are required to fund arts and environmental initiatives.

When we were discussing this possibility, real estate professionals told us again and again that buyers would not go along with it and that we would undoubtedly lose sales. But here we are, twenty years later, and we have never lost a sale!

Currently, Serenbe's transfer fees are designated to our nonprofit organization the Art Farm. Its mission is to cultivate meaningful part-nerships for programming, learning, and outreach while honoring the culture and diversity of our local communities with care for the natural environment. The Art Farm strives to create and maintain environments for world-class performances, artist residencies, thought leadership, and arts incubation. The local arts community knows that this funding exists, so they bring their ideas to Serenbe and together we bring high-quality events, projects, and exhibits into fruition.

Throughout the years the Art Farm, originally called the Serenbe Institute, has sponsored world-class theater productions, live music events, movie nights, comedy shows, visual art installations, dance performances, and much more. A typical season includes something for everyone.

Later in this chapter, I'll share some ideas for long-term arts funding if transfer fees aren't feasible in your community.

Welcome to the Art Farm! A Sampling of What We're Doing in Serenbe

Broadway talent arrives annually for full-scale musical theater productions like *Little Shop of Horrors*. Terminus Modern Ballet Theatre performs in nontraditional venues (often outdoors) with set pieces like raging towers of fire that would be impossible to support in a closed theater environment. And musical touring group Tertulia performs classical chamber music concerts in nature and in cafes around Serenbe.

Recently, Serenbe's Art Farm has offered programming that explores the definition of art and entertainment, celebrating unique forms of expression such as acrobatics, filmmaking, spoken word, and more. The Art Farm is also engaging with the community by hosting several interactive environmental events, as well as a new workshop series that will allow participants to learn directly from experts and create art that is personally meaningful to them.

Other recent events sponsored by the Art Farm include a memoir-writing workshop, a "Movies That Made Me" series led by a world-famous choreographer and creative director, Friday night jazz concerts, drive-in movies in Serenbe's wildflower meadow, and an electrifying circus act under the Big Top. (See photos on page 193.)

Life and Art Intersect in Serenbe

Early on we set the intention of making our Selborne hamlet the center of the community's art scene. We decided to complete the aesthetic by featuring artist-designed public amenities instead of purchasing them from standard catalogues. These would include the hamlet's lamps, benches, trash cans, signs, and handrails. Hiring artists to design these functional works of art and hiring craftsmen to build them sent a message that we honored art, and that further, we lived and practiced the belief that art is central to a healthy, happy life.

The Art Farm at Serenbe has performances throughout the year featuring theater, dance, music, film, and environmental education. *Photos by J. Ashley.*

As part of this collaboration, I commissioned artist Robert Rausch to create many of Serenbe's functional art pieces. The first piece Robert designed was a marketing box that featured a bronze cast of an acorn, which was central to Serenbe's branding from the beginning. (As I shared in chapter 6, this box was sent to early potential buyers and investors.) The oak acorn symbolized a seed of new thought growing into a sturdy hardwood tree, just as I hoped my fledgling plans for Serenbe would eventually grow into a strong, vibrant community.

Robert went on to design unique streetlamps for Serenbe's individual hamlets, reflecting each neighborhood's area of focus. For example, Selborne's commercial focus is on the arts, and its architecture is influenced by styles from the 1920s. Robert's cast-iron streetlights in the shape of Art Deco trees are a perfect fit. For Grange, which has an agricultural focus, Robert designed a double lantern supported by a rustic wooden post. For Mado, the streetlights are metal cones with laser-cut designs. Finally, for Spela, the lampposts are Art Deco–inspired, with branching arms, dangling shades, and handblown crystals shaped like leaves. Over the years, Robert has continued to work closely with Serenbe, both as an artist in his own right and by connecting us to other artists whose work we have commissioned.

Public Art Takes Center Stage

Understanding the need for public art in the community, we determined several locations throughout Serenbe where we would display an assortment of murals, sculptures, and other forms of artistic expression. As residents go about their day, they enjoy paintings on the exterior of our businesses, or lovely sculpted statues thoughtfully placed along walking paths or other public thoroughfares. Some of our public art includes the following.

The Dance, by Martin Dawe. Located in Serenbe's Wildflower Meadow.

When artist Martin Dawe visited Serenbe, he was struck by the balance we achieved on a community-wide scale as we addressed the dynamics of social and physical structures, governance, and cultural life. Dawe said this reminded him of the balance between the "feminine" and "masculine" aspects within all individuals regardless of gender and inspired the sculpture he titled *The Dance*. This powerful piece of art was further inspired by one of Kahlil Gibran's poems from his book *The Prophet*:

Give your hearts, but not into each other's keeping.
For only the hand of Life can contain your hearts.
And stand together yet not too near together:
For the pillars of the temple stand apart,
And the oak tree and the cypress grow
not in each other's shadow.[4]

Methods of Embrace, by Serenbe resident Rachel Garceau. Located at the Mado Pond.

Many Serenbe community members are well-known artists. Rachel Garceau's *Methods of Embrace* is positioned as a portal leading into the woods from the center of the Mado hamlet. Consisting of interlocking porcelain tubes and forms, the sculpture suggests the act of embracing—not just physically but also emotionally—through its delicate and organic design. Garceau says the fragility and strength of porcelain play important roles in symbolizing the human experience, representing both the support and the tenderness involved in human connections. This aspect of the sculpture invites viewers to reflect on their own personal relationships and interactions.

Serenity for Shango, by Curtis Patterson. Located at the entrance of Serenbe.

This work by world-renowned sculptor Curtis Patterson is the result of Serenbe's Public Black Art Project, which supports Black artists by opening a cultural space and sparking important, community-wide dialogue. *Serenity for Shango* is a powerful example of how art can help communicate via the heart while opening the mind to different perspectives and experiences. The primary figurative element in the piece is influenced by Shango, a deity of the Yoruba people of Nigeria who is believed to imbue power and energy. The double-iron shape atop the figurehead

The Dance by Martin Dawe.

Methods of Embrace by Rachel Garceau. *Photo by Rachel Garceau.*

Serenity for Shango by Curtis Patterson.

The Tree by Morgan Boszilkov. *Photo by Mia Yakel.*

is a symbolic element paying homage to those who served as domestic laborers for hundreds of years.

The Tree, by Serenbe resident Morgan Boszilkov. Located in the Selborne hamlet.

This ceramic tile mosaic was commissioned in memory of Shelton Stanfill, former chair of the Art Farm and a powerful voice and influence in the US art world. The tree represents the many branches of art Shelton was involved in and his love of nature.

Serenbe's Artists in Residency Program Gives Artists the Opportunity to Recharge and Create

A walk in the woods is a wellspring for human creativity. It recharges us and enables us to thrive. With such a rich natural environment surrounding us, one of our first artists, Tom Swanston, championed Serenbe as the perfect environment for artists to partake in a residency program that would benefit community members, visitors, and artists alike.

Artists in Residence Need a Residence!

Various Serenbe residents opened their homes and guesthouses to accommodate our first Artists in Residence, but building dedicated cottages to support this program was always the plan. After a few years, we learned that Rural Studio, an architecture program at Auburn University whose mission is to educate students and help build homes for under-resourced communities, was looking for a partner to test the viability of student projects in the real world.

The Serenbe team raised money to build these cottages, recruited builders to bid on the construction documents, permitted the plans, and oversaw the EarthCraft certification. This partnership gave Rural Studio the opportunity to determine the true, real-world cost of building a cottage so that the plans could be shared with other organizations and communities. (Up to this point, Rural Studio's builds had been completed using donated product and student labor as an educational process.) On our end, it was a perfect fit with Serenbe's tradition of working with universities for thought leadership.

In 2015, we broke ground on two cottages. In the end, each Artist in Residence cottage cost around $70,000 total to complete. While a cottage with this price tag certainly falls into the "affordable" range, Rural Studio continues to work toward even more cost-efficient designs.

Scan QR code 11.1 at the end of this chapter to learn more about Rural Studio.

The Artists in Residency program serves twenty-five to thirty artists per year, who stay at Serenbe from two weeks to one month. We invite writers, painters, musicians, sculptors, spoken word artists, and poets to come spend time in nature, recharge their creative energies, and work on their projects. Artists are nominated to attend by partnering organizations as well as by museums in the southeast area. While in residency, they have an opportunity to share their work and talk about their creative practice with the community.

To learn about some of Serenbe's Artists in Residence, scan QR code 11.2 at the end of this chapter.

Artist Spotlight: Serenbe's First Artists in Residence Call Serenbe Home

When married couple Gail Foster and Tom Swanston were deciding where their next home base would be back in the early 2000s, I invited them to come see what we were doing at Serenbe. They were all in! We ultimately traded art for land to reduce the couple's purchase price. They bought two live-work spaces where they would establish their studios and later open Serenbe's first art gallery in 2005.

Around this same time, Tom had been observing the migration of sandhill cranes along with nature's amazing ability to renew itself. Today, much of his work involves themes around migration, the movement through time and space, and ultimately returning home again. This archetypal form resonates with people around the world. Today, Tom's work is found in the United States as well as in faraway places like Hong Kong and Istanbul.

Gail's art has always revolved around change—personal change, changes in relationships, and changes within the relationships to universal powers. Sadly, she passed recently, yet her final work lives on, including elemental photography of "trash to treasure" assemblages, low-VOC (volatile organic compound) acrylic paintings, and mixed media on paper.

To learn more about Gail's and Tom's art, scan QR code 11.3 at the end of this chapter.

Serenbe Collaborates with Terminus Modern Ballet Theatre

Terminus Modern Ballet Theatre is Atlanta's premier contemporary ballet company. When a group of five contemporary dancers decided to leave the Atlanta Ballet Company, they formed Terminus under the capable direction of John Welker. Under the umbrella of Serenbe's Art Farm, Terminus was able to find the support it needed to work through some of its many start-up issues. Today, Terminus is its own 501(c)3 and enjoys performing at Serenbe several times a year, as well as throughout the Atlanta area and at their space in Midtown Atlanta. In addition to performance, they've established an excellent school for young students of ballet.

To learn more about Terminus Modern Ballet Theatre, scan QR code 11.4 at the end of this chapter.

Our Art-Focused Community Attracts Residents Who Are (What Else?) Artists!

By setting our intention and following through with policy and action, we achieved our desired results in an organic way. And in doing so, the creative class from coast to coast has naturally discovered Serenbe over the years. I won't name names, but many well-known people in the film and theater industries now call Serenbe home, and their children are enrolled in Terra School. Others are moving their studios or offices to Serenbe.

All of these elements tie together to make Serenbe a center for the arts. We give artists the foundation (and sometimes the inspiration) they need to work, and they bring the passion and talent to make the art happen.

What Communities Can Do to Support the Arts

Serenbe has created a model for those who seek to live in or visit a place where art and artists are integral parts of daily life. Here are some steps other communities can take to bring arts and culture to the forefront.

Explore Your Funding Options

A transfer fee to fund the arts was a good fit for Serenbe, but it may not be feasible for existing communities and towns. Here are a few alternative options that may work for you:

- Local governments can use a CID (Community Improvement District) fund to establish a commercial mixed-use district. CID funds are special taxes levied on commercial property owners in a designated area, and are typically used to fund services, upgrades, and improvements. Atlanta's Midtown Improvement District, or MID, is a good example of this model. The MID works closely with the Midtown Alliance, a nonprofit membership organization made up of businesses, three residential neighborhoods bordering the area, and community members who are united in their commitment to make Midtown Atlanta a premier destination for commerce, culture, education, and living.

- Some cities choose to establish cultural districts with tax incentives for artists and creative businesses, funded by the resulting economic growth.
- Others implement tourism taxes that allocate a portion of hotel, restaurant, or tourism revenue to arts initiatives.
- A forward-thinking city can even dedicate a percentage of its capital improvement projects budget to public art. If you go this route, I recommend establishing an arts council funded by a portion of annual real estate tax revenues to promote the arts, organize events, and allocate funding.
- Cities can issue municipal or community bonds for arts funding, repaid through community support or project revenues.

These approaches create a sustainable ecosystem for arts funding, blending public, private, and community contributions while advancing broader goals like economic development, cultural enrichment, and social cohesion.

Form a Public Art Committee to Bring Arts to Your Area

Bring together a committee of people educated in and/or well informed about the arts to figure out how to bring initiatives to your community. What can you do to bring art and culture to schools, businesses, and community centers? What existing arts organizations are already in place? How can you support them or help them expand their impact?

Bring Arts Education to the Classroom

There are numerous national and local organizations working to introduce school-aged children to the arts. Scan QR code 11.5 at the end of this chapter to learn more about several prominent arts initiatives for children. Perhaps they (or others like them) might be a good fit for your community.

Communities can also expose schoolchildren to arts and culture through simple projects and programming. Here are a few things schools and communities can do to get kids excited about art:

- Invite working artists into the classroom to talk about their experiences and their work and, if feasible, to lead students in producing their own creative projects.
- Create school events around a famous (or locally famous) artist. For example, during "Frida Kahlo Day," students might learn about Kahlo's life and culture, view her works, discuss her inspiration, and create their own Kahlo-inspired art. Don't limit yourself to visual artists, either—you can do the same with writers, poets, actors, and the like.
- If there is a blank wall at a school or in a public spot in the community, allow students to turn it into a mural. Perhaps a local artist might even lead students in choosing a subject and creating the finished work!
- Feature art on school grounds. Is there a front walk that can become a three-dimensional art installation? Is there an entryway or hallway that might host rotating exhibits of various artists' work? (And yes, posters and prints of famous paintings count!)
- Infuse creativity into recess by allowing students to have fun with sidewalk chalk. If you'd like to take a more structured approach, you might assign one class per week to transform a section of sidewalk into a piece of art based on a prompt.

Include the Community's Artists in the Planning

The arts community likely has a wealth of ideas as well as know-how. Be sure to take advantage of their wisdom. Pull together a group of local artists for a coffee and brainstorming session. Ask them, "What are your ideas for bringing more art to our area?"

Is There a History of Art in the Community? Tell That Story

It's very important to narrate the significance of art in the community so residents begin to understand its impact. Tell your story far and wide. Share these stories in the local paper, in newsletters, and in online posts. Start publishing the reports and statistics associated with your arts initiatives so that the community can see the impact and value of local arts. To view an example of the Art Farm's annual report, scan QR code 11.6 at the end of this chapter.

Highlight the Community's Homegrown Creatives and Share Their Stories

Is there a former student who graduated from the local school and went on to earn a living in the creative world? If so, tell the story, celebrating them and their experience. Maybe a local art teacher or artistic parent inspired them. Or maybe it was the lack of art in their life, and their subsequent thirst and struggle to find it, that drove them to carve out a career as a creative professional in your community. That story can join the tapestry of your community's artistic history.

Create Arts Awareness Through Celebrations

April 15 is National Art Day in the United States. Tie your community's arts culture into occasions like this by creating a slate of arts-focused events. You might hold a school-system-wide art contest, a "pay what you can" night at a local theater, or a series of free concerts and lectures featuring musicians, authors, or poets.

Figure Out Innovative New and Traditional Ways to Create Art

While there are fewer traditional avenues for funding art, you can still tap into the sources that exist, even as you pursue new methods. Can religious communities come together around an art project? Maybe your local church, synagogue, or mosque would house a local community choir, or display a rotation of public art, or put on a musical. Also, be sure to speak with any local philanthropists and make a case for funding one of the arts events conceptualized by the arts committee.

Use Art to Address Tough Topics that Impact Your Community

Art is a powerful way society can grapple with difficult topics because art speaks though the nonjudgmental heart versus the critical (and often reactive) brain. Seek out artistic expression that deals with tough issues such as racism or social justice and use it as a springboard for dialogue, understanding, and positive change. Serenbe's Black Art Project is a good example. To learn more about this project, scan QR code 11.7 at the end of this chapter.

Humans have an intrinsic need for creativity. I see this every day in Serenbe—not just through our community's professional artists, but in the preschooler who stops on the sidewalk to arrange leaves into a pattern and the homeowner who lovingly decorates with meaningful objects.

I believe that art in any form fulfills deep societal needs by revealing important truths and speaking to the heart. Throughout history, regardless of the era or the challenges of the moment, art has possessed a unique ability to transcend and connect. By infusing art into your community's heritage, you will strengthen its identity, showcase its vibrancy, and inspire residents and visitors alike.

Chapter 11 QR Codes

Rural Studio
QR Code 11.1

Artists
QR Code 11.2

Gail & Tom
QR Code 11.3

Ballet
QR Code 11.4

Children
QR Code 11.5

Art Farm
QR Code 11.6

Art Project
QR Code 11.7

Chapter 11
Image Gallery

12

Creating a Community That Attracts a Creative Class of Visitors, Residents, and Businesses

Maybe you live in an established community and are reading this book because you're interested in encouraging your town or city to shift toward a lifestyle that makes people healthier and happier. Or maybe you want to create a biophilic community from scratch, as I did. Either way, at some point on your journey, attracting visitors, new residents, and businesses will become an important part of the process. When you create a place that connects people and nature in a thoughtful and artistic way, you'll find that visitors often become residents and business owners, and that everyone actively engages in community life.

So how do you invite newcomers to plug into a conscious, connected, and curious lifestyle? In this chapter, we'll look at some commonsense ideas and best practices that will welcome and engage people for a day, a week, or a lifetime.

Why Is Serenbe Attractive to Visitors and Residents?

For many visitors and new residents, one of Serenbe's primary draws is the fact that it's an "escape" or "getaway" from city or suburban life. Being here is a way to experience small-town convenience, a slower pace, and nature without giving up conveniences and some of the "finer things." People don't need to leave for the essentials (like food or medical care) or for many add-ons (like various retail options, salon and spa services, a school, etc.). And since Serenbe is walkable with mixed-use zoning, there's no need to drive from one highly developed commercial center to another. Children who live in Serenbe are rarely in a car seat.

For those who feel the need to connect with a larger city, Serenbe is only forty minutes from the heart of downtown Atlanta, twenty minutes from five traditional commercial centers with big-box retail and chain restaurants, and twenty-five minutes from an international airport connecting nonstop to capitals of the world.

"Welcome to Our Community!" How Serenbe Attracts Visitors

I think it's fair to say that we all understand why visitors are an important part of a community's economy. When tourists patronize local businesses, it helps those businesses grow, creates employment opportunities, and brings dollars into the community. (Residents win too, because—especially in a walkable community—they are able to take advantage of retail and hospitality venues that survive due to support from visitors.) Tourism revenue can be reinvested in the community, making it an even more attractive place to visit and live. Plus, satisfied visitors can be a fantastic source of free marketing as they tell others about their positive experiences.

While the economic benefits of attracting visitors might be top-of-mind, there are plenty of other good reasons to bring newcomers into your community. I've always found that the people who visit Serenbe help keep things fresh because they provide a constantly changing connection to the wider world. I love hearing their perspectives, observations, and suggestions as they experience our community. Without visitors, Serenbe could easily become isolated, insular, and inward-focused—none of which would be compatible with our desire to be connected, conscious, and caring citizens.

As Serenbe evolved from my family's farm into a residential community, we have always striven to remain inviting, open, and welcoming to everyone, especially because we aren't in a location that most people would serendipitously stumble upon or happen to drive through. Visitors must make a conscious choice to come to our community in the woods—which means we must make a conscious effort to attract them.

Here, I'll share our approach to doing that, as well as some tips to help your community do the same.

Make the First Move: Invite Visitors In

In order to attract visitors, explicitly invite them in and make them feel welcome. Don't assume that they'll make their way into your community on their own, even if (unlike Serenbe) you tend to get a lot of foot or vehicle traffic. Think about it: How many neighborhoods or towns have you repeatedly traveled through without ever stopping to learn more about them?

First, ensure that you're making it easy for visitors to physically come into your community. Make sure roads and entrances are clearly marked and consider erecting welcome signs. Avoid marks of exclusivity or "checkpoints," such as gating your community or requiring credentials or payment to enter. Second, publicize events, performances, amenities, venues, and businesses that are open to the public. Thanks to social media this is easier and cheaper to do than ever before—although "old school" methods like newspaper and television ads, signage, and direct mail won't hurt.

The good news is that if people have a positive first experience with your community, they'll often be proactive about keeping it on their radar. Again, social media makes this easy—a simple "like" or "follow" can ensure that visitors are notified of future events and opportunities.

In our case, many people who live in the surrounding Chattahoochee Hills and metro Atlanta area frequently take advantage of Serenbe's events, facilities, restaurants, and amenities. We publicize events that are open to the public, whether those have to do with art, performances, the farm, and so on. In fact, between 3,000 and 5,000 visitors come into Serenbe each week.

Look for Reasons Why People Might Want to Visit—Then Leverage Them

As I've mentioned, people need a reason to visit other communities. Chances are, you already have assets, amenities, and features that will draw people in. You don't necessarily need to (and probably shouldn't!) create new attractions right off the bat.

If you haven't done so already, inventory your community's strengths. What makes it unique? What is it known for? What does it do well? Where do people already tend to spend their time and money? What traditions do you have? What do current visitors tend to comment on or seek out?

For example, some of the reasons why people visit Serenbe include:

- Trails and outdoor recreation, including horseback riding and goat yoga
- Regular community events (e.g., trivia night, wine tastings, our annual plant sale, etc.)
- Our working farm and farmers market
- Arts and culture events (exhibitions and installations, musicals and theater, etc.)
- Fitness and wellness opportunities (spa treatments, yoga, Pilates, etc.)
- Standout farm-to-table restaurants

While these elements are the norm for Serenbe residents, they are far enough outside many people's everyday experience to qualify as good reasons for a getaway or vacation. Thus, they are easy for us to leverage.

Your "Reasons to Visit" Don't Need to Look Like Ours!

And they probably won't, because every community is different. For instance, Serenbe has a barn and horses, which we advertise to attract visitors. If you don't have those things, you certainly don't need to build a barn and buy horses. Use our community as a springboard for your own ideas, not as a recipe you must follow exactly.

Be Intentional When Creating New Amenities and Attractions

If you are creating new infrastructure and events with the specific goal of attracting visitors, think about areas where you want to see community growth and what you would like your community to be known for. In other words, what are your values and your brand? Let this vision guide your growth.

For instance, early on we decided that art was an important factor in creating a vibrant, creative community. Chapter 11 describes many of the programs, initiatives, and events that we've established to encourage a thriving arts community in Serenbe. Because of our focused efforts, we've not only created a rich arts culture for our residents; we've also attracted an active visitor population to help support these various entities.

Scan QR code 12.1 at the end of this chapter to learn how other communities across the country have attracted visitors by placing a focus on the arts, agriculture, and the natural world.

Emphasize Hospitality: Create Places to Gather and Stay

Establishing restaurants, retail, meeting spaces, and overnight accommodations is a key to attracting visitors *and* residents. The more there is to see, do, experience, buy, eat, and so on, the more people will want to spend time in a particular community—whether it's for a few hours, a weekend, or a lifetime. (At the risk of sounding cliché: If you build it, they will come.)

A lot has evolved about Serenbe since its early days, but my place-making philosophy has not. While Serenbe is a residential community, it also devotes a lot of resources to providing experiences and accommodations for visitors. It is, more than ever, a place to gather. For instance:

- In addition to taking advantage of the experiences and amenities mentioned throughout this book, visitors can choose to stay at the Inn at Serenbe. They can also rent a cottage or home in the community while enjoying the inn's amenities and services.

- Packages and themed getaways combine accommodations, dining, and activities. At various times of the year, visitors can book overnight packages that feature cooking classes, gourmet wine and food pairings, stargazing, architecture tours, outdoor activities, spa treatments, holiday celebrations, and more.

- Serenbe provides venues that can accommodate a wide range of events. It's probably easy to see why Serenbe would be a fantastic location for, say, a wedding, celebration, or family reunion—but you may be surprised to learn that there is a lot of corporate business during the week. We've fitted out meeting spaces with plenty of flexible seating, projectors, HD displays, and private break areas, and we also offer the services of an events coordinator. We frequently host conferences, corporate retreats, team-building functions, and client entertainment.

The Restaurant in the Woods

During my early career in the hospitality industry, I found that restaurants had the power to transform retail or geographic areas (especially ones that weren't previously popular or trendy) into "places to be." For instance, the 1973 opening of the Pleasant Peasant in Midtown Atlanta was instrumental in transforming a neglected section of Peachtree Street into a popular up-and-coming area. Later, the Peasant on Pennsylvania in Washington, DC, was one of five restaurants recruited to help transform Pennsylvania Avenue between the White House and the US Capitol into the vibrant live-work-play center that it is today.

With those experiences under my belt, I realized early on that one of the first things I needed to do at Serenbe was create a place where people could gather for conversation, food, and drink. That place turned out to be the Blue Eyed Daisy Bakeshop, which opened by the time the fourth resident moved in. Real estate and financial professionals thought I was crazy! They encouraged me to locate the restaurant on a main road, not in the middle of the woods. But my goal wasn't just to get warm bodies into the restaurant; it was to create a destination that would, eventually, attract visitors off the main road and into the woods. I call this placemaking.

This idea has continued to be central as Serenbe has expanded. In each hamlet, there is some type of business where people can gather over food, a cup of coffee, or a glass of wine. As I write this book, Serenbe has twelve hospitality businesses for seven hundred households—and those numbers are growing!

Balance the Needs of Visitors and Residents

Sometimes I'm asked whether Serenbe's residents mind the thousands of visitors who enjoy our community every week. Especially given our closely clustered hamlets and mixed-use development, don't residents get tired of having other people in "their" neighborhood space? Walking on "their" sidewalks? Shopping at "their" neighborhood stores?

By and large, this doesn't tend to be an issue. I believe the main reason is that Serenbe exemplifies placemaking, a process centered on creating vibrant, meaningful spaces that prioritize human experience, community engagement, and connection. For instance, Serenbe's focus on pedestrians means that parking areas don't take center stage and vehicle traffic is limited. Visitors tend to get around on foot too, so residents aren't overly bothered by an abundance of automobiles. Additionally, some of Serenbe's amenities, like our network of trails, are reserved for residents and guests (for instance, of the inn), not day visitors. The swim club requires a membership. There are plenty of retreats for residents!

While placemaking is all about creating quality of place for the people who use it, traditional development tends to be developer-led, top-down, and focused on short-term financial results, efficiency, and regulatory compliance. This can lead to negative impacts like overcrowding, overtourism, and disturbances to locals.

Serenbe's residents are drawn to our intentional approach. They understand and support growth because it brings services, entertainment, and hospitality venues they can walk to, enhancing the community's self-sustainability. Visitors play a vital role in supporting Serenbe's restaurants, shops, and art events, making the community an enduring model of placemaking success.

That said, there have been times when visitors have disrupted Serenbe's local rhythms. For instance, as I'll share in the next chapter, in our earlier years Serenbe hosted events to attract outside visitors. As Serenbe became more well known, resident support for these events dwindled because they *were* so visitor-centric—and we decided not to hold them anymore.

If you are developing a new community, a focus on placemaking will likely prevent visitors and residents from butting heads too fiercely. If you're revamping an existing area, perhaps converting it into a mixed-use zone, these pointers may help you achieve a balanced volume of visitors:

- As I mentioned earlier, I encourage communities not to charge an entrance fee to enter the town or neighborhood itself. However, you *can* charge entrance fees to popular attractions and events—perhaps even limiting the maximum number of visitors or adding timed-entry slots.
- If a certain public space like a town square, art installation, or garden is becoming overwhelmed, follow the lead of cities like Venice, Lisbon, and Amsterdam and charge a tourist tax. These charges can be added to overnight accommodations.
- Focus on walkability. Locate parking on the fringes of your community and in less-visible areas. And be creative with space! Just because a building or shopping center used to have a massive parking lot doesn't mean that still needs to be the case. Turn it into a park or garden instead.
- Try to attract businesses that will be attractive to visitors and residents alike. A boutique with locally made jewelry? Yes! A souvenir shop? Maybe not.

Putting Down Roots: How Serenbe Attracts Residents

Attracting visitors is an important part of developing a vibrant, growth-focused community, but a community's residents are the biggest determining factor in establishing its identity, values, connectedness, goals, and so much more.

No matter what stage you're at in developing your community, attracting residents is something you'll need to consider. If you're building a community from the ground up, bringing in residents will be a main priority early on. Even if your community is currently at residential capacity, sooner or later various properties will go on the market!

Here's the good news: In many ways, attracting more residents to your community is no different than attracting visitors. After all, who better to relocate to a place than people who already know and love it? That has certainly been our experience at Serenbe.

Just like attracting visitors, there isn't a set formula for attracting residents. So much of building a permanent community depends on the relationships, social norms, and traditions that organically grow between residents, businesses, and even their natural and built environments.

While I can't tell you step-by-step how to encourage people to call your community home, I can share how that has played out at Serenbe.

Be Welcoming to All and Banish Notions of Exclusivity

I'm not a proponent of creating homogeneous communities where everyone has the same background and espouses the same political or social ideology. I love communities where everyone is welcomed, where neighbors care about one another, and where all residents are invested in one another's well-being.

The only requirement to live at Serenbe is being able to pay your mortgage or rent and bills. There is no selection committee for potential residents—but residents do tend to self-select. I'll admit that this is a broad generalization, but by and large, when dyed-in-the-wool pessimists, cynics, and critics visit Serenbe, they just don't "get" our ethos and way of life—and they usually aren't tempted to live here. Optimists *do* get it—they feel the positive vibes of hope and engagement.

As we continue to grow, I see Serenbe as a "community without labels." As I've mentioned elsewhere in this book, there are many types of households here: single adults, couples, families with children, and empty nesters. People come from a mix of backgrounds, ethnicities, sexualities, and political viewpoints. Our residents range in age from newborns to elders. They hail from all over the country, and indeed the world.

One thing nearly everyone has in common is that they all believe in Serenbe as a community. They understand the biophilic vision and love how those elements play out in everyday life. Serenbe is a place where they feel comfortable, connected, balanced, and at peace. In fact, multiple people have told me that before moving to Serenbe they would walk in their front door and say, "I'm home." Now, they say the same thing when they drive in Serenbe's front entrance. Home is no longer a house; it's a community.

Just Enough Sandpaper

By and large, Serenbe is a community where everyone's views fit. There is usually coexistence and respect, if not always agreement. That said—just like any gathering of human beings—there is disharmony from time to time. I believe this is a good thing. You need a certain amount of sandpaper to have a fine finish. When we are around people with different perspectives, opinions, and worldviews, it pushes us to reexamine (and perhaps redefine) our own.

Minimize Fees and Requirements

The more fees people have to pay, the more rules and regulations they have to follow, and the more hoops they have to jump through to live in your community . . . the more many of them will be turned off. The ultimate result will be that you'll create an exclusive, homogeneous community of people who *are* willing to follow the rules!

For this reason, we decided that Serenbe would be run more like a town than like a development where residents' HOA fees pay for amenities such as a pool. Our pool, stables, entertainment events, clubs, and more are all self-supporting and not dependent on any assessed fees. For instance, Serenbe Swim Club is privately owned. Residents can choose to purchase a membership or not, depending on their preferences. Serenbe's HOA fees go toward handling the basic maintenance of streets, trails, and landscaping in the common areas, as well as personal yards to the back corner of a house or fence.

We try to minimize the number of community rules, and those that are in place emphasize common sense and basic respect for each other and the natural world. As needs arise, new rules emerge. For example, in the early days we had no rules about leashes for dogs. However, as more residents with dogs (with varying degrees of training!) moved into our community, the need for leash laws became evident.

Instead of Utilizing Traditional Advertising, Consider Letting Your Community Market Itself

In my research on community development, I have noticed that many planned communities self-segregate (as opposed to self-select) because they target a particular demographic in their marketing. I don't think most of these communities have negative intentions, but the fact remains that if you place limits on who knows about your community, you won't have a wide variety of people visiting it, learning about it, and deciding whether or not to live there.

While Serenbe has a marketing team that helps facilitate earned media coverage and manages our social media accounts, we do not utilize traditional advertising. Instead, as I shared earlier in this chapter, we publicize all public events and welcome the wider community to visit our town anytime. This doubles as marketing for our community *without* feeling pushy or exclusionary. We are not advertising; we are simply sharing.

Regarding attracting residents, though, I can only give part of the credit to Serenbe's visitor outreach policy. We've found that when people love where they live, they'll tell their friends, family, and coworkers about it: "You should consider moving here! You'd love the trails/the farm/the restaurants/the art scene," and so on. Word of mouth is responsible for bringing in a lot of potential residents—and the personalized tours they receive from their friends often seal the deal.

Even when interested parties don't have a personal connection to our community (perhaps they learned about Serenbe on social media or via a news article), they quickly see what's special about this place. I can't tell you how many times I've heard potential home buyers comment on how neighbors connect with and care for one another, how children roam "free range" and enjoy their childhoods, how elders are included in community life, and more. Serenbe's sense of community isn't the reason many visitors initially come—but it is the reason many of them stay.

Make It Easy for People to Join Your Community with a Real Estate Office

As Serenbe has grown, my daughter Garnie created a real estate office, and all of its agents are Serenbe residents. Because they live and work here, agents see potential buyers as potential neighbors—and that motivates them to match each future resident with a property where they'll be happy and comfortable.

Serenbe's real estate agents help people buy and sell existing homes. They can also connect people who buy an empty lot with Serenbe's preferred builders. More than a few people who have moved to Serenbe have an origin story that starts like this: "Well, we were just here to visit, and we liked what we saw, so we decided to stop by the real estate office out of curiosity . . . and the rest is history."

Offer a Mix of Residential Options

The more choices people have for their dwellings, the more diverse your community's residents will be. A homogeneous group of homes will lead to a fairly homogeneous group of residents. You may need to become involved in your city's comprehensive plan updates to make sure a variety of home sizes are allowed. Often, there is a minimum square footage required. (Not only does this limit the variety of home sizes; it also isn't conducive to creating a clustered, walkable community.)

As you'll recall from chapter 6, Serenbe has housing options for everyone—tiny homes, townhomes, estate homes, live-works, and more. There are options to rent and to buy. In particular, we've found that mixed-use housing (like carriage house apartments, mother-in-law suites, or lower-level apartments in townhomes) is a great way to get people at various places in the economic spectrum into one community. And because we've mastered the art of mixing architectural styles and home sizes within the same intersection or along the same street, neighborhoods are made up of a mix of personalities, ages, and household sizes that are attracted to the various housing types.

"Onboard" New Residents

In a typical home purchase, the buyer gets the keys at closing, and perhaps also an information packet if there is an HOA or other type of neighborhood organization. After that, they're left to their own devices when it comes to learning about and plugging into their new home. However, this is the perfect opportunity to begin connecting with new residents and welcoming them into your community.

At Serenbe, the real estate office sends a list of closings to the director of community operations, who reaches out to soon-to-be residents via email. They are set up with Serenbe's weekly newsletters and with the Serenbe app, which allows residents to submit tickets for complaints, concerns, requests, questions, and so on. New residents are invited to meet with the director of community operations for what we call "onboarding." Aided by a brief PowerPoint presentation, the director overviews life at Serenbe and answers any questions the new residents might have.

The Way to the Neighbor's Heart Is Through Their Stomach

For our first forty residents, my wife, Marie, delivered a home-cooked meal on their first night in Serenbe. Versions of this welcome meal continue today as people reach out with food and a helping hand to new neighbors on their street.

New arrivals also get an unofficial "onboarding" in their neighborhoods. Current residents welcome them, are genuinely curious to get to know them, and go the extra mile to help them settle in. For example, neighbors often provide a meal for the first night in the house, organize a "get to know you" coffee or cocktail gathering with adjoining homes, or arrange playdates with other kids on the street. Each encounter is shaped by the personalities of the people involved. This is not formally planned or required—it's something people willingly choose to do and has become an ingrained part of Serenbe's identity.

Filling a Need: How Serenbe Creates an Attractive Atmosphere for Businesses

Before I conclude this chapter, there's one particular aspect of attracting people to your community that I'd like to touch on: creating an atmosphere for small businesses. As I mentioned earlier, a community's retail, restaurants, accommodations, and services play a big role in giving people a reason to visit (and potentially relocate); plus, they create a vibrant place to live.

A key principle of biophilic communities like Serenbe to is to connect people, and businesses play an important role in this. They serve as ambassadors to the public by showcasing the community's interests, values, and priorities. For instance, many of Serenbe's shops and markets feature products that are all-natural, sustainable, and responsibly sourced—often from local vendors. This sends a clear message about our ethos.

In some ways, facilitating the development of a thriving business community might seem more daunting than attracting visitors and residents. But again, when you prioritize shared biophilic values and human connection, I think you'll find that this aspect of development soon begins to take care of itself. Here are a few things I've observed at Serenbe.

Mixed-Use Zoning Makes a Big Difference

I've touched on mixed-use zoning several times throughout this book. To review, it integrates residential, commercial, and recreational spaces within close proximity, reducing reliance on cars and fostering dynamic, livable environments.

This model enhances economic activity while promoting environmental sustainability and strengthening community connections. By combining multiple functions within one area or building, it maximizes land use, curbs urban sprawl, and creates vibrant public spaces that host events, markets, and social activities. Additionally, diversified land use provides resilience to market fluctuations; for instance, if retail demand decreases, residential or office components can sustain the area's economic vitality.

Serenbe's business owners tend to appreciate our community's mixed-used zoning, and as you'll soon read, some even take advantage of our live-work buildings. In talking with business owners, I often hear some variation of "I love doing business here and can't imagine relocating elsewhere! Operating a business in Serenbe is like opening your front porch for business and inviting friends and neighbors to drop by for a chat."

However, mixed-use development does present challenges that you should be aware of if you are trying to apply this model in your community. It requires careful planning and collaboration to achieve a thoughtful urban design that balances aesthetics, functionality, and the diverse needs of users. These projects often face stricter zoning and building code requirements, necessitating negotiations with multiple stakeholders to align the interests of residents, businesses, and government agencies in close proximity.

When executed effectively, though, mixed-use zoning has the potential to transform urban and suburban living, delivering long-term social, economic, and environmental benefits.

Many Businesses Are Resident-Run

After coming to Serenbe, more than a few residents have decided to re-create their lives and careers in a way that's simpler, more values-driven, or truer to what they're really passionate about. Almost invariably, these people did not come to Serenbe with the intention of becoming entrepreneurs. Instead, integrating into our community triggered a reevaluation of priorities, prompted a values shift, or reawakened a long-dormant dream of opening their own business.

When residents see a need they can fill in Serenbe's business landscape, they often decide to take the plunge. Following are a few examples.

Raina and her husband occupied one of Serenbe's first five homes. She was a flight attendant, and her husband worked in Atlanta's fire department. Raina had always loved combing through thrift and consignment shops to find treasures, so as Serenbe grew she funneled her passion into opening Honeycomb Consignment, an upscale women's consignment boutique. It's a popular destination for people with an enviable closet that needs culling, as well as for women who want to find a special wardrobe piece that won't break the bank.

Greg represented a spa equipment company and traveled the world to promote its products. One year, a spa industry conference was held in Atlanta, and a tour of Serenbe was part of the post-conference schedule. I later found out that during the tour, Greg called his wife, Amanda, in Philadelphia, where they had lived for twenty years. He suggested that she join him at Serenbe for the weekend. After a second visit, they purchased a townhouse that included a home office space, which Greg equipped with some of his demonstration equipment. Within two years, though, Greg had left the international company so that he and Amanda could open Creek Retreat, which offers personalized, cutting-edge health, wellness, and aesthetic treatments.

Sometimes neighbors come together to combine their passion and talent with a void in the neighborhood's commercial fabric. For example, Charlene is a former pastry chef. Her neighbor Jeff frequently mentioned how much he missed his New York–style bagels, so the two of them started experimenting with recipes in his home kitchen. Around this time, a third neighbor bought a live-work and was exploring what business could occupy the street-level retail space. Soon, Radical Dough sprang to life. This neighborly collaboration offers bagels, pizza, and evening meals.

Similarly, another resident, Jill, bought a live-work in Mado to use as an investment property. One day over coffee with a friend, she wondered aloud about what type of business she could open to augment Mado's wellness focus. As it turned out, Jill's coffee mate, Julie, had been thinking about the best way to put her Doctor of Chiropractic degree and passion for therapeutic Pilates to use. The two came together and created Studio 13, a full-service Pilates studio.

Rachel, a ceramic sculptor, has "done it all" (or at least, a lot!) here at Serenbe. After moving to Serenbe, she was married at our little waterfall, had a son, and opened a studio in a street-facing retail space. Visitors can watch Rachel work and purchase her art. One of her pieces, *Methods of Embrace,* was featured in chapter 11.

The desire to live in—or return to—Serenbe has inspired some to create businesses that enable that return. Meghan and Patrick first visited after seeing Serenbe on the cover of *Cottage Living* magazine. They were instantly captivated and bought a home. After Patrick's promotion at Banana Republic took them to San Francisco, they often eased their homesickness by browsing Serenbe Real Estate's website. This longing led them to return and create Sharp Furniture Co., leaving their jobs to open a storefront shop offering furniture, home accessories, gifts, candles, and coffee table books—a reflection of their deep connection to home design and Serenbe.

On the other side of the coin, some of Serenbe's business owners were already operating in the entrepreneurship space and decided to open their doors here because they were drawn to what our community was doing. This led to many of them becoming residents. Here are a few examples:

- April and Tony were living in Boulder, Colorado, and dreaming about opening a nontoxic household and personal care boutique. When they read about Serenbe, they knew this was the perfect place to open Allchemy: A Biophilic Farmacy, which opened in Mado in the fall of 2024.
- As part of her own health journey, Kelley researched the advantages of cold-pressed juice and was amazed by the healing she experienced. Wanting to share these advantages, she looked for a partner—and found one in my daughter Garnie. Together they opened Bamboo Juices, which makes and bottles raw, organic, cold-pressed juices.

- When veterinarian Erica and her wife wanted a more rural experience for their family, they decided to buy a live-work at Serenbe. Collier Animal Hospital soon opened on the first floor.

Many of Serenbe's businesses have been here for years and are still going strong. Some have even reached "community fixture" status. Scan QR code 12.2 at the end of this chapter to check out Serenbe's podcast, *Serenbe Stories*. In many episodes, Serenbe residents and business owners recount what drew them to our community and what they love about living here.

The Commercial Intention of Each Neighborhood Attracts Businesses in Those Sectors

As I've shared, each of Serenbe's hamlets has a commercial focus. For example, Mado centers on health and wellness. Many wellness entrepreneurs and healthcare providers who have opened their doors here say that of all the locations they could have chosen in the Atlanta area, Serenbe stood out. Entrepreneurs liked that our community is known for embracing wellness practices and that the area is becoming known as a hub of well-being. Business owners knew that at Serenbe they would have a built-in group of potential clients who were *already* predisposed to health and wellness. And since Serenbe is accessible and welcoming to visitors who live across the greater Atlanta area, Mado's entrepreneurs can also tap into a broader pool of clients.

A Snapshot of Serenbe's Business Community

Serenbe's business community is constantly growing and evolving. We have a wide variety of businesses that span arts, education, food and dining, hospitality, retail, health and wellness, and more. To explore Serenbe's business directory, scan QR code 12.3 at the end of this chapter.

As I've said before, places like Serenbe "work" when people care about improving their own (literal and metaphorical) backyards, and when they engage with each other and with the natural world. The principles and practices I've described throughout this book will take root and flourish when the folks who live, work, play, worship, learn, socialize, and shop in your community become part of the process of making them happen.

Chapter 12 QR Codes

Visitors
QR Code 12.1

Serenbe Stories
QR Code 12.2

Businesses
QR Code 12.3

Chapter 12
Image Gallery

13

Events That Bring People Together

L iving in a beautiful community that's nestled in nature and filled with friendly neighbors is a wonderful experience. But even the most contented citizen can get a little restless (and maybe even bored) with their weekday routine. Inevitably they will ask, "So . . . what are we doing this weekend?"

A calendar full of social events is a sure sign that a community is strong and vibrant. "Programming" your community with fun activities is a smart way to bring people together and enrich lives. It gives them "something to do," exposes them to new things, strengthens their relationships with friends and neighbors, and builds a sense of belonging and engagement.

People who live in communities with plenty of things to do experience a higher quality of life. Plus, events help communities solidify and showcase what they stand for. (Remember, Serenbe is built on biophilic principles, one of which *is* community engagement, so our intense focus on events—not to mention the sheer number of them—makes perfect sense for us!)

Here are a few of the ways events build and sustain communities:

- **Events boost the local economy by attracting visitors.** When people come out for events, they spend their money in that community. This might include buying food, experiences, and souvenirs. This spending supports local businesses. Then, if they enjoy their experience, those people will come back and tell their friends that they should visit as well—creating a beneficial economic cycle for the community.

- **They foster connection.** Events give community members a chance to come together and get to know one another on a deeper level. It creates networking opportunities for professionals and gives everyone a chance to talk, make new friends, and strengthen existing friendships.

- **They support mental and emotional wellness.** People need things to do besides eat, work, and sleep. Activities and events give them something to look forward to and a chance to socialize, which supports their mental health and emotional wellbeing. Events are especially important for people who spend long stretches of time at home, such as the elderly.

- **Events help bolster the community's identity.** Well-loved traditions create lasting memories for community members and help the community collectively identify what it values and stands for. Annual events such as festivals and celebrations strengthen the social fabric of communities.

- **They improve quality of life for citizens.** A well-thought-out roster of events and activities makes a community a great place to live or visit. It creates a sense of anticipation, fun, and belonging for everyone.

So you see, events are vital for people's presence and their engagement. Your community building efforts won't be complete without thoughtful and compelling events programming. But you'll need more than good intentions to get your efforts underway. In the next section we'll learn the *who* and the *how* of planning events that will attract people to your neck of the woods.

Programming = People: How Events Attract Visitors and New Residents

We can learn an important lesson about the value of events from communities that are growing and/or revitalizing their downtowns. Programming (creating activities to drive people downtown) is a big piece of their strategy. It gets people to show up, spend time and money, and come back in the future. Not only do events attract visitors on day or weekend trips, but they also encourage people to move in permanently because the downtown is becoming more vibrant and interesting. As the downtown grows, it will also attract new businesses. (You can't expect a business to open downtown if there are no people in the area.) In other words, events become a catalyst for the downtown's overall economic growth. They are the magnetic force that attracts people and makes them excited about being there.

I knew this from my own experience in Atlanta as chairman of the Midtown Alliance in the early 1990s. Our Much Ado About Midtown event, which closed off one mile of Peachtree Street for over 160 performing artists and exhibits, was attended by thousands of people. It brought public awareness to the fact that Midtown Atlanta was home to major museums, theaters, restaurants, and more, and was an early contributor to the revitalization of the area. As you'll see later in this chapter, a similar strategy at Serenbe (albeit on a smaller scale.) created awareness and drew people into our community. Many of them are still here!

Whose Job Is It to Plan Events?

Who should oversee planning events that attract people to a community? In a way, this is everybody's job, so unfortunately, often it is nobody's job. This can be one reason it's sometimes tough to get momentum going in planning and carrying out events.

The good news is, once you get a few people stepping up, the momentum builds. (Reading this book is a good starting point!) But when a community is getting started with offering a lineup of events, community leaders should, well, *lead* the efforts. Here are some insights:

- **Community leaders should get the (events) ball rolling.** It's up to the community leaders to show people how programming, as well as events planning and execution, are done. Depending on the type of community, local business leaders, Chambers of Commerce, or development organizations might take the lead on this.
- **Educate the community on why events matter.** Leaders and organizers should position events as a community value that everyone supports and believes in. Continue getting buy-in by sharing the benefits of events programming (see above).
- **Invite others to join you or take on the mantle of event planning themselves.** Once you have hosted one or two successful events, the spirit of creativity and momentum will spread to others. At this point, invite new people who seem engaged and willing to take a more involved role. Over time, this process becomes more organic because people now want to spend time together and make something great happen. They believe it is important—because they've seen the success and benefit firsthand—and it becomes part of their values.

Back to the Beginning: Early Events at Serenbe

In the early days, the Serenbe Development Company functioned a bit like a cruise ship, planning events to create awareness that there was a great community growing out here in the woods of rural Georgia. Our goal was to attract people to visit and check out what we were doing. Over twenty years later, as residents have taken over the events planning (and have even created their own events), the development team has transitioned away from planning and sponsoring the events around Serenbe.

This evolution speaks to the need for sustainability in planning events. While it may be necessary for a development company or local government to get the ball rolling, it is good to eventually transition the role of planning and carrying out events to the community members themselves. Resident ownership of the process gives it the vitality required to keep events going year after year.

May Day: The Event That Jump-Started Our Programming Efforts

One of the first events Serenbe ever hosted was its May Day celebration. From the beginning, May Day was a big deal in our community because we wanted to celebrate the culinary, visual, and performing arts—and also to celebrate the agrarian meaning of May Day, which historically signified the beginning of the spring planting season. Serenbe's May Day event was a huge draw, attracting visitors from all over the area. We closed down the streets and held an art and food street festival for people of all ages.

The celebration went on for around fourteen years, but Serenbe Development Company eventually stopped producing it. There was no energy from the community to take the reins because it was primarily an attraction for people outside of Serenbe. While residents got a lot from the event in its prime, they decided it was time to move on. This is a good example of keeping in mind who you are trying to serve and knowing when it's time to pivot to something new.

How a July 4 Challenge Became a Time-Honored Tradition

Other Serenbe events started organically and simply needed community support to grow. Our yearly Fourth of July parade is one example. Years ago, a group of residents decided Serenbe should have a holiday parade. They set a challenge for residents to build parade floats. Soon, float-building parties were cropping up in various garages. A neighbor whose family has been in the area for seven generations volunteered his antique tractor. Now, three generations of that family continue to lead the parade each year. Another group organized fireworks, and yet another group took on planning for the afternoon barbecue. This grassroots effort has created a beloved event people look forward to every year.

Today, Serenbe has transitioned to a more mature community with 1,400 residents who take ownership and plan its activities. Most events are organized through various community groups, and the Art Farm has year-round art productions and events. That's the thing about planning fun events: They take on a life of their own. Today, having lots of activities for people of all ages is something Serenbe is known for.

Flash Forward: Summer in Serenbe 2024

Let's fast-forward twenty years (give or take) of community events and activities. Today, there's never a dull moment when Serenbe residents get together and start making plans. Here is a snapshot of three big weekend events—all organized by different groups of residents—that took place on June 1 and 2 of 2024. It just goes to show what is possible when people get engaged and create the programming that they would like to see in their community.

- **Summerfest.** A group of parents decided the community needed to celebrate the end of the 2024 school year. This residents-only festival was held on the ballfield and featured food trucks and organized games for kids, parents, and everyone else to enjoy.
- **Adult Big Wheel Race.** Created by a local retailer to bring attention to their business and involve the community, the annual Big Wheel Race gives grownups a chance to be kids again. In this event, people design their own big wheel vehicles, dress in costumes, and compete in relay races along the streets of Serenbe. The Big Wheel Race has become so popular that it's featured programming on a national sports network. Scan QR code 13.1 at the end of this chapter to watch a teaser for 2024's race, which later aired on ESPN8: The Ocho.

- **Adult Prom.** This fundraiser is sponsored by the Serenbe Social Committee, which was formed to plan and oversee events that the Serenbe Development Company and HOA were not going to sponsor. At this "prom," attendees can dress up in their prom attire from the era of their choosing and dance the night away.

Plenty to Do on the Weekends: Serenbe's Rich Tapestry of Community Events

Now, we'd like to give you a broader glimpse into many of the events that make Serenbe an exciting place to live. We offer many different types of events—so many that we don't have room to list them all here! Some are meant to showcase our community and attract visitors, while others provide fun and unique ways for local folks to connect with each other, soak up some culture, and celebrate nature and the glory of the seasons.

Here is an overview of the rich menu of things to do at Serenbe:

- The Art Farm regularly hosts music, dance, theater, and spoken word performances, as well as comedy nights, film viewings, and more.
- Serenbe's businesses have established weekly events like Farmhouse Fridays (live music on the restaurant's porch), Austin's Saturday jazz nights, General Store's Saturday wine tastings, Thursday night trivia at Halsa, and more. Serenbe Yoga + Bodyworks even offers Saturday morning goat yoga! Businesses also sponsor seasonal or annual events, like Hamlin's Big Wheel Race.
- Various community groups organize regular events like neighborhood potlucks, as well as beloved annual traditions like the Serenbe Olympics, an Easter Egg Hunt, the Fourth of July Parade, and a Halloween costume contest.

Serenbe Event Spotlight: ChattHills Porchfest

ChattHills Porchfest is one of my favorite Serenbe events because it shines a light on the talents of our residents and regional artists. During the annual Porchfest music festival, residents offer their front porches for different musicians—either someone local from the neighborhood or, increasingly, visiting musicians. It doesn't matter how "professional" the artists; the point is to provide a showcase of creativity while connecting neighbors with one another (and, in some cases, revealing their hidden talents). Porchfest is completely organized by Serenbe's residents. As people walk through Serenbe's streets, they can connect with neighbors and visitors. In addition to the live music, there is an art walk, food trucks, and children's bake sales. Every year, participation grows as we all celebrate the richness of music of all types, bringing our community together and appreciating the artists who live among us.

- Serenbe Farms hosts regular events ranging from the farmers market and farm tours to gardening classes and farm volunteer days.
- Serenbe's HOA organizes a series of hikes and nature walks, new resident parties, and monthly Coffee Talks that highlight various aspects of our community's biophilic values and vision.
- Athletically inclined residents can participate in community sports leagues and compete against their neighbors in scheduled soccer, softball, and kickball matches.
- Serenbe's facilities often play host to other organizations' events. A few good examples are Wholesome Wave Southern Chefs Potluck, the Ray C. Anderson Foundation's Ray Day, and Atlanta Les Dames d'Escoffier International's Afternoon in the Country.

Serenbe Event Spotlight: Fast Bananas Trail Race

Once a year you'll see large groups of people—some of whom are dressed as bananas—running Serenbe's trails. No, we haven't gone crazy. This is the Fast Bananas Trail Race, which offers a 5k, a 10k, or a one-mile fun run for kids. The Fast Bananas Trail Race is a beloved annual tradition and supports many of Serenbe's biophilic priorities, like health and fitness, a connection to nature, and community engagement.

The Fast Bananas Trail Race is owned and organized by Dr. Kate Mihevc Edwards, founder of Precision Performance & Physical Therapy. Dr. Edwards initially opened an office in Serenbe's One Mado building thinking she'd operate from this location once a week, but today that office's hours have expanded to four days a week—and it's the only location where Dr. Edwards personally sees patients. She and her family have also become full-time Serenbe residents.

Dr. Edwards designed the Fast Bananas Trail Race to bring fun to Serenbe while celebrating fitness, nature, and wellness in an engaging and supportive environment. I'd say she has more than met her goal! Best of all, just about any community could organize an event like this to promote fun and health, and to draw in visitors. (Plus, races are a great fundraiser idea!)

- While many of Serenbe's events are open to residents of all ages, some are designed specifically for our youngest community members. These include children's gardening classes, cooking classes, martial arts classes, pottery classes, drama club, chess club, sports leagues and lessons, horseback riding, and much more. In the summer, kids can participate in a variety of outdoor adventures at Camp Serenbe.

Scan QR code 13.2 at the end of this chapter to see a current list of events happening at Serenbe.

These events should inspire you and help you visualize what's possible. But don't feel you need to replicate Serenbe's lineup. Every community is different. Talk to your residents and ask them what they feel should be celebrated. Build events and activities around what your community values. Each event may not be an instant hit, but eventually you will discover what brings your community the most joy and connection.

How to Create Great Events in Your Community

Here are some pointers to help leaders and community residents create a mindset around planning events to bring the community together. Remember, it's not about scheduling the perfect mix of events; it's about creating the right atmosphere by bringing people together and making it easy for them to engage and contribute. If you do that, the passion and talent of your community members will take over. People who have something to contribute will rise to the occasion and find ways to make great things happen.

- **Start small and grow from there.** You don't have to create a full events roster right away. Start by choosing one event to carry out, so as not to overwhelm people. For example, plan a Spring Fling festival. Once that event is finished, people will say, "That spring event was really fun. Let's plan an outdoor movie night for the fall." Gradually the community will build momentum. Even if some events aren't hits, that's okay. Move on and try something else.

- **Set a goal of self-sustainability.** Your initial events may need a sponsor (such as a development company), but make it your goal for events to ultimately be self-supporting and organic. It's important for the community members to think, "We are doing this ourselves," rather than "The city/developer/etc. is funding this." Always be moving toward supporting events via ticket sales and donations.

- **If there's something you really believe in, find a way to fund it!** You may be able to get creative to allocate funds for your upcoming events. Serenbe funds its robust art program through a transfer fee. For every home purchased in Serenbe, 1 percent of the sale goes toward arts and culture events. Transfer fees of this nature spread out the cost and make people feel a sense of ownership. It works because if you're helping to pay for an event, you're far more likely to attend it yourself.

- **Be prepared for conflict.** One of the pitfalls of having the community organize its own events is managing conflict. This can be tough to handle, especially if planning the event isn't really your "job." In these cases, it's easy to get frustrated, to disengage, or to quit altogether. Therefore, try to solve conflicts in a healthy way. Always assume good intent from the people making waves. Try to understand each other's perspectives. At the end of the day, all parties usually want the same thing—a successful event.

- **Support the people stepping up to lead.** Let the organizing team know that you see the time, effort, and energy they're putting into these events. A heartfelt thank you goes a long way.

- **Get involved in a leadership position yourself!** If you don't like the way an event was carried out, volunteer to chair the event committee next year. Or if you have ideas on how to make something better, share your feedback.

- **Don't reward complainers (but don't be surprised by them either).** Unfortunately, it is socially popular to be negative, to complain, and to air our grievances in public. In fact, negativity is some people's go-to for getting engaged. Create a culture where complaining is *not* popular. You might counter complaints and negativity by providing examples of—and expressing appreciation for—what *is* going well in the community. When people learn that negativity won't get them anywhere, they are far more likely to get engaged in finding solutions. Nudge them toward getting active in building the community programming they want to see more of.

- **Make events appealing for all ages.** Plan events that will make everyone happy, from kids to parents to senior citizens. There should be something for people at every age and stage of life—because all ages are important for a healthy community. Doesn't that make common sense?

- **Keep asking, "Are we creating a great place to live?"** If your answer is yes, you're on the right track. Talent always follows place, and investment follows talent. If you create a great place to live with vibrant programming and events, people and businesses will find you. While people once followed money and jobs around the country, they are now putting down roots where they want to be and finding a job in that place. The work you do to make your community a great place to be will ensure that it keeps getting better for years to come.

Getting Started: Simple Event Ideas for Communities

You might be thinking, "Is this a call to become an event planner?" Not at all—unless that excites you! Instead, think of events as opportunities to solve everyday challenges or bring a little joy to life. Just think about what could happen in your own backyard, on your street, in a local park, or in any community spot where people could gather.

Are your kids bored or driving you crazy? Collaborate with a few other parents for a simple, fun activity. Feeling curious about something new, whether that's a hobby, book, or topic? Call a neighbor and brainstorm a gathering. Maybe new families have moved into the neighborhood—organize a casual get-together. Did someone take a trip to a place you'd love to learn about? Invite them to share their experience with a small group. Who in your community has a unique hobby or skill? Why not suggest they share it with others? The possibilities are endless.

To spark your imagination, here are some ideas organized around popular themes. Remember, while there's nothing wrong with elaborate events, they don't have to be complicated to be fun. Especially when you're first getting started, keeping it simple can be the way to go.

Food and Drink

- **Potluck dinners:** Make it exciting with fun themes like international cuisine, comfort food, or dishes that can only be eaten with your hands.
- **Coffee or tea meetups:** Host a warm and cozy gathering at home or partner with a local cafe for a relaxed morning or afternoon get-together.
- **Outdoor barbecues:** Keep it simple and classic—organize a grill-out with neighbors bringing side dishes, desserts, or drinks to share.
- **Pumpkin-carving parties:** Perfect for fall, these can be as simple or elaborate as you like and don't need to be tied to Halloween.
- **Ice cream socials:** Celebrate summer with a sundae bar, tasting competition, or creative topping contest.
- **Pie contests:** Showcase seasonal harvests like apples, berries, or pumpkins with a friendly pie-making or tasting competition.
- **Seasonal festivals:** Think corn festivals, tomato tastings, or even a gourd-growing contest—simple ways to celebrate the harvest while connecting with neighbors.

Outdoor Activities

- **Neighborhood walks or hikes:** These are simple ways to connect and enjoy nature. No special equipment or prior preparation required!
- **Block party:** Close a street or gather in a green space for games, food trucks, and music.
- **Outdoor movie night:** Set up a projector for a family-friendly film or use a dual-screen setup for kids and adults.

Games and Competitions

- **Trivia night:** This is a perfect event for a backyard, community room, or even a coffee shop.
- **Scavenger hunt:** Tailor it for kids, adults, or mixed groups for a fun challenge.
- **Yard games:** Cornhole, bocce, or croquet can be a hit with all ages.

For Families and Kids

- **Chalk art festival:** Decorate sidewalks together with colorful creations.
- **Parades:** Organize bike, pet, or costume parades with festive flair.
- **Board game night:** This is a relaxed and inclusive option for all ages that encourages connection and communication.

Creative and Interactive Activities

- **Art in the park:** Gather with art supplies for an afternoon of creativity.
- **Book or recipe swap:** Share favorite reads or culinary ideas.
- **DIY workshops:** Candle-making, painting, or gardening—there's always a skill to share.

Community Service

- **Neighborhood cleanup:** Beautify parks or shared spaces together.
- **Charity drives:** Collect goods for local causes while fostering goodwill.
- **Garden or tree-planting day:** Work together to enhance the environment. Bonus points for planting edible and/or native species!

Seasonal and Holiday Celebrations

With more than thirty holidays and observances throughout the year, plus other annual remembrances that might be unique to your community, there's no shortage of reasons to celebrate. By leveraging these holidays and observances, you can create meaningful, fun, and engaging opportunities to bring neighbors together. Whether it's through food, games, creativity, or service, each event strengthens community bonds and makes everyday life richer. Here are some ideas for activities:

Federal Holidays

- **New Year's Day (January 1):** Resolution-setting parties, a polar plunge, or neighborhood walks
- **Martin Luther King Jr. Day (Third Monday in January):** Community service projects, unity walks, or educational sessions on diversity
- **Presidents' Day (Third Monday in February):** American history trivia night, patriotic crafts for kids, or a movie marathon featuring US history
- **Memorial Day (Last Monday in May):** Flag-raising ceremonies, decorating graves of veterans, BBQs, or hosting a moment of silence event
- **Juneteenth (June 19):** Freedom-themed events, cultural festivals, or discussions on history and progress
- **Independence Day (July 4):** Parades, fireworks, a block party with red, white, and blue themes, or patriotic games
- **Labor Day (First Monday in September):** Community picnics, sports tournaments, or organizing a relaxing neighborhood gathering
- **Columbus Day/Indigenous Peoples' Day (Second Monday in October):** Cultural exchange events, storytelling about Indigenous heritage, or themed cooking nights
- **Veterans Day (November 11):** Thank-a-vet card drive, parades, or a community ceremony honoring local veterans
- **Thanksgiving (Fourth Thursday in November):** Gratitude-themed events, potluck dinners, turkey trot, or community pie-sharing
- **Christmas Day (December 25):** Caroling, tree-lighting ceremonies, cookie swaps, or hosting a toy drive for children in need

Major US Holidays

- **Valentine's Day (February 14):** Card-making for neighbors, dessert swaps, or a romantic movie night for couples
- **St. Patrick's Day (March 17):** Green-themed parties, scavenger hunts for "gold," or Irish music and dance events
- **Easter (Varies—Spring):** Egg hunts, bonnet parades, or spring-themed picnics
- **Mother's Day (Second Sunday in May):** Brunch gatherings, flower arranging workshops, or a special tea party
- **Father's Day (Third Sunday in June):** BBQs, sports games, or a neighborhood "dad joke" contest
- **Halloween (October 31):** Trick-or-treating, costume contests, haunted house tours, or pumpkin-carving parties
- **Hanukkah (Dates vary in December):** Dreidel games, menorah lighting ceremonies, or latke-tasting nights
- **Kwanzaa (December 26–January 1):** Candle-lighting ceremonies, storytelling, or cultural feasts
- **New Year's Eve (December 31):** Countdown parties, fireworks displays, or a neighborhood toast

Cultural and Observational Days

- **International Women's Day (March 8):** Celebrations of women in the community, storytelling sessions, or mentorship events
- **Pi Day (March 14):** Pie-baking contest, math trivia night, or pie-eating competition
- **April Fool's Day (April 1):** Comedy nights, prank competitions (friendly ones!), or laughter yoga sessions
- **National Siblings Day (April 10):** Photo contests, family history sharing, or sibling games
- **Earth Day (April 22):** Neighborhood cleanup, tree planting, or recycling drives
- **Arbor Day (Last Friday in April):** Planting trees, garden workshops, or outdoor education sessions

- **Cinco de Mayo (May 5):** Mexican culture celebration with themed potlucks, mariachi music, or dance lessons
- **Flag Day (June 14):** Patriotic displays, flag-making crafts, or a flag-raising ceremony
- **National Night Out (First Tuesday in August):** Safety-focused gatherings, meet-the-police events, or community BBQs
- **Grandparents' Day (First Sunday after Labor Day):** Organized storytelling events, photo-sharing sessions, or a family-focused brunch
- **Patriot Day (September 11):** Candlelight vigil, remembrance walk, or community service projects
- **National Neighbor Day (September 28):** Community potluck, yard games, or "get-to-know-your-neighbor" meetups

Seasonal Celebrations
- **Spring Equinox (Around March 20):** Planting flowers, kite flying, or picnic potlucks
- **Summer Solstice (Around June 21):** Outdoor yoga, nature walks, or a bonfire gathering
- **Fall Harvest (October–November):** Pumpkin festivals, apple-picking trips, or corn mazes
- **Winter Solstice (Around December 21):** Candlelight ceremonies, storytelling, or cozy hot cocoa gatherings

Other Fun Observances
- **National Pet Day (April 11):** Pet parades, meet-and-greet for pets, or a pet costume contest
- **National Gardening Day (April 14):** Gardening workshops, plant swaps, or landscaping meetups
- **Teacher Appreciation Week (First Full Week of May):** Appreciation breakfast, gift-making workshops, or thank-you card drives
- **National Ice Cream Day (Third Sunday in July):** Ice cream socials, tasting competitions, or "make-your-own-sundae" parties

You see the possibilities—there are so many ways to bring people together, spark joy, and foster a sense of connection. As humans, we thrive in community, but sometimes it takes a simple event to remind us of that. Isn't that just common sense?

Chapter 13 QR Codes

**Big Wheel
QR Code 13.1**

**Events
QR Code 13.2**

14

Getting Started

Planting the seeds of Serenbe and watching the community grow and thrive has been an amazing experience. Living here for the past twenty-two years has been even better. Not only have my family and I reaped immeasurable rewards, it's also been so gratifying to see the lives of our friends and neighbors slowly transform in ways both big and small.

If you have read this far, I hope you're feeling inspired. While this book has focused on building a community, my larger goal in writing it has been to send a message about self-determination and self-reliance. When we aren't happy with something in our life, we can take charge and change it for the better. Many times it's a matter of looking at the situation from a different angle and applying commonsense thinking. As I mentioned earlier in this book, changing the world begins with changing one's own backyard—literally and metaphorically. When I internalized this truth, it liberated me—and I wish the same for you.

That said, perhaps the "backyard" you want to change is, indeed, your own built environment and you're wondering how you might create a "Serenbe" of your own. (By the way, I don't mean that literally. Every community is different and that's a good thing, but the elements that make Serenbe so appealing are wonderfully transferrable.)

I'm about to offer a few simple strategies and tactics for those who are ready to change. First, I will speak to those readers wishing to improve the community they currently live in. Whether you're a local government official, nonprofit or civic leader, business owner, or simply an engaged citizen who wants a better life, I hope I can provide some helpful inspiration and guidance. Then I will address those readers who want to build a biophilic community from scratch.

Let's get started.

For Existing Communities

Start Putting Together a Great Team

What, specifically, is bugging you? Who controls the issues around the aggravating issue? What will it take to make changes? You may not know the full answers to all the questions right now, but you probably know enough to start putting together some alliances. You need a solid team of people on your side with knowledge and—perhaps even more important—a genuine passion for change. (As I alluded to a few paragraphs ago, this applies to all kinds of transformation, but for now let's stick to community building.)

In the opening to this book, I named a few individuals who were instrumental in getting Serenbe off the ground. Of course, there were many others! Placemaking is a collaborative effort. As you seek to build out your own team, throw a broad net. Don't just look at real estate development types (often their thinking is in a rut). Consider bringing in landowners, business leaders, civic leaders, academic organizations, environmental institutes, and others.

It is almost better to include people with no preconceived ideas. Recall the story of Serenbe's unique wastewater management system.

Had we gone with the conventional "experts," we wouldn't have prom-goers posing on the boardwalk in the middle of the treatment center!

ASSESS Before You ADDRESS

It always makes sense to diagnose before treating. You are doing this for your people, so find out what they most want and need before they start. This is a two-pronged effort:

Quality of life survey: Reach out to the people in your area and ask them how they feel about where they live. Are they happy with all aspects of their community? What elements are missing that they'd like to see? Businesses? Green spaces? Different types of housing? Your survey might include questions on community services, social activities/connectivity, access to healthful food, the arts, and the state of your local education.

I recommend that you engage a polling professional for the survey(s). Questions can be asked via phone, email, mail, or in-person meetings, or a combination of any of the above. I like in-person meetings because they allow you to do real-time attitude assessments and challenge stale beliefs. There are now apps that allow people to vote on their phones and see real-time results from their peers.

One helpful technique is to use written questions followed up with the same questions accompanied by visual images. This allows people to see how their ideas would actually look in reality.

Health assessment: The other piece of the puzzle is assessing the health of residents (physical and mental). There are a couple of ways to approach this. You can do an anonymous survey around general health issues. The key is persuading them to participate by providing hope that change is possible. Again, a professional polling firm can advise you—and may also be able to word things in a way that reassures respondents that feed-back will not be shared inappropriately. (You might even offer a material reward in exchange for participation.)

Another option is to look at local statistics on percentages of people in your area who have asthma, are overweight, or have been diagnosed with cancer, as well as stats around behavioral issues, depression, anxiety, addiction/substance abuse, and other mental health problems. (Many of these statistics may be available via your state or city health department.)

As we've discussed throughout this book, biophilic living is beneficial and healing for a variety of issues and conditions because so many of them are intertwined. This multipronged solution—encompassing social connecting, healthful foods, exercise, fresh air, and so forth—improves mental and physical health in general. The purpose of the health assessment and local data gathering is mostly to build a case that change is needed. Too many people deny that problems exist in their world . . . or they think they are the only ones dealing with an issue . . . or perhaps they have just lost hope.

Between these two assessments—quality of life and health—a picture should start to come together around what your community's most pressing wants and needs might be.

Know Where to Start

You can't change everything at once. What you can do is use the results of the assessments to guide you on where to start.

Let's say the survey tells you the community's top priority is having better access to healthful foods. You could start by looking to create a community garden or a weekly farmers market. You might partner with a local community college to offer cooking classes. Eventually, you might try to attract food-related businesses such as restaurants, kitchen retail stores, or a commercial kitchen with spaces to rent by the day or season.

If the survey shows that people are missing out on human connection, you might consider creating central places for mail delivery (rather than having mailboxes at the end of the driveway). You could sprinkle in neighborhood gathering spots: a Ping-Pong plaza, an in-ground trampoline, a gazebo with rockers. You could replace common area landscaping with edible plants open to everyone: blueberry bushes, fig trees, herb gardens, and the like. Or, if there are lots of large fenced-in yards, consider a master plan to remove the fences and join up the backyards for more of a common green space with a central path down the center.

As you can see, there are tons of possibilities. Pick one or two ideas (again, based on what people say they care most about) and get to work on them. Remember, I've included some practical tips you can begin implementing at the end of most chapters.

Understand Change Management Basics

It is important to realize that people inherently resist change—even "good" change. It is just human nature. People fear what they don't know. ("What if the community's gain means a loss for me personally?") Perhaps they've been let down before. Perhaps there are conflicts of interest. There are many possibilities. The point is realizing that change will not always be comfortable, but knowing that up front will make things easier.

There are many wonderful books and articles on change management. I suggest doing some reading so you will know what to expect. While this is way too big a subject to cover here, I would like to share a few helpful hints:

- **Set realistic goals.** If a goal is too big, people won't believe they can do it. The goal will fail, discouragement will set in, and momentum will stall.
- **Appeal to the heart, not just the mind.** Humans are emotion driven. If you can paint a vivid picture of a community that will improve the lives of their children and perhaps their aging parents—and make them see that it can be done—they will get on board.
- **Certain people will never get on board.** Don't try to sway the stalwart resisters. This will drain your energy and get you nowhere. Focus your efforts on the groups who seem undecided and/or convincible.

- **Be aboveboard and honest—always.** Explain what you are doing and why. Don't be evasive. Remember that trust is vital and precious—don't squander it.

Tackle the Practical Barriers and Look for Areas of Opportunity

There may be legal or development issues you need to address up front. For example, is rezoning needed so that commercial properties can be placed within walking distance of housing? As you're working on these issues, you can also be looking for opportunities. Is there an area bound to be redeveloped that could be repurposed as a community benefit? Is there a vacant piece of property (infill land) nearby or open land on the edge of the community?

Educate the Community

I believe that most people want better lives. They realize something is not right about the way they're living. However, they don't know what the possibilities are. When you can educate people on what you want to change—and more to the point, *why*—they are more likely to get on board. Part of this is about creating a common language so that people can talk the ideas. For example: *What is biophilia? What do we mean when we say green infrastructure? What does it mean to be a walkable community? Why is it so important to have good local food supply?* Bring in speakers to give presentations and encourage the community to attend. The more they can see and understand your vision, the better.

Another piece of the education might focus on the health assessment I mentioned earlier. Here's where you deploy the results—for example: "Statistics show 60 percent of our town's citizens are classified as obese or overweight. This puts us at risk for diabetes, heart disease, and cancer, all of which are extremely costly. I know that everyone wants better for themselves and their families. We can help work toward solutions by creating a community garden to shore up a local source of fresh veggies and build a network of walking paths to encourage exercise."

Create Your Narrative and Start Building a Common Sense of Purpose

What are your guiding principles? What do you want your community to be known for? Wellness? Conservation? Human connectedness? A better way for children to grow up? Figure out what you want your message to be and hone it until it's clear, simple, and easy to repeat. Connect it to the objective data gathered in your assessments.

Figure out the WIIFM factor (WIIFM stands for "What's In It For Me?"). Factor for different audiences: residents, government, business owners, and so on. This will allow you to build your case in a way that connects to their wants and needs. The more people you get on board, the more likely your plans will succeed.

Get Super Focused on Engaging Residents

As I've mentioned earlier, Serenbe residents have an exceptionally high level of engagement. They don't "outsource" things like education, elder care, or even food production. They make it a point to stay connected to the rich and meaningful parts of life, and this has made the community successful in many areas. This is what community engagement looks like—and it needs to start early in the change process.

Here are a few tips for engaging people:

- Talk to lots of different groups: business owners, civic organizations, parents, young people. Ask them for feedback. Solicit their help.
- Again, focus on education. The more you can teach people about what you're trying to do, and how it benefits them, the more likely they'll become engaged, enthusiastic supporters.
- Make the most of social media. Educate people, ask for their feedback, ask for their ideas. Post updates on projects as often as possible to keep the excitement and energy going.
- Recognize and profusely thank your volunteers. It is rare to bring about community change (or any kind of change) without

a lot of help. You might have volunteers who educate citizens, campaign for local officials who are friendly to your cause, create fliers and post on social media, plant community gardens, and so on. Be sure to publicly recognize and thank them. Gratitude goes a long way.

One Change at a Time

It is almost always better to start small, with a single project or goal, before moving on to bigger changes. "Too much too fast" overwhelms people and sets you up to fail. On the other hand, small successes build confidence.

Celebrate Small Wins

So you got that new store opened, those bike trails built, or the fall festival kicked off? Make a big deal out of it. Create a big splash on social media, posts lots of pics, and offer your sincerest thank-yous to the community and others involved. This generates a lot of enthusiasm and people will want more wins. One success builds on another one. This is how you generate momentum and create the critical mass it takes to get big projects over the finish line.

Keep the Communication Going

With a few victories under your belt, you might think you can let up. Don't. Continue to provide regular updates to the community. Keep repeating your narrative and the "why" behind your efforts. Keep any metrics and survey results in front of people. A steady flow of information builds trust, which is so important to keeping people's support.

Don't Lose Patience—Change Takes Time

Healthy communities are living organisms. They keep on growing and evolving. What this means is you'll never be "done" creating a better community. The good news is, if you're passionate about it, you'll never want to be.

For New Communities

It may be that this book has inspired you to start your own community based on biophilic principles. I won't mince words: It's a massive undertaking. Yet I cannot imagine a more exciting, worthwhile, and richly rewarding one. That's why I have made it my life's work to help people exactly like you.

In our commitment to support new communities and those seeking change, my family and I have founded a consulting company to help guide these efforts. I invite you to visit Nygren Placemaking at www.NygrenPlacemaking.com. As a global consultancy, we collaborate with developers, builders, and dreamers in order to shape, enhance, and bring their development ideas to life.

Our offerings bring people together to explore ideas about building places that organically connect humans to each other and nature. Our goal is to help others create healthier and more vital lives for themselves, their loved ones, and their neighbors. The Nygren Placemaking team shares valuable lessons to integrate the environment, technology, arts, and biophilia to build resilient wellness communities. Our commonsense approach to thoughtful development provokes new ways of planning for a sustainable future. In particular, we model beneficial ways to both preserve and develop land by focusing on the twelve biophilic development principles that are implemented in the Serenbe community.

You will see on our website that we provide consultations and in-depth project engagements that include land planning, streetscapes, plan books, and more.

Finally, we offer a placemaking conference onsite at Serenbe each year in the fall. Attendees learn the nuts and bolts of planning and building a walkable community where residential, retail, and farming thrive. They discover how Serenbe's unique model conserves natural resources and provides greater financial returns for the developer and the homeowner while creating a thriving, in-demand wellness lifestyle.

Photo by J. Ashley.

I'd like to close with a few words to readers who wish to make any other kind of change in their life or career or the world around them: Go for it. Life is short—and it can and should be sweet. Don't settle for a gray and mediocre existence. Don't settle for someone else's dream (or even worse, settle for what they settled for). There is simply too much joy to be had, wonder to be experienced, and connectedness to be savored *not* to craft a life that works for you.

Thank you for reading. I wish for you success in your journey, sunshine on your skin, and a life filled with the glories of nature, art, delicious food and drink, and the magic of friendship and love. With awe, I encourage you to embrace the wonder of each sunrise and sunset . . . and the miracle of life itself.

ACKNOWLEDGMENTS

The idea of writing a book has been on my mind for quite some time. However, as someone who isn't the best speller and struggles with punctuation, I resisted putting pen to paper. Fortunately, I discovered that good editors and agents can take care of those details, so thanks to Sandi Mendelson, Dottie DeHart and the team at BenBella, this book is a reality—if you're reading this, they made it happen.

One significant edit I want to acknowledge is the replacement of "we" with "I" throughout most of the pages. The various references to "we" were often too complex to untangle, as they encompassed many different groups. When organizing five hundred landowners to preserve the rural character of the land, there were numerous key people I considered part of our team.

More than twenty years ago, we broke ground on Serenbe—a community within our newly formed town of Chattahoochee Hills. Many individuals have played pivotal roles in bringing Serenbe to life. Phill Tabb, formerly the head of the architecture department at Texas A&M, became our unexpected land planner and now calls Serenbe home. Robert Rausch, who encouraged new creative ideas, designed all the streetlights. Monica Olsen, a marketing executive for national brands, moved to Atlanta from Los Angeles when her husband was recruited by Turner Broadcasting. Years ago, they found Serenbe when their children were young (now they're in college). Today, she serves as our chief marketing officer and was instrumental in encouraging me to write this book.

Gil Mathis, an insurance actuary, moved his family to Serenbe seeking peace in nature and discovered a fulfilling challenge in helping to create a new way of living—he now serves as our chief financial officer. Amy Peterson has held various roles over the past twelve years and currently manages our HOA. Matt Collins, a young engineer working with our civil team, joined us as the development manager. Thomas Peters, our dedicated horticulturist, and John Whitney, our maintenance manager, have both played key roles. And, of course, the many hospitality managers, farmers, artists, shopkeepers, and team members who all breathe life into Serenbe and give me the stories to share.

Throughout this journey, my family has been an integral part of every "we" that has now become an "I" in the book. My wife, Marie, has been the ultimate hostess—ensuring food and hot coffee were always available during community meetings as we worked to form our town. In the early years, she even prepared home-cooked meals for every new resident for their first night at Serenbe.

Our daughter Garnie turned down opportunities in the hotel industry after graduating from Cornell, returning home just as the first house foundations were being poured. She now serves as our chief operations manager and is a serial entrepreneur, creating businesses wherever there is a need. Our daughter Kara, with a degree in psychology and early childhood education from the University of Colorado, initially joined Garnie in the real estate office but soon followed her nurturing instincts to create Camp Serenbe, which she continues to run while also managing our Nygren Placemaking consulting firm.

Quinn, our youngest daughter, once thought the farm was too dirty and the family business too intense. However, after earning her art history degree from the University of Colorado and gaining design experience in Los Angeles and Atlanta, she found her way back home a decade ago and now serves as our director of branding.

Even our sons-in-law have become part of Serenbe's fabric. Matt, a professional chef, owns Serenbe Foods. Micah transitioned from a career in mental health to help manage the real estate office. Lucas, with his passion for wine, owns the Serenbe Wine Shop.

The greatest reward of creating Serenbe is that all seven of our grandchildren live here, and I have the joy of seeing them daily.

Life's rewards can be truly magical when you embrace the radical commonsense idea of following your heart into the unknown.

NOTES

Introduction

1. Kasanoff, Bruce. "How to Be Relentlessly Positive." LinkedIn. September 14, 2016. www.linkedin.com/pulse/how-relentlessly-positive -bruce-kasanoff/.

Chapter 1

1. Helliwell, John F., Richard Layard, Jeffrey D. Sachs, Jan-Emmanual De Neve, Lara B. Aknin, and Shun Wang. "World Happiness Report 2024." *University of Oxford: Wellbeing Research Centre*. 2024. happiness -report.s3.amazonaws.com/2024/WHR+24.pdf.
2. Moniuszko, Sara. "U.S. Drops from Top 20 Happiest Countries List in 2024 World Happiness Report." Edited by Paula Cohen. CBS News, March 20, 2024. www.cbsnews.com/news/happiest-countries -world-list-2024-united-states-gallup/.
3. CDC. "Adult Obesity Facts." May 14, 2024. https://www.cdc.gov /obesity/adult-obesity-facts.
4. Kochhar, Rakesh, and Stella Sechopoulos. "How the American Middle Class Has Changed in the Past Five Decades." Pew Research Center. April 20, 2022.
5. "Mental Health By the Numbers." NAMI. April 2023. www.nami.org /About-Mental-Illness/Mental-Health-by-the-Numbers/.
6. Kochhar, Rakesh, and Stella Sechopoulos. "How the American Middle Class Has Changed in the Past Five Decades." Pew Research Center. April 20, 2022.

7. Feinberg, Richard A., and Jennifer Meoli. "A Brief History of the Mall." In Rebecca H. Holman and Michael R. Solomon (eds.), *Advances in Consumer Research* 18 (1991): 426–27.

8. David, Donald R., Melvin D. Epp, and Hugh D. Riordan. "Changes in USDA Food Composition Data for 43 Garden Crops, 1950 to 1999." *Journal of the American College of Nutrition* 23, no. 6 (May 2004): 669–82. doi: 10.1080/07315724.2004.10719409.

9. Smith, Matthew R., and Samuel S. Myers. "Impact of Anthropogenic CO2 Emissions on Global Human Nutrition." *Nature Climate Change* 8 (August 27, 2018): 834–39. doi: 10.1038/s41558-018-0253-3.

10. Kobylińska, Milena, Katarzyna Antosik, Agnieszka Decyk, and Katarzyna Kurowska. "Malnutrition in Obesity: Is It Possible?" *Obesity Facts* 15, no. 1 (January 2022): 19–25. doi: 10.1159/000519503.

11. Katona, Géza, and Janos Juhasz. "The History of the Transport System Development and Future with Sharing and Autonomous Systems." *Communications—Scientific Letters of the University of Zilina* 22, no. 1 (January 2020): 25–34. doi: 10.26552/com.C.2020.1.25-34.

12. Zimmer, John. "The Third Transportation Revolution: Lyft's Vision for the Next Ten Years and Beyond. Medium.com. September 18, 2016. medium.com/@johnzimmer/the-third-transportation-revolution -27860f05fa91.

13. Warnick, Melody. "The Porch Puzzle: The Desire to Be Neighborly Butts Up Against the Desire to Be Left Alone." Curbed.com, June 23, 2020. www.curbed.com/article/porch-design-history-porching.html.

14. Fogarty, Amelia. "The American Backyard as We Know It Developed After World War II." Smithsonian, May 22, 2018. www.si.edu/stories /invention-american-backyard.

Chapter 4

1. Klepeis, Neil E., William C. Nelson, Wayne R. Ott, John P. Robinson, Andy M. Tsang, Paul Switzer, et al. "The National Human Activity Pattern Survey (NHAPS): A Resource for Assessing Exposure to Environmental Pollutants." *Journal of Exposure Science & Environmental Epidemiology* 11 (2001): 213–52. 10.1038/sj.jea.7500165.

2. Kemp, Simon. "Digital 2024: Global Overview Report." DataReportal, January 31, 2024. datareportal.com/reports/digital-2024-global -overview-report.

3. United States Census Bureau. "Nation's Urban and Rural Populations Shift Following 2020 Census," December 29, 2022. www.census.gov /newsroom/press-releases/2022/urban-rural-populations.html.

4. Bettmann, Joanna E., Kort C. Prince, Kamala Ganesh, Kelsi F. Rugo, AnnaBelle O. Bryan, Craig J. Bryan, et al. "The Effect of Time Outdoors on Veterans Receiving Treatment for PTSD." *Journal of Clinical Psychology* 99, no. 9 (September 2021): 2041–56. doi: 10.1002 /jclp.23139; Kuo, Frances E., and Andrea Faber Taylor. "A Potential Natural Treatment for Attention-Deficit/Hyperactivity Disorder: Evidence From a National Study." *American Journal of Public Health* 94, no. 9 (September 2004): 1580–86. doi: 10.2105/AJPH.94 .9.1580.

5. Frumkin, Howard and Richard Louv. "The Powerful Link Between Conserving Land and Preserving Health." Land Trust Alliance, 2007. arachnid.biosci.utexas.edu/courses/THOC/Readings/Nature-Health .pdf.

6. Boere, Katherine, Kelsey Lloyd, Gordon Binsted, and Olave E. Krigolson. "Exercising Is Good for the Brain but Exercising Outside Is Potentially Better." *Scientific Reports* 13, no. 1 (January 20, 2023): 1140. doi: 10.1038/s41598-022-26093-2.

7. Arendt, Randall. "More Benefits of Conservation Design." Landchoices .org. Accessed October 1, 2024. www.landchoices.org/conservation subs/moreadvant.htm.

8. Arendt, Randall. "Advantages of Conservation Subdivisions (Conservation Development) for Developers." Landchoices.org. Accessed October 1, 2024. www.landchoices.org/conservationsubs/advnt_consubs _devel.htm.

9. Arendt, "Advantages of Conservation Subdivisions."

10. "The Facts About Lawn Chemicals." United States Environmental Protection Agency. Accessed October 1, 2024. cfpub.epa.gov/npstbx /files/marc_lawnchemicals.pdf.

11. WaterSense: An EPA Partnership Program. "Outdoor Water Use in the United States." United States Environmental Protection Agency, January 2017. 19january2017snapshot.epa.gov/www3/watersense/pubs /outdoor.html.

12. "Yard Trimmings: Material-Specific Data." United States Environmental Protection Agency, November 22, 2023. www.epa.gov/facts -and-figures-about-materials-waste-and-recycling/yard-trimmings -material-specific-data.

Chapter 6

1. Bratman, Gregory N., Gretchen C. Daily, Benjamin J. Levy, and James J. Gross. "The Benefits of Nature Experience: Improved Affect and Cognition." *ScienceDirect* 138 (June 2015): 41–50. doi: 10.1016 /j.landurbplan.2015.02.005; Magsamen, Susan. "Your Brain on Art: The Case for Neuroaesthetics." *Cerebrum* 2019 (2019); Abbas, Sarah, Nathalie Okdeh, Rabih Roufayel, Hervé Kovacic, Jean-Marc Sabatier, Ziad Fajloun, et al. "Neuroarchitecture: How the Perception of Our Surroundings Impacts the Brain." *Biology* 13, no. 4 (March 2024): 220. doi: 10.3390/biology13040220.

2. "Serotonin." Cleveland Clinic, March 18, 2022. my.clevelandclinic.org /health/articles/22572-serotonin.

Chapter 7

1. Hales, Craig M., Margaret D. Carroll, Cheryl D. Fryar, and Cynthia L. Ogden. "Prevalence of Obesity Among Adults and Youth: United States, 2015–2016." *National Center for Health Statistics Data Brief* no. 288. October 2017. www.cdc.gov/nchs/data/databriefs/db288.pdf.

2. Lauby-Secretan, Béatrice, Chiara Scoccianti, Dana Loomis, Yann Grosse, Franca Bianchini, and Kurt Straif. "Body Fatness and Cancer— Viewpoint of the IARC Working Group." *New England Journal of Medicine* 375, no. 8 (August 25, 2016). doi: 10.1056/NEJMsr1606602.

3. Blumberg, Perri Ormont. "What Experts Really Think About Diet Soda." Time.com, April 9, 2024. time.com/6964018/diet-soda -health-effects/; Debras, Charlotte, Mélanie Deschasaux-Tanguy,

Eloi Chazelas, Laury Sellem, Nathalie Druesne-Pecollo, Younes Esseddik, et al. "Artificial Sweeteners and Risk of Type 2 Diabetes in the Prospective NutriNet-Santé Cohort." *Diabetes Care* 46, no. 9 (July 25, 2023): 1681–90. doi: 10.2337/dc23-0206; Swithers, Susan E. "Artificial Sweeteners Produce the Counterintuitive Effect of Inducing Metabolic Derangements." *Trends in Endocrinology & Metabolism* 24, no. 9 (n.d.): 431–41. doi: 10.1016/j.tem.2013.05.005; "Aspartame Hazard and Risk Assessment Results Released." World Health Organization, July 14, 2023. www.who.int/news/item/14-07 -2023-aspartame-hazard-and-risk-assessment-results-released.

4. "The Heat Is On: A Trust for Public Land Special Report." Trust for Public Land. Accessed October 1, 2024. www.tpl.org/wp-content /uploads/2020/09/The-Heat-is-on_A-Trust-for-Public-Land_special -report_r1_2.pdf.

5. Chang, Chia-chen, Brenda B. Lin, Xiaoqi Feng, Erik Andersson, John Gardner, and Thomas Astell-Burt. "A Lower Connection to Nature Is Related to Lower Mental Health Benefits from Nature Contact." *Scientific Reports* 14, no. 6705 (March 20, 2024). doi: 10.1038 /s41598-024-56968-5.

6. "Understanding Spirituality and Mental Health." McLean Hospital, August 31, 2023. www.mcleanhospital.org/essential/spirituality.

7. Balboni, Tracy A., Tyler J. VanderWeele, Stephanie D. Doan-Soares, Katelyn N.G. Long, Betty R. Ferrell, George Fitchett, et al. "Spirituality in Serious Illness and Health." *Journal of the American Medical Association* 328, no. 2 (July 12, 2022): 184–97. doi: 10.1001 /jama.2022.11086.

8. "The Heat Is On."

9. "Urban Sprawl: A Growing Problem." Yale Ledger, March 16, 2021. campuspress.yale.edu/ledger/urban-sprawl-a-growing-problem/.

10. Ulrich, Roger S. "View Through a Window May Influence Recovery from Surgery." *Science* 224, no. 4647 (May 1984): 420–21. doi: 10.1126 /science.6143402.

11. Diette, Gregory B., Noah Lechtzin, Edward Haponik, Aline Devrotes, and Haya R. Rubin. "Distraction Therapy with Nature Sights

and Sounds Reduces Pain during Flexible Bronchoscopy: A Complementary Approach to Routine Analgesia." *CHEST Journal* 123, no. 3 (March 2023): 941–48. doi: 10.1378/chest.123.3.941.

Chapter 8

1. Boothby, Suzanne. "Victory Gardens Revisited As Pandemic Gardens." Nama. May 2021. namawell.com/blogs/journal/victory-gardens -revisited-as-pandemic-gardens.

2. Tarr, Delaney. "Two New Savi Provisions Shops Are Heading to Atlanta Food Deserts." Saporta Report, December 19, 2024. saportareport.com/two-new-savi-provisions-shops-are-heading-to -atlanta-food-deserts/.

3. Frerick, Austin. "Fixing Our Food System—and Reviving Rural America—Means Breaking Up Big Ag." Civil Eats. February 28, 2019. civileats.com/2019/02/28/fixing-our-food-system-and-reviving -rural-america-means-breaking-up-big-ag/.

4. Kobylińska, Milena, Katarzyna Antosik, Agnieszka Decyk, and Katarzyna Kurowska. "Malnutrition in Obesity: Is It Possible?" *Obesity Facts* 15, no. 1 (January 2022): 19–25. doi: 10.1159/000519503.

5. FAO, IFAD, UNICEF, WFP and WHO. 2021. "The State of Food Security and Nutrition in the World 2021." doi: 10.4060/cb4474en.

6. "Food Waste FAQs." U.S. Department of Agriculture. Accessed October 1, 2024. www.usda.gov/foodwaste/faqs.

7. McGough, Matthew, Aubrey Winger, Shameek Rakshit, and Krutika Amin. "How Has U.S. Spending on Healthcare Changed over Time?" Health System Tracker. December 15, 2023. www.health systemtracker.org/chart-collection/u-s-spending-healthcare-changed -time/.

8. US Department of Agriculture, Economic Research Service, Food Expenditure Series. "Budget Share for Total Food Remained 11.2 Percent in 2023." June 27, 2024. www.ers.usda.gov/data-products/chart -gallery/gallery/chart-detail/?chartId=76967.

9. Myers, Iris. "EWG's Dirty Dozen Guide to Food Chemicals: The Top 12 to Avoid." Environmental Working Group, September 19,

2024. www.ewg.org/consumer-guides/ewgs-dirty-dozen-guide-food
-chemicals-top-12-avoid.

10. "What Is Happening to Agrobiodiversity?" Food and Agriculture
Organization of the United Nations. Accessed December 16, 2024.
www.fao.org/4/y5609e/y5609e02.htm.

11. "Food Waste FAQs."

Chapter 9

1. Murthy, Vivek H. "Our Epidemic of Loneliness and Isolation: The
U.S. Surgeon General's Advisory on the Healing Effects of Social
Connection and Community." Office of the Surgeon General, 2023.
www.hhs.gov/sites/default/files/surgeon-general-social-connection
-advisory.pdf.

2. Wang, Fan, Yu Gao, Zhen Han, Yue Yu, Zhiping Long, Xianchen
Jiang, et al. "A Systematic Review and Meta-Analysis of 90 Cohort
Studies of Social Isolation, Loneliness and Mortality." *Nature
Human Behavior* 7 (August 2023): 1307–19. doi:10.1038/s41562-023
-01617-6.

3. Klepeis, Neil E., William C. Nelson, Wayne R. Ott, John P. Robinson, Andy M. Tsang, Paul Switzer, et al. "The National Human Activity Pattern Survey (NHAPS): A Resource for Assessing Exposure to
Environmental Pollutants." *Journal of Exposure Science & Environmental Epidemiology* 11 (2001): 213–52. doi: 10.1038/sj.jea.7500165.

4. Poon, Linda. "City Life Is Too Lonely. Urban Planning Can Help."
Bloomberg.com. December 14, 2023. www.bloomberg.com/news
/features/2023-12-14/how-to-design-a-city-that-fights-loneliness.

5. Kopf, Jennifer. "Welcome to the Porch Capital of America." Country Living. April 12, 2016. www.countryliving.com/life/travel/g3211
/serenbe-georgia/.

6. Alake, Tope. "Seven Projects to Reclaim NYC Space from Cars."
Bloomberg.com. July 11, 2023. www.bloomberg.com/news/articles
/2023-07-11/nyc-adds-bike-lanes-and-pedestrian-plazas-to-reclaim
-space-from-cars; "Pearl Street Mall." Wikipedia, May 29, 2024.
en.wikipedia.org/wiki/Pearl_Street_Mall.

7. "Green NYC: Parks." Mike Bloomberg. Accessed October 1, 2024. www.mikebloomberg.com/mayoral-record/green-nyc/parks/.
8. Münzel, Thomas, Frank P. Schmidt, Sebastian Steven, Johannes Herzog, Andreas Daiber, and Mette Sørensen. "Environmental Noise and the Cardiovascular System." *Journal of the American College of Cardiology* 17, no. 6 (February 2018): 688–97. doi: 10.1016/j.jacc.2017.12.015.

Chapter 10

1. "Screen Time and Children," *American Academy of Child & Adolescent Psychiatry* no. 54 (May 2024). www.aacap.org/AACAP /Families_and_Youth/Facts_for_Families/FFF-Guide/Children -And-Watching-TV-054.aspx.
2. "Health Benefits and Tips." National Wildlife Federation. Accessed December 17, 2024. www.nwf.org/Kids-and-Family/Connecting-Kids -and-Nature/Health-Benefits-and-Tips.
3. "Children in Nature: Improving Health by Reconnecting Youth with the Outdoors." National Recreation and Park Association. Accessed December 17, 2024. www.nrpa.org/uploadedFiles/nrpa.org/Advocacy /Children-in-Nature.pdf.
4. Dadvand, Payam, Jesus Pujol, Dídac Macià, Gerard Martínez-Vilavella, Laura Blanco-Hinojo, Marion Mortamais, et al. "The Association between Lifelong Greenspace Exposure and 3-Dimensional Brain Magnetic Resonance Imaging in Barcelona Schoolchildren." *Environmental Health Perspectives* 126, no. 2 (2018). doi: 10.1289/ EHP1876.
5. Kuo, Frances E., and Andrea Faber Taylor. "A Potential Natural Treatment for Attention-Deficit/Hyperactivity Disorder: Evidence from a National Study." *American Journal of Public Health* 94, no. 9 (September 2004): 1580–86. doi: 10.2105/AJPH.94.9.1580.
6. Moore, Robin C. "The Need for Nature: A Childhood Right." *Social Justice* 69, 24, no. 3 (1997): 203–20. www.jstor.org/stable/29767032.
7. Hartig, Terry, Richard Mitchell, Sjerp de Vries, and Howard Frumkin. "Nature and Health." *Annual Review of Public Health*, 35 (March 2014): 207–28. doi: 10.1146/annurev-publhealth-032013-182443; Christian,

Haley, Stephen R. Zubrick, Sarah Foster, Billie Giles-Corti, Fiona Bull, Lisa Wood, et al. "The Influence of the Neighborhood Physical Environment on Early Child Health and Development: A Review and Call for Research." *Health & Place* 33 (May 2015): 25–36. doi: 10.1016/j.healthplace.2015.01.005; Wolch, Jennifer, Michael Jerrett, Kim Reynolds, Rob McConnell, Roger Chang, Nicholas Dahmann, et al. "Childhood Obesity and Proximity to Urban Parks and Recreational Resources: A Longitudinal Cohort Study." *Health & Place* 17, no. 1 (January 2011): 207–14. doi: 10.1016/j.healthplace.2010.10.001.

8. Wells, Nancy M., and Gary Evans. "Nearby Nature: A Buffer of Life Stress Among Rural Children." *Environment and Behavior* 35, no. 3 (May 2003): 311–30. doi: 10.1177/0013916503035003001; Corraliza, JosŽ A., Silvia Collado, and Lisbeth Bethelmy. "Nature as a Moderator of Stress in Urban Children." *Procedia: Social and Behavioral Sciences* 38 (April 19, 2012): 253–63. doi: 10.1016/j.sbspro.2012.03.347.

9. Pagels, Peter, Anders Raustorp, Antonio Ponce De Leon, Fredrika Mårtensson, Maria Kylin, and Cecilia Boldemann. "A Repeated Measurement Study Investigating the Impact of School Outdoor Environment upon Physical Activity Across Ages and Seasons in Swedish Second, Fifth and Eighth Graders." *BMC Public Health* 14 (August 2014). doi: 10.1186/1471-2458-14-803.

10. Razani, Nooshin, Kian Niknam, Nancy M. Wells, Doug Thompson, Nancy K. Hills, Gail Kennedy, et al. "Clinic and Park Partnerships for Childhood Resilience: A Prospective Study of Park Prescriptions." *Health & Place* 57 (May 2019): 179–85. doi: 10.1016/j.healthplace.2019.04.008.

11. Lieberman, Gerald A., and Linda L. Hoody. "Closing the Achievement Gap: Using the Environment as an Integrating Context for Learning. Results of a Nationwide Study." *State Education and Environmental Roundtable*, San Diego, CA, 1998. digitalcommons.unomaha .edu/slcek12/64/; Chawla, Louise. "Benefits of Nature Contact for Children." *Journal of Planning Literature* 30, no. 4 (2015): 433–52. doi: 10.1177/0885412215595441; Berezowitz, Claire K., and Andrea B. Bontrager Yoder. "School Gardens Enhance Academic Performance

and Dietary Outcomes in Children." *Journal of School Health* 85, no. 8 (August 2015): 508–518. doi: 10.1111/josh.12278; Williams, Dilafruz R., and P. Scott Dizon. "Impact of Garden-Based Learning on Academic Outcomes in Schools: Synthesis of Research Between 1990 and 2010." *Review of Educational Research* 83, no. 2 (June 2013): 211–35. doi: 10.3102/003465431347582; Wells, Nancy M., Beth M. Myers, Lauren E. Todd, Karen Barale, Brad Gaolach, Gretchen Ferenz, et al. "The Effects of School Gardens on Children's Science Knowledge: A Randomized Controlled Trial of Low-Income Elementary Schools." *International Journal of Science Education* 37, no. 17 (November 2015): 2858–78. doi: 10.1080/09500693.2015.1112048.

12. Faber Taylor, Andrea, Frances E. Kuo, and William C. Sullivan. "Views of Nature and Self-Discipline: Evidence from Inner City Children." *Journal of Environmental Psychology* 22, no. 1–2 (March 2002): 49–63. doi: 10.1006/jevp.2001.0241; Mårtensson, F., C. Boldemann, M. Söderström, M. Blennow, and J.-E. Englund. "Outdoor Environmental Assessment of Attention Promoting Settings for Preschool Children." *Health & Place* 15, no. 4 (December 2009): 1149–57. doi: 10.1016/j.healthplace.2009.07.002; Wells, Nancy M. "At Home with Nature: Effects of 'Greenness' on Children's Cognitive Functioning." *Environment and Behavior* 32, no. 6 (2000): 775–95. doi: 10.1177/00139160021972793; Berto, Rita, Margherita Pasini, and Giuseppe Barbiero. "How Does Psychological Restoration Work in Children? An Exploratory Study." *Journal of Child and Adolescent Behavior* (April 2015). doi: 10.4172/2375-4494.1000200.

13. Faber Taylor, et al. "Views of Nature and Self-Discipline," 49–63; Ruiz-Gallardo, José-Reyes, Alonso Verde, and Arturo Valdés. "Garden-Based Learning: An Experience with 'At Risk' Secondary Education Students." *Journal of Environmental Education* 44, no. 4 (August 2013): 252–70. doi: 10.1080/00958964.2013.786669.

Chapter 11

1. van Gogh, Vincent. January 1874. www.vangoghmuseum.nl/en/highlights/letters/17.

2. Neville, Helen, Annika Andersson, Olivia Bagdade, Ted Bell, Jeff Currin, Jessica Fanning, et al. "Effects of Music Training on Brain and Cognitive Development in Under-Privileged 3- to 5-Year-Old Children: Preliminary Results." *Learning, Arts, and the Brain* (2008): 105-116. University of Oregon.

3. Cohen, Gene D., Susan Perlstein, Jeff Chapline, Jeanne Kelly, Kimberly M. Firth, and Samuel Simmens. "The Impact of Professionally Conducted Cultural Programs on the Physical Health, Mental Health, and Social Functioning of Older Adults." *Gerontologist* 46, no. 6 (December 2006): 726–34. doi: 10.1093/geront/46.6.726.

4. Gibran, Kahlil. "On Marriage." Poem. In *The Prophet*. Alfred A. Knopf, 1923. poets.org/poem/marriage-3.

ABOUT THE AUTHOR

Climbing the corporate ladder and running fast on the treadmill of life, **Steve Nygren** found it hard to effect large-scale change on the social and cultural challenges all around him. Making a radical decision he sold his company and retreated to the countryside on the edge of Atlanta to raise his family. Six years into this peaceful retirement, Steve realized the issues from his past he fought so hard to change were inching closer and closer to destroying the rural paradise he had built. Rather than withdraw even further, he launched an effort to save his own backyard, eventually expanding the effort to the surrounding 40,000 acres. Now, that land is a living laboratory for change, offering solutions and hope to communities around the world who are curious about a better future.

Want to start in your own backyard?

Want to inspire your team, membership or board? Invite Steve to your next gathering to spark motivation and embrace radical common sense in your own backyard.

Interested in implementing our biophilic planning principles into your project? Book a half, full or multi-day consulting charette through Nygren Placemaking.

For more Radical Common Sense:
Watch the Radical Common Sense video shorts, listen to the Start In Your Own Backyard podcast series and dive deeper into Serenbe's history with the Serenbe Stories podcast.

stevenygren.com

Follow Steve on social @stevenygren